THE HISTORY
OF
WORLD
WAR II

A German 37mm anti-tank gun in action during the
early part of the Russian campaign.

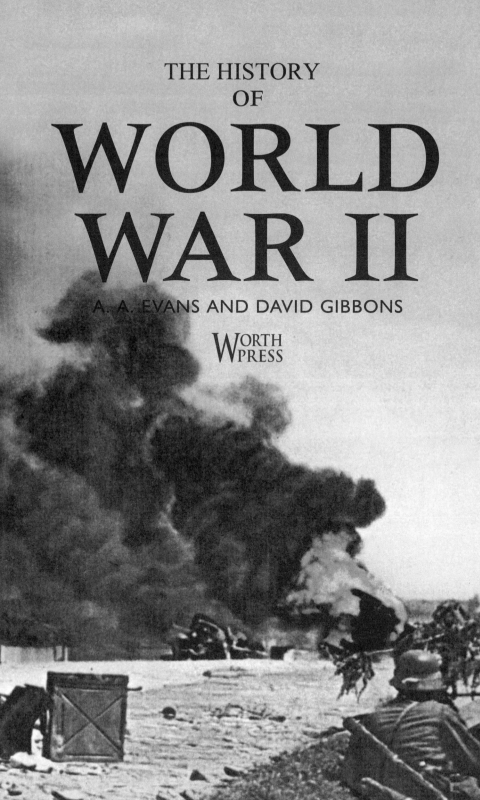

THE HISTORY
OF
WORLD
WAR II

A. A. EVANS AND DAVID GIBBONS

WORTH
PRESS

First published 2017 by Worth Press Ltd., Bath, England
worthpress@btconnect.com

British Library Cataloguing in Publication Data
A catalogue record for this book is available from the
British Library

ISBN: 978-1-84931-140-3

10 9 8 7 6 5 4 3 2 1

Publisher's Note Every effort has been made to ensure
the accuracy of the information presented in this book.
The publisher will not assume liability for damages caused
by inaccuracies in the data and makes no warranty
whatsoever expressed or implied. The publisher
welcomes comments and corrections from readers,
emailed to worthpress@btconnect.com, which will be
considered for incorporation in future editions. Every
effort has been made to trace copyright holders and seek
permission to use illustrative and other material. The
publisher wishes to apologize for any inadvertent errors
or omissions and would be glad to rectify these in future.

Designed and produced by
DAG Publications Ltd., London.

Printed and bound in China.

Illustrations *Illustrated London News*: Marks, Lenin and
Stalin, Franco, Bren-gunner, Panzer IV, Hirohito, Tunisia
Tiger, Mussolini Munich Conference, D-Day, Mao
Zedong. *National Museum of the USAF*: Me 262, Fw 190,
Mosquito, P-61. *Signal* magazine: Anti-tank gunners,
Mannerheim, Blitzkrieg, Hitler, Fallschirmjäger, Ju 87,
PzKpfw III, German infantryman, Hitler, Rommel, Bren
Gun Carrier, Manstein, Do 17. *United States Department
of Defense*: Hitler Sudetenland, Rotterdam, Evacuees, St
Paul's, Thames, London Blitz, German soldier, Hitler in
Paris, Rommel, Roosevelt, Pearl Harbor, Banzai!, Marine,
Midway, Montgomery, Marines Guadalcanal, Japanese
dead, Mount Suribachi, Marines Bouganville, Marine
Guam, 'Torch' landings, Marine Okinawa, Santa Cruz
Battle, depth-charge, USS *Pennsylvania*, Molotov and
Stalin, dead at Chungking, New Guinea, Jewish
resistance, US 155mm gun, Bougainville, Ebansee, Burma
campaign, Nimitz, Shipyard welders, Irrawaddy River,
Marshall Islands, Balikpapan, US infantryman, 10th
Infantry Battalion, Bradley, Stilwell, Nijmegan, Prato, SS
soldier, USS *Bunker Hill*, MacArthur, Eisehhower, P-40,
Chiang Kai-shek, periscope, Japansese destroyer, US
submarine, P-38, B-25, Red Beach, 37mm anti-tank gun,
crossing Rhine, German town, Okinawa, concentration
camp, Refugees, American dead, *Enola Gay*, Nagsaki,
Japanese surrender, Nuremberg, Ichigaya, 60th Infantry
Regiment. Other illustrations PageantPix and compilers'
collections. While every effort has been made to trace
copyright holders and seek permission to use illustrative
material, the Publishers wish to apologize for any
inadvertent errors or omissions and would be glad to
rectify these in future editions.

Front endpaper: British 3.7-inch anti-aircraft guns in action as ground support
against the German Gothic Line in Italy, during the late summer of 1944.

Back endpaper: September 1944. US troops, protected by a tank, advance
cautiously into a Belgian town. The vehicle is an M-4 Sherman equipped with a
Prong, also known as the Cullin Hedgerow Device. This was originally fitted to tanks
in order to break through the thick hedges of the Bocage country in Normandy.

CONTENTS

CONTENTS

INTRODUCTION

The aim of this book is to provide the reader with a concise but detailed chronological narrative of World War II, with sufficient background detail and illustrations to enable an understanding of this great conflict and to provide a basis for further reading.

Rather than presenting the events of the war on a day-by-day basis; the timeline takes the form of a series of chronological sections, each dealing with a specific theater or campaign, these sections running sequentially through the five-year timeline from the autumn of 1939 to the autumn of 1945. This preserves the continuity of the narrative within each campaign, while progressing the course of the war overall.

The timeline is on the right of each spread, and facing this are features expanding upon the events listed and providing background information. Specific battles are explained in more depth, with maps and illustrations, while there are also brief biographies of the generals, admirals and political leaders and data concerning weapons, tanks, aircraft and warships. Overall themes are not neglected, including resistance movements, civilians at war, the Holocaust and war trials, while there are also sections detailing specific armies and weapon types.

Preceding the timeline is a summary of events between this World War and its predecessor, followed by reference maps showing the overall strategic moves of the war; and at the end of the book is a useful guide to further reading.

Below: Allied armor going aboard Landing Ships Tank en route to the invasion of Sicily in July 1943. The tanks, M-4 Shermans, are equipped with deep-wading gear, allowing their engines to breathe while the tanks make their way through the shallow water from the LST ramps to the beach.

1914–1918 World War I is the greatest conflict yet fought by mankind. Millions die, and it changes the map of the world forever
1919 The Treaty of Versailles alters many borders, dismembers the Austro-Hungarian and Turkish Empires, creating new states, and places the blame for the war on the Central Powers (Germany and Austria-Hungary). Germany loses territory and its colonies, a heavy indemnity is imposed by the victors, and her armed forces are restricted
1920s Germany seethes with resentment at these measures, many Germans feeling betrayed; social unrest is rife and the

Above: Lenin (left) and Joseph Stalin.

Left: During the 1920s Germany experienced hyperinflation, and the Mark lost almost all its value. Here children play with bundles of worthless bank notes.

economy collapses. In these circumstances, opinion polarizes between Communists and right-wing Nationalists. They fight out their differences on the streets, each playing on the public's fear of the other. Several coup attempts fail
Oct 1922 In Italy, the Fascist Party led by Benito Mussolini attains power after a campaign characterized by violence and bloodshed
Nov 9, 1923 Munich putsch. Ex-soldier Adolf Hitler, backed by Erich Ludendorff, formerly Chief of Staff to Hindenburg during World War I, attempts a coup. It fails and Hitler is imprisoned for 9 months, during which time he writes his political manifesto, Mein Kampf
1924 Death of Vladimir Lenin, leader of the

his successor and sets about the creation of a totalitarian, industrialized state
1930 Hitler's political party, the National Socialists (Nazis), becomes the second largest party in the German Reichstag after a campaign of violence and street fighting
1932 Field Marshal von Hindenburg defeats Adolf Hitler in the German presidential election
1932 The Nazis become the largest party in the German Reichstag
1932–4 International Disarmament Conference at Geneva fails to achieve anything
Jan 30, 1933 After a political impasse, Hitler is appointed Chancellor (prime minister) of Germany
Feb 27, 1933 Reichstag fire in Berlin fuels fear of a communist uprising in Germany
March 23, 1933 The German parliament passes an Enabling Bill granting Hitler powers that allow him to rule by decree. Germany now becomes a one-party, Nazi state
Aug 2, 1934 President von Hindenburg dies. Hitler combines the roles of president and chancellor, naming himself 'Führer'
1935–6 Mussolini's Italy conquers Abyssinia, in the face of world opinion. But international action against the aggressor is limited. The League of Nations, established after World War I to avoid international conflict, is insufficiently supported, the USA

1936–9 Spanish Civil War. The European dictators – Hitler, Mussolini and Stalin – interfere despite international attempts to prevent this

Left: *General Francisco Franco (1892–1975), victor of the Spanish Civil War and, keeping Spain out of World War II, the only one of the pre-war European dictators to continue in power after 1945.*

Above: *'Peace in our Time', – British Prime Minister Neville Chamberlain returns from Munich brandishing what he claims to be a binding agreement with the German dictator over Czechoslovakia.*

March 7, 1936 Hitler begins his campaign to reassert Germany's position in the world and sends troops to take control of the Rhineland, occupied by the Allies since World War I

Nov 1, 1936 Rome-Berlin Axis signed by Hitler and Mussolini, an alliance between the two Nationalist dictators

March 13, 1938 *Anschluss*. Hitler achieves his aim of uniting the two German-speaking nations of Europe by annexing Austria to Germany

Sept 29, 1938 Munich Agreement. After much diplomatic activity, Britain and France agree to Hitler's demands to incorporate the German-speaking area of Czecho-slovakia (Sudetenland) into Germany. In return he promises that this will be his final territorial demand

October 1938 Hitler demands the restoration of Danzig to Germany and communications rights in the 'Danzig Corridor' of Polish territory that separates Germany and the province of East Prussia

April 7, 1939 Italy invades Albania

Summer 1939 Tensions mount as Hitler pursues his claims on Poland. The Poles refuse to negotiate with Germany. Britain and France publicly state their support for Poland

Below: *Hitler enters the Sudetenland in triumph, September 1938.*

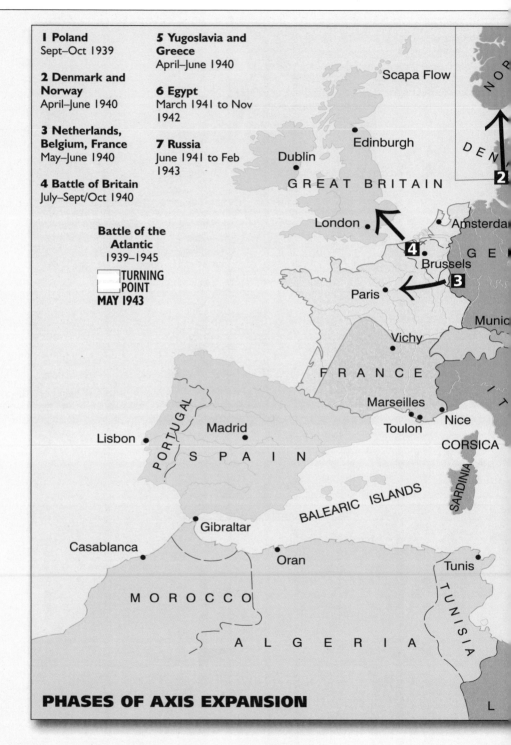

1 Poland
Sept–Oct 1939

2 Denmark and Norway
April–June 1940

3 Netherlands, Belgium, France
May–June 1940

4 Battle of Britain
July–Sept/Oct 1940

5 Yugoslavia and Greece
April–June 1940

6 Egypt
March 1941 to Nov 1942

7 Russia
June 1941 to Feb 1943

Battle of the Atlantic
1939–1945

TURNING POINT
MAY 1943

PHASES OF AXIS EXPANSION

SWEDEN
Stockholm
Leningrad
Tallinn
ESTONIA
Riga
LATVIA
LITHUANIA
openhagen
Moscow
1
rlin
Warsaw
RUSSIA
NY
POLAND
Prague
7
Kiev
Stalingrad
ECHOSLOVKI
Vienna
Budapest
TURNING POINT
STALINGRAD
SEPT 1942 TO FEB.
1943
HUNGARY
ROUMANIA
YUGOSLAVIA
Belgrade
Bucharest
Sarajevo
Dubrovnik
BULGARIA
Sofia
Constantinople
ALBANIA
GREECE
TURKEY
Athens
Corinth
CRETE
CYPRUS
TURNING POINT
ALAMEIN
OCT-NOV 1942 *Suez Canal*
Jerusalem
Tobruk
Alamein
Alexandria
6
Benghazi
Cairo
A
El Agheila
EGYPT

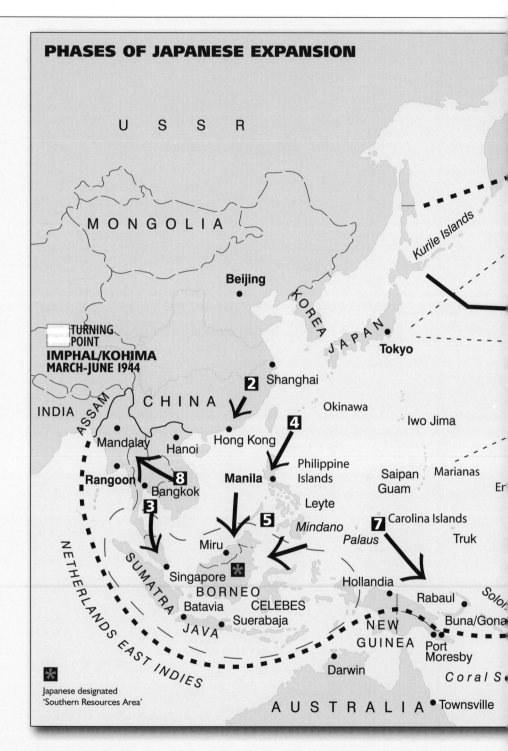

PHASES OF JAPANESE EXPANSION

U S S R

MONGOLIA

Beijing

TURNING POINT
IMPHAL/KOHIMA
MARCH–JUNE 1944

ASSAM

INDIA

CHINA

KOREA

JAPAN

Kurile Islands

Tokyo

Shanghai

Okinawa

Iwo Jima

Mandalay

Hanoi

Hong Kong

Philippine
Islands

Saipan   Marianas
Guam   Er

Rangoon

Bangkok

Manila

Leyte

Carolina Islands

Mindano

Palaus

Truk

SUMATRA

Miru

Singapore

BORNEO

Batavia   CELEBES
        Suerabaja

Hollandia

Rabaul

Buna/Gona

Solo

NETHERLANDS EAST INDIES

JAVA

NEW
GUINEA   Port
Moresby

Darwin

Coral S

Japanese designated
'Southern Resources Area'

AUSTRALIA • Townsville

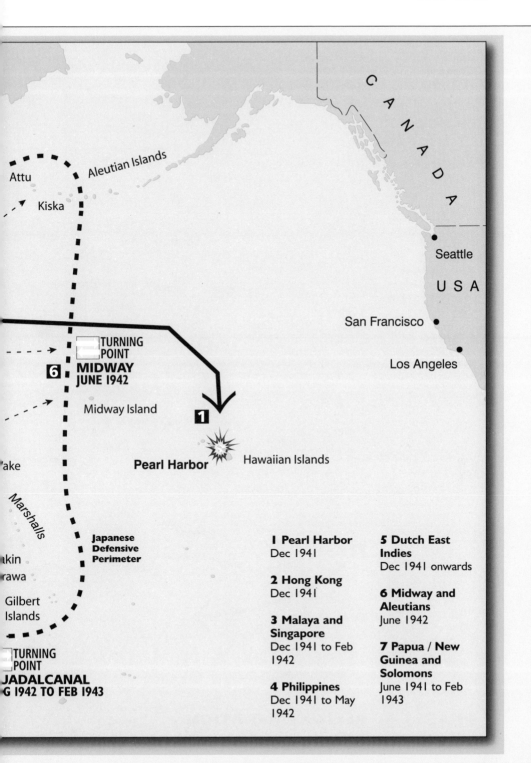

CANADA

Aleutian Islands

Attu

Kiska

Seattle

USA

San Francisco

Los Angeles

TURNING POINT
6 **MIDWAY JUNE 1942**

Midway Island

1

Pearl Harbor 💥 Hawaiian Islands

ake

Marshalls

Japanese Defensive Perimeter

akin

awa

Gilbert Islands

TURNING POINT
JADALCANAL G 1942 TO FEB 1943

1 Pearl Harbor
Dec 1941

2 Hong Kong
Dec 1941

3 Malaya and Singapore
Dec 1941 to Feb 1942

4 Philippines
Dec 1941 to May 1942

5 Dutch East Indies
Dec 1941 onwards

6 Midway and Aleutians
June 1942

7 Papua / New Guinea and Solomons
June 1941 to Feb 1943

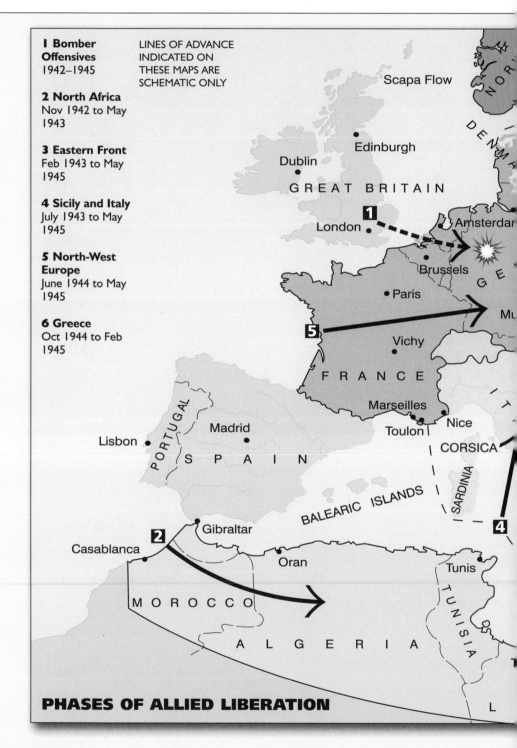

1 Bomber Offensives
1942–1945

2 North Africa
Nov 1942 to May 1943

3 Eastern Front
Feb 1943 to May 1945

4 Sicily and Italy
July 1943 to May 1945

5 North-West Europe
June 1944 to May 1945

6 Greece
Oct 1944 to Feb 1945

LINES OF ADVANCE INDICATED ON THESE MAPS ARE SCHEMATIC ONLY

PHASES OF ALLIED LIBERATION

SWEDEN

Stockholm

Leningrad

Tallinn
ESTONIA

Riga
LATVIA

openhagen

LITHUANIA

Moscow

N

Berlin

Warsaw

R U S S I A

3

P O L A N D

Kiev

Stalingrad

Prague

ZECHOSLOVKI

A

Vienna

Budapest

HUNGARY

R O U M A N I A

YUGOSLAVIA

Belgrade

Bucharest

Sarajevo

B U L G A R I A

Dubrovnik

Sofia

ALBANIA

Constantinople

GREECE

T U R K E Y

Athens

6

LY

Corinth

CRETE

Middle East
April-May 1941 Allies secure Iraq
May-July 1941 Allies secure Syria

Tobruk

Suez Canal

Benghazi

Alamein

Alexandria

2

Cairo

Y

El Agheila

E G Y P T

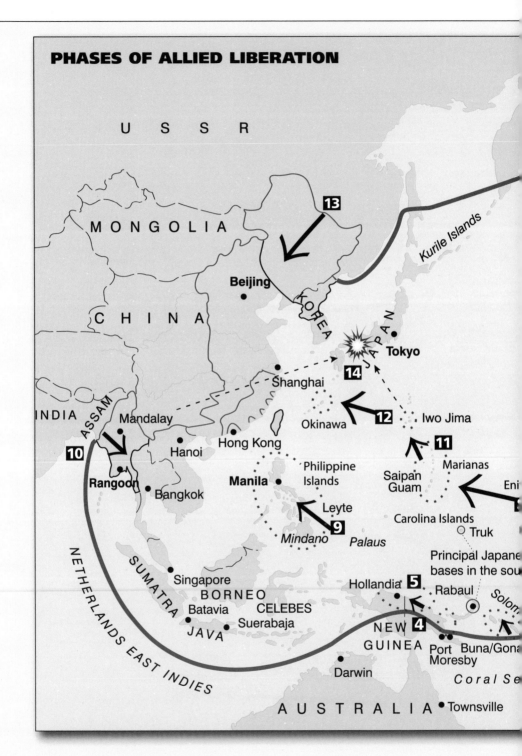

PHASES OF ALLIED LIBERATION

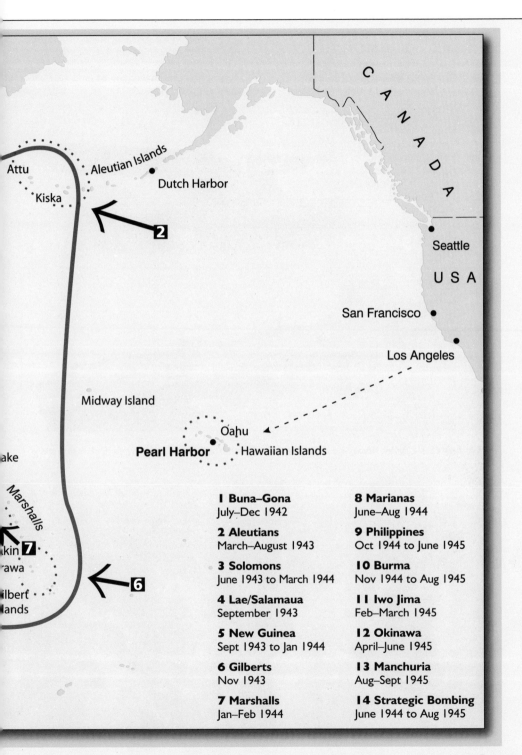

Attu

Kiska

Aleutian Islands

Dutch Harbor

2

CANADA

Seattle

USA

San Francisco

Los Angeles

Midway Island

Oahu

Pearl Harbor · Hawaiian Islands

ake

Marshalls

akin **7**

awa

ilbert

lands

6

1 Buna–Gona July–Dec 1942	**8 Marianas** June–Aug 1944
2 Aleutians March–August 1943	**9 Philippines** Oct 1944 to June 1945
3 Solomons June 1943 to March 1944	**10 Burma** Nov 1944 to Aug 1945
4 Lae/Salamaua September 1943	**11 Iwo Jima** Feb–March 1945
5 New Guinea Sept 1943 to Jan 1944	**12 Okinawa** April–June 1945
6 Gilberts Nov 1943	**13 Manchuria** Aug–Sept 1945
7 Marshalls Jan–Feb 1944	**14 Strategic Bombing** June 1944 to Aug 1945

POLISH ARMED FORCES

The Polish Army on September 1, 1939 was less than 300,000 strong, though it had a large number of reservists. It was made up of 30 infantry divisions and 11 cavalry divisions, but only two mechanised brigades. Polish cavalry units were only just beginning to be mechanised. The Germans, on the other hand, had more than 100 divisions, including five powerful Panzer divisions and eight mechanised or motorised divisions, totalling some 2.5 million well-trained soldiers. The Polish Air Force had only 154 bombers and 159 fighters but, apart from some bombers, these were mostly obsolescent aircraft. The Germans had over four times that number and all modern, state-of-the-art warplanes.

Top: the PZL P.11 fighter. *Above:* the submarine Orzel. *Below:* Polish cavalry, no match for tanks and artillery.

The Poles fought bravely, but bravery is often not enough. They quickly succumbed to the better-equipped and far more numerous foe. Moreover, the Germans had a much better appreciation of modern, fast-moving, mechanised warfare.

Seventeen days after the campaign began Soviet troops also invaded eastern Poland. Germany and the USSR then proceeded to carve up Poland between them once organised Polish resistance had ended on October 6, 1939.

Some 100,000 Polish soldiers would escape and form the Free Polish Brigade in France and then England, where they would continue to fight the Nazis on land, sea and in the air.

On the eve of war most of the major Polish Navy ships, had been sent for safety to the British Isles. The Polish Navy fought with great distinction alongside the other Allied navies in many important and successful operations, including those conducted against the German battleship, *Bismarck*.

Above: *Polish 7 TP light tanks*

Above: *Polish troops with Bofors 37mm anti-tank guns*

Aug 23, 1939 Non-Aggression Pact signed between Germany and the Soviet Union
Aug 25, 1939 Formal alliance signed between Poland and Britain

GERMAN CONQUEST OF POLAND
Poland has had just two decades of independence since the peace treatries of World War I, having been repeatedly partitioned by Russia, Prussia and Austria during the eighteenth and nineteenth centuries. During World War II, Poland will become a place of horror, the site for extermination camps as the Nazi Holocaust engulfs the Jews of Europe
Sept 1, 1939 Germany invades Poland
Sept 12, 1939 Battle of the River Bzura: Polish Poznan Army attempts to break out of its encirclement. The offensive fails by 18th; 170,000 surrender
Sept 15, 1939 German armies surround Warsaw
Sept 17, 1939 Soviet armies invade Poland from the east

Above: *German infantry during the conquest of Poland*

Following the years of appeasement by the Western powers, lamentably abused by the German invasion of Czechoslovakia, the German campaign against Poland at last provoked a military response, and what became a world war began.

Hitler's demands on Poland – essentially Danzig and the 'Polish Corridor' that separated East Prussia from the rest of Germany – were several times refused. Even at the last minute, Britain and France tried to persuade the Poles to negotiate, but war was inevitable.

The attack on Poland began without declaration of war. Although fully prepared for the conflict, the Poles were not ready for the nature of the onslaught that came on September 1. The Polish linear deployment of troops was ideal for *blitzkrieg*, enabling rapid penetration and envelopment by the panzers, which cut through the thinly spread Polish formations. Speed was of the essence, since the bulk of the German army was committed to Poland, leaving the French front lightly guarded.

Within three days, the Luftwaffe's 1,600 aircraft had destroyed practically the entire Polish Air Force. Air superiority then enabled terror bombing of the cities and communications centers as well as bombardment of the surrounded Polish armies. Between 9/12th and 12/18th, the Polish Poznan Army, which had been deployed west of the capital, failed to break free of the surrounding Germans at the Battle of the Bzura. Meanwhile the concentric German advance reached Warsaw, which was now subjected to a massive bombardment from land and air.

The bulk of the Polish armed forces having been destroyed or captured, the Soviet invasion on September 17 encountered less resistance. Surrounded Polish formations were gradually forced to surrender, and Warsaw itself capitulated on 27th. Poland, partitioned by its conquerors, now entered a nightmare period of occupation by two of the most vicious régimes in history.

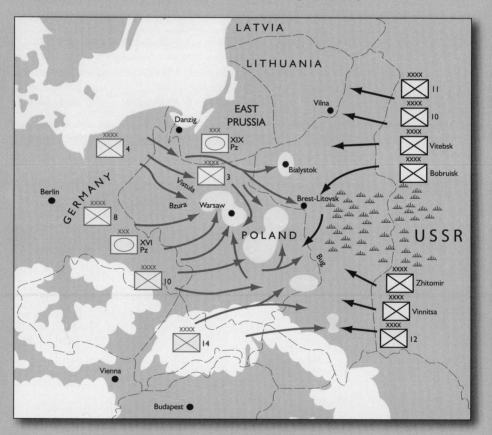

POLAND – OPPOSING FORCES

	GERMANY	POLAND
Infantry Divisions	40	30
Tank Divisions	11	1 brigade
Bomber Aircraft	850	210
Fighter Aircraft	400	150

Above: The diminutive Panzer II was the main German tank during the Polish campaign.

POLAND: LOSSES

	GERMANY	POLAND
Killed	8,000	70,000
Wounded	27,300	130,000

Above: The Royal Castle in Warsaw burning, after coming under German shellfire 17 September 1939.

Sept, 19, 1939 Meeting of German and Soviet invading armies at Brest-Litovsk
Sept 22, 1939 Soviet troops take Lvov
Sept 27, 1939 Warsaw surrenders
Sept 28, 1939 Modlin area: 10 Polish divisions, encircled for 18 days, surrender
Oct 6, 1939 End of Polish resistance

Western Theater General Events
Sept 2, 1939 Britain and France issue an ultimatum to Germany: withdraw from Poland within 12 hours
Sept 3, 1939 No response is forthcoming from Germany. Britain and France declare war on Germany
Sept 3, 1939 British liner *Athenia* sunk by *U-30*, the U-boat captain believing his target to be an auxiliary cruiser. 28 Americans are among the dead. Britain sees this as the start of unrestricted submarine warfare by the Germans and instigates a system of convoys
Sept 4, 1939 British aircraft make first attack of the war on German coast near entrance to the Kiel Canal. It is not successful and 7 aircraft are lost
Sept 5, 1939 USA declares its neutrality
Sept 6, 1939 South Africa declares war on Germany
Sept 7, 1939 French troops enter German Saarland but withdraw by Oct 4
Sept 9, 1939 British Expeditionary Force begins crossing to France
Sept 10, 1939 Canada declares war on Germany
Sept 17, 1939 British aircraft carrier *Courageous* sunk by German U-boat *U-29* southwest of Ireland. The submarine is sunk by the carrier's escorting destroyers
Sept 25, 1939 Royal Navy begins mining English Channel
Sept 29, 1939 German foreign minister von Ribbentrop and his Soviet counterpart Molotov meet in Moscow to agree on spheres of influence in Eastern Europe. Germany takes all ethnic Poland; Russia is given a free hand in the north-east Baltic

FRENCH ARMED FORCES

On September 3, 1939 France declared war on Germany and the French armed forces spent the next eight months, 'safe' behind the Maginot Line, in relative inactivity. The Drôle de Guerre (Phoney War) was suddenly broken on May 10, 1940 when the Germans invaded, and in less than six weeks France was conquered.

Numerically the French Army was superior to that of the Germans. Their tanks were good and they had more of them. The French High Command was, however, geared towards static warfare, the concept of defence and the Maginot Line. The Army was let down by tactics that were outdated and uninspired.

The French Air Force had inadequate equipment, and fewer than half of its 2,200 aircraft could be considered modern. Consequently it was annihilated by the Luftwaffe.

Right: *A French 155mm howitzer.*

Below: *Morane-Saulnier MS.406 fighter.*

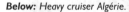

Below: *Heavy cruiser Algérie.*

The French Navy was highly respected in 1939–40. It was the fourth largest in the world and many of its ships were modern. Until the collapse it had operated with distinction, but the French warships at Mers el-Kébir would not join with the British to continue the fight against the Germans so, reluctantly, the Royal Navy had to attack them in order to stop these powerful vessels from falling into German hands. As a consequence French ships were sunk and many French sailors lost their lives. 140,000 personnel of the Free French Forces, commanded by Charles de Gaulle, stood alongside the Allies. They continued the fight against the Germans and following D-Day and the victory in Normandy in 1944 they were the troops that liberated their capital, Paris, from the Nazi oppressors.

Above: *The Char B heavy tank was armed with a 47mm gun in the turret and a 75mm howitzer in the hull and, for its time, was a heavily armed tank. They did destroy a number of German tanks, but were too poorly coordinated with infantry and artillery to be fully effectively.*

states and takes Belorussia and Ukrainian Poland

Sept 30, 1939 General Sikorski forms Polish government-in-exile in Paris

At the outbreak of war, German commerce raiders *Deutschland* and *Graf Spee*, both 'pocket battleships', are already at sea and awaiting activation. *Deutschland* is in the North Atlantic; *Graf Spee* in the South Atlantic. There are also 16 of the Kriegsmarine's 57 U-boats at sea

Sept 30, 1939 German raider *Graf Spee* makes her first kill, the merchantman *Clement*, off the coast of Brazil

Sept/Oct, 1939 Germans lay magnetic mines in British coastal shipping lanes British naval forces are deployed to the South Atlantic in search of *Graf Spee*

Oct 12, 1939 Russia opens discussions with Finland, in effect making territorial demands in the sphere of influence now ceded to the USSR by Germany

Oct 14, 1939 U-boat *U-47* enters the supposedly secure British fleet anchorage of Scapa Flow and sinks the battleship *Royal Oak* with the loss of over 800 crew. The U-boat returns to Germany, and the commander, Leutnant Günther Prien, and crew are fêted

Oct 16, 1939 German aircraft open hostilities against the British Isles, raiding the Firth of Forth and damaging the cruisers *Edinburgh* and *Southampton*

Nov 7, 1939 Netherlands and Belgium offer their services as mediators between the warring nations

Nov 8, 1939 Attempt to assassinate Hitler in Munich fails

Nov 21–7, 1939 First North Atlantic commerce-raiding cruise of German battlecruisers *Scharnhorst* and *Gneisenau*

Nov 23, 1939 British auxiliary cruiser (armed liner) *Rawalpindi* sunk defending convoy against *Scharnhorst* and *Gneisenau*

RUSSO-FINNISH WAR ('The Winter War')
Nov 30, 1939 Soviet troops invade Finland, having broken off diplomatic relations the

FINNISH ARMED FORCES

The Soviet Union crossed the border with democratic Finland on November 30, 1939. The inadequately equipped Finnish Army consisted of ten divisions with fewer than 200,000 soldiers, but it was prepared for the Soviet invasion, utilising the sub-zero temperatures, the deep snow and the densely wooded terrain which greatly favoured defense. The Finns lacked modern communications equipment, anti-tank guns, anti-aircraft guns and motor transport. The well-trained and aggressive Finnish ski-troops could move freely through the snow-bound wilderness, and, even though greatly outnumbered, they fought particularly well. The Soviets would use 26 divisions consisting of 1,200,000 troops supported by 1,500 tanks and 3,000 aircraft.

The Finns' main defence was the Mannerheim Line, which managed to hold out until February 12, 1940. When it was finally breached the Finns had no alternative but to sue for peace, and they lost about 10% of their territory. The Finns had inflicted huge numbers of casualties on the Red Army, estimated at about 200,000. Finnish losses were about 25,000 killed and 45,000 wounded.

The Finnish Air Force had 200 aircraft, of

Right: *Britain supplied 30 Gloster Gladiator fighters to Finland.*

Below: *Finnish ski troops.*

RUSSO-FINNISH WAR – FORCES

	USSR	FINLAND
Divisions	26	10
Tanks	1,500	—
Aircraft	3,000	c.100

which only about half were operational. Despite its weakness, it fought very well and inflicted heavy losses on the Soviet Air Force, estimated at over 200 aircraft.

Sweden aided her neighbor by contributing a squadron of aircraft and two battalions of infantry.

The Finns regained the lost territory when they joined with the Germans in the attack on the USSR in 1941. In an armistice concluded in September 1944 the Soviets demanded heavy reparations from Finland but the Finns did manage to save themselves from Soviet occupation and their democracy remained intact.

Above: Finnish machine-gun team in action.

Above: The Finnish C-in-C, Field Marshal Mannerheim.

previous day. They attack up the Karelian isthmus. They are held by the Finnish defenses, the Mannerheim Line

Nov 30, 1939 to Jan 8, 1940 *Battle of Suomussalmi.* Soviet attacking forces on the central front are surrounded and destroyed by the Finns in blizzard conditions and temperatures of –40°F. 27,000 Russians are killed or freeze to death; 50 tanks are destroyed

Dec 3, 1939 Finnish forces pull back behind the Mannerheim Line defenses which stretch across the isthmus

Dec 6, 1939 Soviet attacks against the Mannerheim Line begin. These and subsequent attempts fail

Dec 29, 1939 Finns make a successful counterattack north of Lake Ladoga

Jan 7, 1940 Stalin appoints Timoshenko to command Soviet forces in Finland. He regroups and reinforces preparatory to a renewed major offensive

Jan 8, 1940 Finns make another successful counterattack, this time on the central front

Feb 1, 1940 Timoshenko launches a major attack across Viipuri Bay, which is covered by ice, attempting to outflank the Mannerheim Line

Feb 11–13, 1940 Mannerheim Line breached. Finns withdraw to a second line of defense

Feb 23 Soviet ultimatum to Finland making territorial demands including a 30-year lease on the strategically important Hango peninsula; the ultimatum expires on March 1

Feb 28–9 Soviets break through the Finnish second line of defense

March 3 Huge Soviet attack on the southern front

March 4 Viipuri threatened by the Soviet advance

March 8 Viipuri falls

March 8 Finns seek armistice

Western Theater General Events
Dec 1, 1939 In Moscow Russia establishes a puppet Finnish government under Otto Kuusinen

NETHERLANDS AND BELGIAN ARMED FORCES

During World War I the neutrality of the Netherlands had been respected, but in April 1940 the Dutch armed forces mobilised because of the strong possibility that this time it would not be. Certain German officers who had misgivings about invading the neutral Netherlands warned the Dutch of the exact date of the forthcoming invasion – May 10, 1940.

The Dutch field army when fully mobilized was made up of eight divisions and eight brigades and numbered 270,000 including reservists. Because of a strong Dutch pacifist movement within the country, the Army was not allowed to modernise or train properly. It did not possess a single tank and only a few armored cars. The artillery was made up of totally outdated guns. Unsurprisingly, despite many valiant acts of bravery, the Army was incapable of resisting the Germans.

The Dutch Air Force did not fare any better. It had just 175 aircraft, of which only 72 were modern. It was opposed by 1,100 modern German aircraft.

The small but modern Navy was primarily employed to defend the Dutch East Indies, which it did until 1942, when it was annihilated by the Japanese.

Below: A Dutch 1894 model 57mm light gun deployed for action.

After the heavy bombing and the destruction of the center of Rotterdam by the Luftwaffe, the Dutch government felt compelled to capitulate. The invasion and conquest of the Netherlands had taken just five days.

In May 1940 the Belgian Army had 22 divisions of 550,000 troops. Unfortunately it

Above: The desolate centre of Rotterdam after the bombing by the Luftwaffe.

possessed only ten tanks and few anti-aircraft guns. Of the 250 aircraft at its disposal, only 50 could be considered modern.

The tenacity of Belgian soldiers surprised the Germans, but after 18 days of very bitter fighting the King decided to surrender in the face of total German military superiority.

Below: One of the few Belgian tanks, a Carden-Loyd M1934.

Dec 7, 1939 Neutrality declarations by Sweden, Norway and Denmark
Dec 12, 1939 British submarine *Salmon* damages German cruisers *Leipzig* and *Nürnberg* in the North Sea
Dec 13, 1939 *Battle of the River Plate:* British cruisers *Exeter*, *Ajax* and *Achilles* find *Graf Spee* and a two-hour gun-battle ensues, the heavier armament of the German ship inflicting damage on two of the British. *Graf Spee* puts into the neutral Uruguayan port of Montevideo for repairs while British reinforcements concentrate. Before they arrive, however, the German Captain Langsdorff is bluffed into thinking himself trapped in the River Plate. **Dec 17** he scuttles his ship and commits suicide
Dec 14, 1939 Russia expelled from the League of Nations
Dec 18, 1939 Disastrous RAF daylight bombing attack on the Schillig Roads; 12 of 24 bombers are lost
Polish, British and French cryptanalysts penetrate the Luftwaffe 'Red' Enigma codes until May

THE PHONEY WAR
A period of waiting, tension and expectation on the Western Front as troops and aircraft deploy, each side eyeing the other warily but neither side initiating significant military action. On April 5 British Prime Minister Chamberlain broadcasts to the nation that 'Hitler has missed the bus', having delayed offensive action in the west too long and thus allowing the Allies to deploy fully. He will soon be proved in error

Western Theater General Events
Feb 5, 1940 Britain and France plan to send an expeditionary force to aid the Finns, but on 23rd Sweden refuses to allow troops to cross the country
Feb 16, 1940 British destroyer *Cossack* enters Norwegian waters to rescue British prisoners taken by *Graf Spee* from the raider's supply ship *Altmark*. This is a violation of

NORWAY AND DENMARK CAMPAIGN

On April 9, 1940, when the Germans invaded, Denmark's small army was a meagre 14,000 strong and her tiny Navy consisted of two small coastal defence vessels. Her Navy/Army Air Force consisted of just 50 aircraft, mostly obsolete. The Germans were offered only token resistance by the Danes, who suffered 26 dead. The invasion was a total success for the Germans.

The Norwegians, who had enjoyed over 100 years of uninterrupted peace, could only field an army of about 100,000 men, but they still put up a stubborn defense against the German invaders. Norway did not have any tank units, because of the very mountainous terrain, and relied on infantry and artillery.

Norway's tiny navy also gave a very good account of itself despite the fact that most of its vessels were obsolete. The Norwegian merchant fleet, totalling four million tons (and 1,000 ships), had been requisitioned by the Norwegian government in April 1940. Because this government was in exile, residing in Britain, these ships went on to play an indispensable part in the Allied cause during the Battle of the Atlantic.

A large part of the Norwegian Air Force was equipped with the semi-modern Gloster Gladiator fighter, but with just 76 aircraft there was little that could be done, especially as the Luftwaffe had all but destroyed them on the opening day of the fighting.

After two months of heavy fighting, and despite the aid of British, French and Free Polish forces, Norway capitulated on June 9, 1940.

Above right: Danish artillery. Below: Norwegian soldiers on exercise.

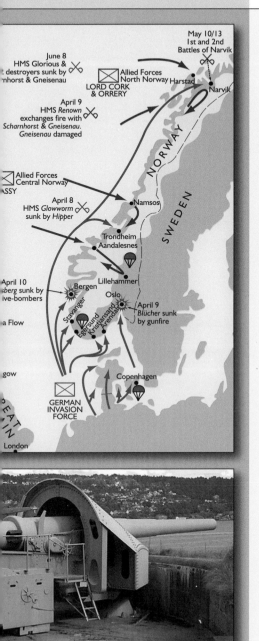

April 9
HMS *Renown*
exchanges fire with
Scharnhorst & Gneisenau.
Gneisenau damaged

May 10/13
1st and 2nd
Battles of Narvik

June 8
HMS Glorious &
destroyers sunk by
nhorst & Gneisenau

Allied Forces
North Norway Harstad
LORD CORK
& ORRERY

Narvik

Allied Forces
Central Norway
ASSY

April 8
HMS *Glowworm*
sunk by *Hipper*

Namsos

NORWAY

SWEDEN

Trondheim
Aandalesnes

April 10
sberg sunk by
ive-bombers

Lillehammer

Bergen

Oslo

a Flow

Stavanger

Egersund

Kristiansand

Arendal

April 9
Blücher sunk
by gunfire

gow

Copenhagen

GERMAN
INVASION
FORCE

EAT
IN

London

Above: One of the two guns used in the sinking of German heavy cruiser Blücher outside Oscarsborg Fortress, Oslofjord, Norway, in 1940.

Norway's neutrality by both sides

March 12, 1940 Peace signed in Moscow. Finland loses the Karelian isthmus including Viipuri, which the Soviets rename Vyborg; parts of east Karelia; and are forced to cede Hango on a 30-year lease

March 16, 1940 Scapa Flow bombed

March 18, 1940 Brenner Pass meeting of Hitler and Mussolini. Italy pledges to enter the war

March, 19/20, 1940 Sylt bombed

March 20, 1940 Reynaud replaces Daladier as Prime Minister of France. He promises Britain not to make a separate peace with Germany

March 31/April 1, 1940 *Atlantis* is first of the German auxiliary cruisers (raiders disguised as merchantment) to set out; *Orion* follows six days later

April 5–8, 1940 Britain and France begin mining Norwegian waters (Operation 'Wilfred') in order to interdict the shipping of iron ore from northern Sweden to Germany

April 9, 1940 German battlecruisers *Scharnhorst* and *Gneisenau* encounter British battlecruiser *Renown* off Lofoten islands. *Gneisenau* sustains damage before the German units escape

GERMAN CONQUEST OF NORWAY AND DENMARK

April 9, 1940 Germans take Copenhagen

April 11, 1940 British expeditionary force sails for Norway

April 15, 1940 British forces land near Narvik

April 16, 1940 British and French forces land at Namsos

April 18, 1940 A third British force lands at Andalesnes

April 24, 1940 Norwegian counterattack repulsed by Germans south of Narvik

April 24, 1940 French troops reinforce the Andalesnes bridgehead

April 29, 1940 British ships take the King of Norway and government to Tromsö

Following the campaign in Poland, during the period of the 'Phoney War', when nothing seemed to be happening and ordinary people fervently hoped that it would all fizzle out, the Allied armies had deployed in northern and eastern France. Neither the British nor the French governments had cohesive plans for offensive action, and the outlook was almost entirely defensive. The French manned their massive Maginot Line, a vastly expensive complex of blockhouses, bunkers and forts that ran from the Alps to the Belgian border just west of Luxembourg. In the event of a German offensive, it seemed not improbable that the Germans would repeat their strategy of 1914 and invade via Belgium. To meet this threat, the British and French Plan 'D' was to advance into Belgium and defend the line of the Dyle and Meuse Rivers. The Belgians and Dutch, meanwhile, had placed their trust in neutrality, and had failed to enter into a joint defensive strategy with the British and French.

The German strategy was archetypal blitzkrieg (see page 32) – a powerful armored thrust through the forested Ardennes (considered by the Allies to be bad terrain for tanks) across the Meuse and straight to the English Channel, dividing the Allied armies in two and then destroying them in detail.

The plan worked spectacularly. Despite flooding much of the countryside, the Netherlands held out for no more than five days, bludgeoned into surrender by threats of massive aerial bombardment of their densely-populated

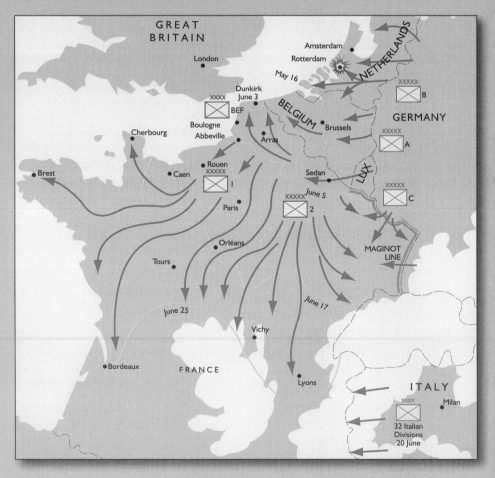

cities, this was chillingly demonstrated on 14th by the destruction of part of Rotterdam by the Luftwaffe. In Belgium, the Germans advanced, and the Belgian army withdrew to the Dyle, reinforced from the west by British and French armies. But while the Allies were thus lured forward into Belgium, the panzers were emerging from the Ardennes, crossing the Meuse at Sedan on May 13–15 and then driving a wedge through the Allied formations some 20–50 miles wide. Behind the tanks the infantry poured through the gap. By May 20 the panzers were at the coast west of Abbeville on the Somme, and the Allied armies had been split in two.

Demoralised and confused, the Allies were everywhere in retreat, the few cohesive counterattacks, such as that mounted by the BEF at Arras on 21st, quickly contained. On the 19th Gamelin was replaced in command of the French armies by Weygand, but the French were already half beaten, despite flying visits by Churchill (now Britain's prime minister) urging resistance.

On May 23 the German armor halted to regroup after its 250-mile thrust to the sea, before wheeling north against the Channel ports. Meanwhile the Allies trapped to the north were being squeezed from the east by the German Sixth and Eighteenth Armies. On the 25th the BEF began to fall back on Dunkirk. Hitler now ordered the panzer divisions to halt and entrusted the final destruction of the surrounded Allied forces to the Luftwaffe. This decision (over which historians have ceaselessly argued) gave time for the almost wholesale evacuation of the BEF and substantial numbers of French and Belgians. By June 4, when the Germans entered Dunkirk, more than 338,000 troops had been taken off the beaches by steamers, destroyers and a flotilla of small craft that has passed into legend. Above the beaches, the RAF fought to keep the Luftwaffe away.

The northern 'pocket' having been eliminated, the Germans struck south on June 5 from the line of the Somme and Aisne Rivers. On the 14th they entered Paris without resistance and on the 22nd the French surrendered. Two days later they also signed an armistice with Germany's ally, Italy, which had cautiously waited until June 10 to declare war and cross the border into Provence.

April 30, 1940 Andalesnes bridgehead evacuated
May 2, 1940 Namsos bridgehead evacuated
May 28, 1940 Allies capture Narvik

Western Theater General Events
Spring/early summer, 1940 Lull in the Battle of the Atlantic as U-boats are redeployed to Norway
April 10 or 11, 1940 German cruiser *Lützow* damaged by British submarine-launched torpedo
April 11, 1940 Stavanger bombed
April 8, 1940 Off Trondheim, Norway, the British destroyer *Glowworm* encounters part of the forces already at sea to support the German invasion of Norway. Massively outgunned, *Glowworm* rams the cruiser *Admiral Hipper* before being sunk
April 9, 1940 German cruiser *Blücher* sunk by coastal guns in Oslo Fjord
April 9–10, 1940 German cruisers *Karlsruhe* and *Königsberg* sunk during Norway operations
April 10, 1940 First Battle of Narvik Fjord: in a destroyer action, each side loses two ships
April 13, 1940 Second Battle of Narvik Fjord: 7 German destroyers sunk by British destroyers and battleship *Warspite*

BLITZKRIEG IN THE WEST:
Belgium, France and the Netherlands
May 10, 1940 Germany invades the Netherlands and Belgium
May 10, 1940 BEF and 3 French armies enter Belgium to deploy along the Dyle–Meuse line. French Seventh Army, having entered the Netherlands, is ordered back to the Scheldt
May 10, 1940 German paratroops secure the Eben Emael fortress, key to the defence of Liège
May 13, 1940 Germans cross Meuse near Sedan
May 14, 1940 Dutch fall back to Amsterdam–Rotterdam–Utrecht

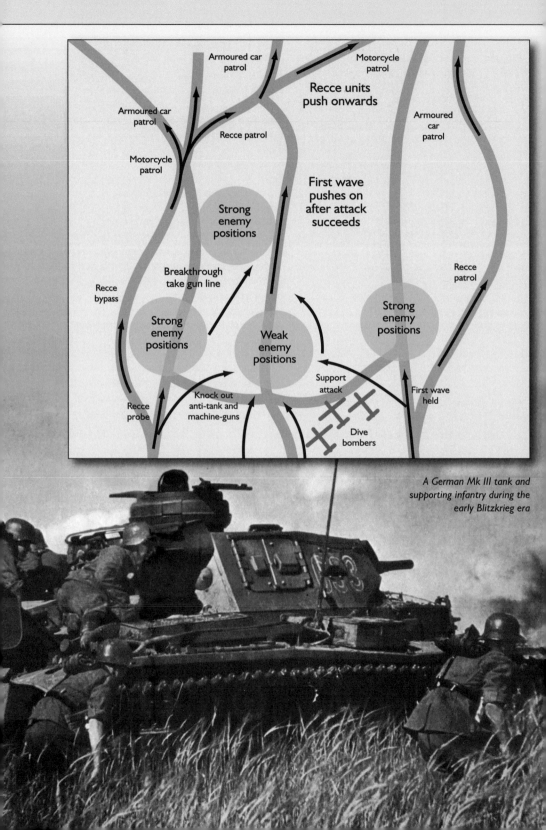

Armoured car
patrol

Motorcycle
patrol

Recce units
push onwards

Armoured car
patrol

Armoured
car
patrol

Recce patrol

Motorcycle
patrol

First wave
pushes on
after attack
succeeds

**Strong
enemy
positions**

Breakthrough
take gun line

Recce
bypass

Recce
patrol

**Strong
enemy
positions**

**Weak
enemy
positions**

**Strong
enemy
positions**

Support
attack

First wave
held

Recce
probe

Knock out
anti-tank and
machine-guns

Dive
bombers

*A German Mk III tank and
supporting infantry during the
early Blitzkrieg era*

The creator of the German tank forces, General Heinz Guderian, set out his theories on tank warfare in his book *Achtung–Panzer!* in 1937. Speed, surprise, flexibility and concentration of force were the essence of the tactic. It combined air power and fast-moving, powerful tank and mechanised infantry units which would thrust deep into enemy-held territory. These units would be supported by mobile artillery, assault engineers and dive-bombers. Strong enemy positions would be contained or bypassed, while the centre of the attack (*Schwerpunkt*) was directed at the weakest point of the enemy's defenses. Good radio communications were vital to the fast-moving assaults. The enemy positions that had been bypassed or contained would be dealt with by slower-moving follow-up formations. The opposing forces would continue to be outpaced and enveloped as attacks would continue after the break-through, generating disorder and terror among the enemy troops. Airborne troops could also be utilised by landing on vital centres in the rear of the front, holding them until relieved by more conventional units.

The Blitzkrieg ('lightning war') was first used during the Polish campaign in September 1939. After the success of this and the Scandinavia campaigns, it was used much more dramatically in the conquest of Belgium, the Netherlands and France, where the concept worked better than anyone could expect. In early 1941 came the taking of Yugoslavia and Greece. Initially the advance into Russia went well, but with very long lines of communication it was found that the Germans were unable to maintain the necessary momentum. The tactic would later be used by the Soviet forces against the Germans.

A brilliant advocate of the Blitzkrieg was General Erwin Rommel. He had commanded the 7th Panzer Division with stunning success during the Battle for France in 1940. Then he took command of the Afrika Korps in the spring of 1941, and came very close to defeating the British Eighth Army even though he was always outnumbered. Eventually he was stopped by much larger and better equipped Allied forces after nearly two years of combat in North Africa.

May 14, 1940 Germans bomb Rotterdam in error after the city has surrendered

May 14, 1940 Dutch Queen Wilhelmina and government evacuate to London

May 15, 1940 Germans break out of Meuse/Sedan bridgehead

May 15, 1940 Surrender of the Netherlands

May 16, 1940 Allies begin to pull back from Belgium as the threat to their south grows

May 17, 1940 Germans enter Brussels

May 17, 1940 De Gaulle's French 4th Armored Division counterattacks unsuccessfully near Laon

May 20, 1940 Germans reach the mouth of the River Somme and split the Allies in two

May 21, 1940 British counterattack at Arras fails

May 23, 1940 German armor halts to regroup, having cut off the BEF, French First Army and Belgian Army

May 23, 1940 British 1st Armored Division begins landing at Cherbourg

May 25, 1940 BEF begins withdrawal to Dunkirk

May 25, 1940 Hitler approves Göring's plan to destroy the trapped Allied armies from the air

May 26 to June 4, 1940 Evacuation of trapped Allied troops from Dunkirk

May 27, 1940 Germans take Calais

May 28, 1940 Belgium surrenders

May 29, 1940 Hitler switches main German operations to the south

June 4, 1940 Germans take Dunkirk

June 5, 1940 Germans attack south

June 6, 1940 Germans reach River Aisne

June 12, 1940 51st Highland Division and 4 French divisions surrender between Dieppe and Le Havre

June 12, 1940 Germans take Paris

June 12, 1940 From London, General de Gaulle makes his first broadcast to the French

June 20, 1940 Italy invades France

June 22, 1940 Franco-German armistice

June 24, 1940 Armistice between France

PzKpfw IV

PzKpfw IV	
Weight	25 tons
Crew	Five
Armament	One 75mm gun and two 7.92mm MG 34 machine-guns
Armor	Max: 80mm. Min: 10mm
Engine	Maybach, 300hp, speed 26mph
Dimensions	Length: 19ft 5in. Width: 9ft 7in. Height: 8ft 6in
Production	8,500

PzKpfw V PANTHER	
Weight	44.8 tons
Crew	Five
Armament	One 75mm gun and two 7.92mm MG 34 machine-guns
Armor	Max: 120mm. Min: 15mm
Engine	Maybach, 690hp, speed 34mph
Dimensions	Length: 29ft 1in. Width: 10ft 10in. Height: 9ft 8in
Production	5,500

PzKpfw V Panther

Left: *Jagdpanther tank destroyer, a derivative of the Panther tank.*

Below: *PzKpfw 38(t).*

PzKpfw VI TIGER I	
Weight	54.1 tons
Crew	Five
Armament	One 88mm gun and two 7.92mm MG 34 machine-guns
Armor	Max. 120mm Min. 26mm
Engine	Maybach, 694hp, speed 23mph
Dimensions	Length: 27ft 9in. Width: 12ft 3in. Height: 9ft 6in
Production	1,354

PzKpfw VI Tiger

Determined not to repeat the stalemate of the trenches of World War I, the German Army made tanks a high priority. The first Panzer (armored) division was formed in 1935, and these units operated independently of more conventional formations. Panzer divisions spearheaded the Blitzkrieg concept of fast, mobile, offensive warfare that dominated the first half of the war.

The first Panzer was the PzKpfw I of 1934, armed only with machine-guns and weighing just 5 tons. By the end of the war the Germans were operating the heaviest tanks of the war, Tiger IIs of 70 tons armed with one of the most powerful tank guns of the war, the 88mm L/71.

In addition to the various marks of tanks built (PzKpfw I, II, 35/38(t), III, IV, V and VI), there were numerous armored assault guns and tank destroyers. Built on the same hulls as the tanks, but easier to construct, these turretless combat vehicles proved particularly useful in the defensive role that the German Army was forced to adopt during the later years of the war.

and Italy

Western Theater General Events

May 10, 1940 Winston Churchill becomes Prime Minister of Britain on the resignation of Chamberlain

May 11, 1940 Lord Beaverbrook, newspaper magnate, appointed British Minister of Aircraft Production

May 11/12, 1940 Mönchengladbach bombed

May 15/16, 1940 Ruhr bombed

May, 19, 1940 General Weygand replaces Gamelin as CinC French forces and Marshal Henri Pétain becomes Deputy Prime Minister of France

June 3–8, 1940 Allies evacuate remaining forces from Norway; King Haakon goes with them

June 8, 1940 German battlecruisers *Scharnhorst* and *Gneisenau* encounter British carrier *Glorious* returning from Norway. The carrier and her two escorting destroyers are sunk

June 10, 1940 Italy enters the war

June 11/12, 1940 Genoa, Turin bombed

June 11, 1940 Italians begin bombing Malta

June 16, 1940 British liner *Lancastria* sunk evacuating troops from France. 3,000 are lost

June 11, 1940 British raid into Libya near Fort Capuzzo opens the war in North Africa

June 12, 1940 Defenses against German invasion of the British Isles are planned and construction of anti-tank ditches, pillboxes, etc., begun

June 18, 1940 French battleship *Richelieu* leaves Brest for Dakar

June, 19, 1940 French battleship *Jean Bart* leaves St-Nazaire for Casablanca

June 24/5, 1940 British Commandos make their first raid, on the coast of France

June 28, 1940 De Gaulle is recognised by Britain as leader of the Free French

June 28, 1940 The USSR demands Bucovina and Bessarabia from Roumania. Germany acquiesces and the Soviets enter the country

ANTI-TANK WEAPONS

Early in the war anti-tank guns ranged in caliber from 37mm to 45mm, firing a projectile weighing approximately 2lb. At first these weapons apeared adequate, but very quickly, with increases in armor protection on tanks, it became obvious that their caliber and power needed to be increased. The next step was 50–57mm caliber and this quickly rose to 75–76mm. One of the best Allied anti-tank guns of the later war period was the British 17pdr (77mm), which was able to knock out the Germans' heavily armored Tiger tank at a range of 1,000 yards. The most feared weapon was the German 88mm. This was developed from the high-velocity 88mm anti-aircraft gun. These weapons had been pressed into service

Above: A Russian 45mm anti-tank gun, typical of the relatively small weapons used during the early part of the war.

by the German Army to operate as long-range anti-tank guns when their 37mm guns were proving inadequate for the job. The '88' could defeat the armor of any wartime tank – their only drawback was the weight of the weapon.

These guns were supplemented by a range of hand-held infantry anti-tank weapons such as the anti-tank rifle, panzerfaust and bazooka.

Below: The mighty German 88mm PaK 43, the most potent anti-tank gun of the war.

Right: The British Boys anti-tank rifle was typical of weapons in other armies at the begining of the war. It had a caliber of 0.551 inches (13.9mm). Bolt-action with a 5-round detachable box magazine, it was able to penetrate 20mm armor at 100 yards. It soon became obsolete as tank armor increased in thickness.

Right: The German Panzerfaust saw service later in the war. It was an inexpensive, recoilless anti-tank weapon consisting of a small, disposable pre-loaded launch-tube firing a shaped charge warhead. It had a nominal maximum range of between 60 and 100 meters, and the big warhead was able to penetrate 200mm of armor.

Right: The Bazooka was jokingly named after a strange musical wind instrument of the time. It first saw service in late 1942. The weapon had a weight of 13¼lb and a caliber of 2.36 inches, firing a rocket that could penetrate 80mm of armor with its shaped-charge warhead. It had a maximum range of 400 yards, but the accuracy fell off rapidly after 100 yards.

Cunningham   *Somerville*

Andrew Cunningham was the very essence of a fighting admiral with the Nelsonian spirit, once signalling to his ships, 'Sink, burn and destroy: let nothing pass.' He joined the Royal Navy as a cadet in 1897, serving in the

CUNNINGHAM

Rank attained	Admiral of the Fleet
Dates	1883–1963
Background	Career sailor, training HMS *Britannia*
Commands	C-in-C Mediterranean Fleet, 1939–42; First Sea Lord, 1943

Boer War and World War I. He became C-in-C Mediterranean Fleet in 1939. In November 1940 his naval aircraft carried out the spectacular raid on the Italian fleet at Taranto, and in May 1941 his fleet inflicted heavy damage on the Italian fleet at the Battle of Cape Matapan. During the battle for Crete, even though suffering heavy losses through lack of air cover, his ships managed to rescue 75% of the 22,000 Allied troops trapped on the island, and his fleet helped keep the island of Malta supplied during its three-year 'siege'. Appointed First Sea Lord, he played a major part in all operations until the war's end. An outstanding commander, he was well liked and respected by Churchill and Eisenhower but most of all by the seamen who served under his command.

SOMERVILLE

Rank attained	Admiral
Dates	1882–1949
Background	Career sailor
Commands	Commander of Force H, 1940; Eastern Fleet, 1942

Born in New Zealand, James Somerville was promoted to Vice-Admiral in 1937 then placed on the retired list in 1939. Returned to active duty after the declaration of war, he was appointed C-in-C of Force H in 1940 based at Gibraltar. After the fall of France his ships were obliged to attack French warships at Mers el-Kébir because the French admiral would not hand over this fleet to continue the fight against the Nazis, and because of the fear that they would fall into the hands of the Germans. One French battleship was sunk, two were heavily damaged and one escaped. In May 1941, Somerville's force was in action against *Bismarck*, aircraft from *Ark Royal* inflicting torpedo damage on the German ship and causing the steering problems that led to her being sunk by British warships. As commander of Force H Somerville was instrumental in getting convoys through the Mediterranean in order to keep the British forces in North Africa supplied. He was selected to command the hastily organized British Eastern Fleet in the spring of 1942 after Japan entered the war, and in 1945 Somerville became head of the British Naval Mission in Washington.

TOVEY

Rank attained	Admiral of the Fleet
Dates	1885–1971
Background	Career sailor, training HMS *Britannia*
Commands	C-in-C Home Fleet, 1940–43; First Sea Lord, 1943

John Tovey served during World War I, including the Battle of Jutland. During World War II he was a Vice-Admiral and second-in-command of the Mediterranean fleet, leading the action against the Italians off Calabria in July 1940 and ten days later sinking the Italian cruiser *Bartolomeo Colleoni*. At the end of 1940 he was appointed C-in-C Home Fleet and was in charge of the strategy that hunted down and sank *Bismarck* in May 1941. In 1943 he relinquished the Home Fleet command and

Tovey   *Ramsay*

became Commander-in-Chief at the Nore, preparing for the Allied invasion of Sicily and the 'Overlord' invasion of Normandy.

RAMSAY

Rank attained	Admiral
Dates	1883–1945
Background	Career sailor, Naval War College
Commands	Dover Command, 1940; Eastern Task Force, Sicily Invasion, 1943; Allied Expeditionary Force, Normandy Invasion, 1944

In World War I, Bertram Ramsay served in the Grand Fleet and the Dover Patrol. In 1938 he resigned and was put on the retired list but in 1939 was recalled to take over the Dover Command. With the collapse of the British and French armies in 1940, he was put in charge of Operation 'Dynamo', the evacuation of over 300,000 British and French troops from Dunkirk, which he handled superbly. An expert in amphibious warfare, Ramsay assisted in the planning of the 'Torch' landings in North Africa and was Naval Commander of the Eastern Task Force for the invasion of Sicily (Operation 'Husky'). He later played a major part in the planning and execution of Operation 'Overlord', the D-Day invasion of Europe, being Chief of Operational Command for the landings. Ramsay's last operation was the Allied attack on Walcheren, the taking of which allowed the port of Antwerp to be used by the Allies. In January 1945 he was killed in an air crash. Eisenhower considered Ramsay an exceptionally able commander. He was a modest but tough man, much admired by his colleagues.

June 28, 1940 General Graziani succeeds Marshal Balbo (killed accidentally) as Italian Governor General of Libya

June 30/July 1, 1940 Germany occupies Channel Islands

July 1/2, 1940 Kiel (first RAF use of 2,000lb bomb on *Scharnhorst*)

NEUTRALIZING THE FRENCH NAVY

July 3, 1940 Concerned with the possibility of the French Navy falling into German hands, Britain seizes all French ships in British ports, including 2 battleships and 9 destroyers

July 3, 1940 Operation 'Catapult': At Oran / Mers el-Kebir British demands that French naval units there join Britain or be demobilized are met with defiance. The British open fire, sinking the battleship *Bretagne* and damaging two others. But the battlecruiser *Strasbourg* escapes to Toulon with 5 destroyers

July 7, 1940 Admiral Godfroy at Alexandria with the battleship *Lorraine*, 3 heavy cruisers, 1 light cruiser, 3 destroyers and a submarine agrees to demobilize his ships

July 7/8, 1940 An ultimatum to French ships at Dakar is rebuffed. The battleship *Richelieu* is attacked by small craft and damaged by an aerial torpedo from the carrier *Hermes*

Western Theater General Events

July 4, 1940 Italian incursion into Sudan, taking border posts of Kassala and Gallabat

July 5, 1940 Diplomatic relations between the Vichy French government and Britain are severed

July 6, 1940 Lorient U-boat base operational, the first in France

July 9, 1940 Battle of Punta Stilo: indecisive first encounter between Italian and British fleets in the Mediterranean

BATTLE OF BRITAIN

July 10, 1940 First RAF/Luftwaffe dogfight

LUFTWAFFE AIRCRAFT

Initially the Luftwaffe operated purely in a tactical capacity as the Wehrmacht swept all before it. The first setback was defeat during Battle of Britain in the summer of 1940. But its tactics continued to be successful in the skies over the Balkans, North Africa and Russia until 1942/1943, when the Allies slowly began to wrest air superiority.

The main failing of the German Air Force was that it did not have the correct aircraft – i.e., heavy bombers – to operate successfully at the strategic level as did the RAF's Bomber Command and the USAAF Eighth Air Force.

Messerschmitt Bf 109

Messerschmitt Bf 109E-1	
Weight	5,875lb (fully loaded)
Crew	One
Armament	Two 20mm cannon and two 7.92mm machine-guns
Range	400 miles
Engine	Daimler-Benz, 1,100hp, max. speed 354mph
Dimensions	Length: 28ft 4in Wing span: 32ft 4in Height: 8ft 2in
Production	30,500 (all marks)

Junkers Ju 87D-1 Stuka	
Weight	5,875lb (fully loaded)
Crew	Two
Armament	Three 7.92mm machine-guns, 3,968lb max. bomb-load
Range	950 miles
Engine	Junkers Jumo, 1,400hp, max. speed 255mph
Dimensions	Length: 37ft 8in Wing span: 45ft 3in Height: 12ft 9in
Production	9,700 (all marks)

Junkers Ju87 Stuka

Below: *Heinkel He 111*

Heinkel He 111H-16	
Weight	30,865lb (fully loaded)
Crew	Five
Armament	One 20mm cannon and 4 or 5 7.92mm machine-guns, 7,000lb max. bomb-load
Range	1,200 miles
Engines	Two Junkers Jumo, 1,350hp, max. speed 252mph
Dimensions	Length: 53ft 9in Wing span: 74ft 1in Height: 13ft 1in
Production	7,300 (all marks)

Even so, such aircraft as the Bf 109, the formidable Focke-Wulf 190 fighter, and the multi-role Ju 88 were equal to the best the Allies had to offer. Indeed, German aviation technologists were developing more advanced aircraft, including the Me 262, the world's first operational jet combat plane, which could have turned the tide in the Luftwaffe's favour had it entered the fray earlier. As it was, much research and development was wasted on often futuristic projects that would have appeared too late to make a difference.

Messerschmitt Me 262

Focke-Wulf Fw 190D-9	
Weight	10,670lb (fully loaded)
Crew	One
Armament	Two 20mm cannon and two 13mm machine-guns, 1,102lb max. bomb-load
Range	520 miles
Engine	One Junkers Jumo, 1,770hp, max. speed 426mph
Dimensions	Length: 33ft 5½in Wing span: 34ft 5½in Height: 11ft 0¼in
Production	19,500 (all marks)

Messerschmitt Me 262A-1a	
Weight	14,108lb (fully loaded)
Crew	One
Armament	Four 30mm cannon
Range	525 miles
Engines	Two Junkers Jumo jets, 1,980lb thrust, max. speed 540mph
Dimensions	Length: 34ft 9½in Wing span: 40ft 11½in Height: 12ft 7in
Production	1,400 (all marks)

Below: *Focke-Wulf Fw 190*

THE BATTLE OF BRITAIN

Having forced the surrender of France and the evacuation of a battered British Expeditionary Force from Dunkirk, Hitler saw Britain as ripe for invasion in the summer of 1940. A prerequisite, quite apart from the construction and equipment of suitable landing barges, was air superiority over Britain and – just as important – over British waters. The Luftwaffe must be free to prevent the overwhelming force of the Royal Navy intervening in the Channel. The Battle of Britain was the result of the German attempt at domination of British skies.

Phase 1, July 10 to August 12, was preparatory, with small-scale probing attacks and air-mining of British coastal shipping routes. July 10 saw the first big dogfight over the English Channel, with more than 100 aircraft in combat.

Phase 2, August 13 ('Adlertag', 'Eagle Day') to September 6, was the main phase of the battle, with sustained and heavy bombing raids on British airfields and radar stations.

Phase 3, September 7 to October 1, saw the Luftwaffe turn on London. The crescendo of the bombing came on the 15th, with more than 1,000 bombers and 700 fighters making sorties over the city. On September 30 the Luftwaffe made their last major daylight raid.

Phase 4, October 1 to November 1, was the period of the night blitz. Initially docks and industries were targeted, but the campaign soon became an outright attempt by the Germans to terrorise the population of London and reduce the city to rubble.

Bad weather inhibited operations towards the end of October, and by then Hitler's attention had turned elsewhere. On September 17, after a series of minor postponements, Hitler postponed indefinitely the invasion of Britain. In July he had announced to his generals his intention to invade Russia, and by the beginning of 1941 the re-deployment of air units to the east was under way.

The repulse of the Luftwaffe onslaught was due not only to the bravery and skill of the RAF pilots. The British radar system gave early warning of from where and when attacks were coming, and ground control enabled fighters to be concentrated at the right place to meet each attack. The German dispersion of effort, and the decision to switch from bombing airfields to striking at cities were crucial, allowing the RAF to recuperate.

DOWDING

Rank attained	Air Chief Marshal
Dates	1882–1970
Background	Royal Military Academy Woolwich; Royal Flying Corps
Commands	C-in-C Fighter Command, 1940

Hugh Dowding joined the newly created Royal Flying Corps in 1914 from the Royal Artillery, ending World War I with the rank of brigadier-general. In 1936 he became C-in-C RAF Fighter Command and set about preparing Britain's air defenses, including the construction of the chain of radar stations around the coasts. He was firm in his belief that the defense of Britain should not be threatened by the dispersal of precious squadrons to Norway and France during those campaigns, the period when their loss was inevitable, and Fighter Command was still heavily outnumbered during the Battle of Britain. He maintained tight control of this pivotal battle, which he commanded from his headquarters at Bentley Priory, while also visiting Fighter Command units in the evenings to discuss tactics and means of countering the German night-bombers. Dowding clashed with other senior officers with regard to tactics, particularly the use of the 'Big Wing', which he

opposed, but was overruled. His austere personality did not help. He was replaced in November 1940 and was sent to the USA to represent the ministry of aircraft production. This was not a success, and he retired in July 1942.

CHAIN HOME RADAR
During the Battle of Britain, this chain of radar stations allowed the detection of incoming German aircraft and direct fighters to intercept them. It was a vital tool in the direction of the battle. Information from the radar stations was passed to Fighter Command's operations rooms, which then vectored the defenders to meet the raiders.

with over 100 aircraft
July 10 to Aug 12, 1940 The preparatory phase of the Battle of Britain is character-ized by relatively small-scale attacks on shipping and night-time aerial mining of the coastal shipping lanes. Losses: Luftwaffe 261; RAF 127
Aug 11, 1940 Dover and Portland bombed
Aug 13, 1940 Adlertag ('Eagle Day'), official German opening of the Battle of Britain, postponed from 9th. Luftwaffe flies nearly 1,500 sorties in 24 hours
Aug 13 to Sept 6, 1940 Central phase of the Battle of Britain as Luftwaffe attacks RAF airfields. RAF increasingly suffers a shortage of pilots. Losses: Luftwaffe 629, RAF 385
Aug 15, 1940 Heaviest dogfights thus far. Losses: Luftwaffe 79, RAF 34
Aug 18, 1940 Heavy attacks on RAF air-fields. Losses: Luftwaffe 69, RAF 39
Aug 25/6, 1940 RAF bombs Berlin in response to German accidental bombing of London the previous night

Western Theater General Events
July, 19, 1940 General Brooke appointed CinC British Home Forces
July, 19, 1940 Hitler makes a 'peace offer' to Britain in a Reichstag speech. It is rejected by Britain on July 22
July 22, 1940 Establishment of SOE, Special Operations Executive, to foment resistance in Nazi-occupied Europe
July 23, 1940 British Local Defence Volunteers, established on May 14, becomes the Home Guard
July 23, 1940 In London, former President Eduard Benes forms a Czech government in exile
July 26, 1940 British coastal convoys are suspended during daylight
July 30, 1940 Exiled Emperor Haile Selassi of Abyssinia arrives in Khartoum from Britain to prepare for the reconquest of his country from the Italians
August 1, 1940 Hitler's Directive for the

Rdefault AF Fighter Command started the war with two very good fighters, the Hurricane and the Spitfire. The Spitfire was progressively updated and improved and went through a total of 24 marks. At first the RAF bomber force was equipped with a diverse collection of bombers. Apart from the Wellington, these aircraft – Battle, Blenheim, Whitley and Hampden – were a disappointment, and all were only light or medium bombers.

As the war progressed capable new fighters joined the fray, such as the Hawker Typhoon, the Tempest and the Allies' first jet, the Gloster Meteor. When the big four-engined bombers started to join Bomber Command, firstly the Stirling then the Lancaster and Halifax, the RAF had the ability to bring about the devastation of Germany's cities and her industry.

The de Havilland Mosquito was one of the first truly multi-role warplanes. Largely built of wood, this aircraft could operate as a high-speed bomber, fighter and night-fighter reconnaissance type.

Supermarine Spitfire

Supermarine Spitfire Mk IX

Weight	9,500lb (fully loaded)
Crew	One
Armament	Two 20mm cannon and four .303in machine-guns
Range	980 miles
Engine	Rolls-Royce Merlin, 1,565hp, max speed 408mph
Dimensions	Length: 31ft 0in. Wing Span: 36ft 10in. Height: 12ft 7in
Production	20,351 (all marks)

Hawker Hurricane

Hawker Hurricane Mk I

Weight	6,218lb (fully loaded)
Crew	One
Armament	Eight .303in machine-guns
Range	525 miles
Engine	Rolls-Royce Merlin, 1,030hp, max speed 308mph
Dimensions	Length: 31ft 4in Wing Span: 40ft 0in Height: 13ft 4in
Production	14,232 (all marks)

Avro Lancaster Mk I

Weight	65,000lb (fully loaded)
Crew	Seven
Armament	Eight .303in machine-guns, bomb-load 18,000lb
Range	2,500 miles
Engine	4 Rolls-Royce Merlins, 1,640hp, max speed 245mph
Dimensions	Length: 69ft 6in. Wing span: 102ft 0in. Height: 21ft 0in
Production	7,378 (all marks)

Below: *Avro Lancaster.*

Vickers Wellington

Vickers Wellington IC

Weight	28,500lb (fully loaded)
Crew	Five/six
Armament	Six .303in machine-guns, bomb-load 4,500lb
Range	2,550 miles
Engines	Two Bristol Pegasus, 1,000hp, max speed 235mph
Dimensions	Length: 64ft 7in. Wing Span: 86ft 2in. Height: 17ft 5in
Production	11,461 (all marks)

Above: *An early Mk I Hurricane being loaded with .303 ammunition*

Above: *A Wellington bomber being bombed-up.*

An ace is a pilot who has managed to shoot down five or more enemy aircraft. Most fighter pilots of the various air forces did not achieve this honour.

The very high scores credited to German fighter pilots were achieved mostly on the Eastern Front, where they had a very rich target environment, particularly during the first eighteen months of the fighting – a case of quality over quantity. Against Western pilots they achieved far fewer. No limit was put on the number of combat missions or hours German pilots could fly. In the long run, this policy hampered the Luftwaffe's ability to turn out large numbers of well-trained pilots later in the war. While British and US pilots scored fewer individual kills, when they finished their tours of duty they then went on to train new pilots, giving them the full benefit of their combat experience.

The highly-trained Japanese fighter pilots carried all before them early in the war but this very élite group was gradually whittled down. The Samurai philosophy inspired most not to

Erich Hartmann, highest scoring ace

carry a parachute as this implied weakness, so they paid the price. The Japanese training schools could not cope with demand and therefore standards had to be lowered.

The Soviet fighter pilots during the early years were poorly trained and badly equipped, but later the situation did improve. Altogether there were over 200 Soviet aces, some of them women. The top female ace was Lilya Litvak, who had thirteen victories to her credit.

As the war progressed, the pilot training schemes of the British and American air forces began to tell. The ever-increasing numbers of pilots they produced meant fewer opportunities for scoring individual victories over the steadily dwindling numbers of German pilots sent up to oppose them. Over Europe, most RAF pilots

TOP SCORING ACES, BY NATION

BRITAIN AND THE DOMINIONS		JAPAN	
M. T. St J. 'Pat' Pattle	51	Tatsuzo Iwamoto	94
J. E. 'Johnnie' Johnson	37	Hiroyoshi Nishizawa	87
W. 'Cherry' Vale	31	Shoichi Sugita	70
G. F. Beurling	31	Saburo Sakai	64
A. G. 'Sailor' Malan	30	Takeo Okumura	54
CZECHOSLOVAKIA		**NORWAY**	
Jan Gerthofer	33	Svien Heglund	14
DENMARK		**POLAND**	
Kaj Birksted	10	Stanislaw Skalski	21
FINLAND		**USA**	
E. I. Juutilainen	94	R. I. 'Dick' Bong	40
		T. B. McGuire	38
FRANCE		D. McCampbell	34
Marcel Albert	23	F. S. 'Gabby' Gabreski	28
		G. 'Pappy' Boyington	28
GERMANY			
Erich Hartmann	352	**USSR**	
Gerhard Barkhorn	301	Ivan Kozhedub	62
Günther Rall	275	Aleksandr Pokryshkin	59
Otto Kittel	267	Grigoriy Rechkalev	56
Walter 'Nowi' Nowotny	258	Nikolai Gulaev	53
		Arseniy Vorozheikin	52
HUNGARY			
Deszö Szentgyörgyi	34	**YUGOSLAVIA**	
		Cvitan Galic	36
ITALY			
Adriano Visconti	26		

achieved ace status early in the war, and by 1943, with some exceptions, they jostled for aerial targets, as did their US allies. In the meantime, in the Pacific the US pilots were cutting a swathe through the Japanese. The 'Great Marianas Turkey Shoot' (Battle of the Philippine Sea) sounded the death knell of the Japanese Navy air arm, as the well-honed US Navy and Marine Corps pilots swept them from the sky. One US Navy pilot, David McCampbell, claimed seven in a single day.

Many pilots who had escaped from the countries of German-occupied Europe fought on in the air forces of the Allies or free air forces and went on to become aces.

BADER

Rank attained	Wing Commander
Dates	1910–1982
Background	RAF fighter pilot.
Commands	No. 242 Squadron; 1940; Tangmere Wing, 1940

Douglas Bader was a British fighter pilot who became a legend in his own life-time. In 1931 he lost both legs in a flying accident and was invalided out of the RAF. He was fitted with artificial legs and managing to overcome his physical disability. He was readmitted to the RAF for flying duties in 1939 and by February 1940 he was with No. 19 squadron. Flying with No. 222 Squadron he got his first kill, a Bf 109, on 1 June 1940. Later that month he was given command of No. 242 Squadron, which was manned by Canadians. During the Battle of Britain he was given a Wing, three squadrons, because of his outstanding leadership qualities. He often disagreed about tactics with Fighter Command Headquarters especially with regard to the use of the 'Big Wing'. In August 1941 he collided with an enemy aircraft over Belgium and was captured. He spent the rest of the War as a POW. After escape attempts the Germans eventually sent him to the high security prison at Colditz. Before capture he shot down a total of 23 enemy aircraft.

GALLAND

Rank attained	Lt General
Dates	1912–1996
Background	Career Pilot
Commands	Gruppen III./JG 26, 1940; Geschwader JG 26, 1940; Fighter Arm, 1941; Jagdverband 44, 1945

Adolf Galland was a leading German fighter pilot and a key Luftwaffe commander. Learning to fly gliders in Germany in the early 30s he then received fighter training in Italy then joining the Luftwaffe in 1934. He volunteered for the Condor Legion in 1937, serving with Nationalist forces during the Spanish Civil War. After his service there he served in Germany as a director of ground support operations. He was serving with a ground support unit when the war began. Later he transferred to a fighter squadron for the 1940 Campaign in the West, shooting down down his first aircraft. He was then promoted to a Gruppenkommandeur and fought in the Battle of Britain, for a time he was Germany's leading ace. In 1941 he was promoted to General of the Fighter Arm at 29 years of age, the youngest general in the German services. He commanded the German fighter forces in the west for the rest of the war and was responsible for many technical innovations in aerial combat. He consistently advocated greater emphasis on the fighter arm, but was always overruled by Göring and Hitler. During the final weeks of the war he was dismissed from his post by Göring and he then organized a unit flying Me 262 jets where he was joined by a number of other German aces. He shot down seven aircraft while flying jet fighters, bringing his total to 103 aircraft.

BRITAIN'S HOME GUARD

In Britain the Local Defence Volunteers (LDV) were raised on May 14, 1940 and within 24 hours 250,000 men had volunteered. 'Dad's Army', as it was affectionately called, allowed men too old, exempt or unsuitable for general military duty to 'do their bit' for King and country.

At first equipment was very scarce, weapons improvised and organisation haphazard. The Home Guard, as it was now renamed, had received large quantities of weapons from the USA by July 1940 just as the justifiable fears of invasion were at their most intense. They performed the useful, if somewhat humble tasks, of guarding factories, the coastline and of establishing roadblocks. Some even experienced the excitement of rounding up Luftwaffe crews whose aircraft had been shot down. This allowed the Regular Army, after Dunkirk, to re-form and concentrate on re-equipping and training.

Uniforms and equipment started to filter through, and by the summer of 1943 the Home Guard was a well-equipped force with a strength of 1¾ million and an average age of under 30. Many manned anti-aircraft batteries, thereby playing an active combat role. The Home Guard was useful training for boys aged 17 and 18 before joining the regular armed forces.

When the Home Guard stood down in December 1944 many members were

disappointed that it had to finish – it had become a way of life for many as well as a form of hobby.

Below: LDV at rifle practice.

Above: Standard Beaverette light reconnaissance cars manned by members of the Home Guard.

Above: Home Guardsmen about to communicate by carrier pigeon.

invasion of Britain: the Luftwaffe is to gain air supremacy over the British Isles as the first phase of the plan while the Kriegsmarine assembles vessels for the amphibious operation

Aug 4–17, 1940 Italians invade and over-run British Somaliland from Abyssinia, thus threatening Aden and the southern Red Sea

Aug 8, 1940 First 'bombe' developed by Alan Turing at Bletchley Park becomes operational and can read 'Red' Enigma again

Aug 13, 1940 Anglo-American Lend-Lease Treaty: Britain leases naval bases to the US in return for 50 World War I destroyers

Aug 17, 1940 Hitler proclaims maritime blockade of Britain, neutral vessels to be sunk without warning

Aug 22, 1940 A large convoy of reinforcements for Egypt, including 150 tanks, sails from Britain, routed around the Cape of Good Hope to avoid Italian attack in the Mediterranean

THE BLITZ ON BRITAIN

Sept 4, 1940 Hitler vows to destroy Britain's cities in reponse to RAF attacks on German cities

Sept 7, 1940 Turning-point of the Battle of Britain: Luftwaffe changes strategy to all-out assault on London

Sept 15, 1940 Göring sends in a massive series of attacks on London, marking the climax of the battle. This day is commemorated in Britain as 'Battle of Britain Day'. Losses: Luftwaffe 56, RAF 29.

Sept 16, 1940 The Germans now see that they have not achieved the air supremacy over Britain necessary for the invasion; on 17th Hitler postpones the operation indefinitely and abandons it on Oct 12

Sept 23/4, 1940 Major RAF raid on Berlin

Sept 27, 1940 London and Bristol raids repelled. Losses: Luftwaffe 55, RAF 28.

Sept 30, 1940 London and Yeovil (Westland Aircraft factory) raids repelled. Losses: Luftwaffe 46, RAF 18. This sees the last of the large daylight raids; Germany

The Luftwaffe bombing campaign known as the Blitz was intended to break the morale of the British civilians by terror and destruction. Between the wars, bombing had been seen as one of the great horrors to come – the bombing of Guernica during the Spanish Civil War providing plenty of evidence of just how devastating ruthlessly deployed aerial assault could be. The doom-laden axiom that 'the bomber will always get through' fed the fears of the popular imagination. In preparation, shelters had been built, and air raid contingency services established, but the anticipated gas attacks, which necessitated the whole British population being issued with gas masks, never materialized.

The Blitz actually overlapped with the Battle of Britain, beginning in earnest on 7 September. Three days earier Hitler had made a speech vowing to destroy all Britain's cities in revenge for RAF raids on German cities – but, in fact, both sides had been attacking the other's cities and ports since the outbreak of the war. In contrast to these attacks on industry and dock facilities, the Blitz was a series of large-scale raids intended to destroy both infrastructure and British morale. Once again, civilians were in the front line.

By mid-November nearly 60 major raids had been launched on London, making some quarter of a million Londoners homeless. The principal bombing effort was made during the hours of darkness: during 24 nights in September, more than 5,000 tons of high-explosive bombs were dropped on Britain's capital, Londoners taking to cellars, shelters and even the underground 'tube' netword for protection.

The Luftwaffe made more than 33,000 sorties, ingenious new navigation devices beginning the 'battle of the beams' as radio navigation took over from celestial navigation – throughout the war, target-finding was a serious problem for the bomber forces – and British electronic countermeasures fought back.

More than 180,000 people were killed or injured by the time the campaign ended, on 10/11 May with a particularly heavy raid. Other British cities suffered too, notably Coventry on 14/15 November, which tore the heart out of the ancient city. The Blitz ended as Luftwaffe units (which lost some 500 aircraft in the campaign) redeployed for the Balkan campaign and then the invasion of Russia.

This picture, taken during the first mass air raid on London, 7 September 1940, shows the scene in London's dock area. Tower Bridge stands out against a background of smoke and fires.

Scenes from the Blitz, including a member of the Observer Corps, vigilant on a roof in the City of London, with St Paul's Cathedral in the background (opposite page); firemen working axhausting hours to put out fires started by the bombs (above); damage to the John lewis store in Oxford Street (left); and a building ablaze in Sheffield (below).

WINSTON CHURCHILL

On the outbreak of World War II Churchill was appointed First Lord of the Admiralty. When Germany invaded and took Norway it was a major setback for the British Prime Minister Chamberlain. There was a vote of censure and Chamberlain resigned, and on May 10, 1940, Churchill was appointed prime minister. He then formed a coalition government, including the leaders of the opposition in key positions. Churchill developed a strong personal relationship with Franklin D. Roosevelt. The 'Lend-Lease' agreement of March 1941 allowed Britain to 'borrow' or acquire war materials and weapons on credit from the US. He kept the morale of the British people high even though during the first three years of the war it continued to go badly for Britain. He would regularly broadcast to the people whenever a serious situation arose, providing them with inspiration. He was a brilliant orator and a great source of strength to people. There were two votes of no confidence in Parliament against his leadership and they were both overwhelmingly defeated. He did have a tendency to meddle in military matters and sometimes his judgement can be called into question – as with the Greek expedition in 1941, which greatly weakened Allied forces fighting in North Africa. When the USA entered the war he worked even closer with Roosevelt to ensure victory over both Germany and Japan. He always treated his ally Stalin with suspicion, and he was

CHURCHILL	
Dates	1874–1965
Background	Soldier; politician
Offices	Major cabinet offices; Prime Minister

Above: Winston Churchill inspecting the bomb damage on Merseyside.

vindicated during the postwar years, but even so the Allies did successfully develop a united strategy against the Axis powers. There was strong pressure from Stalin to land Allied troops in France during 1943, but Churchill rightly insisted on delay, the D-Day landings not taking place until June 6, 1944. Even though highly regarded and much loved by the British people, who looked to Churchill as the wartime leader they needed, the July 1945 election resulted in the Labour leader, Attlee, winning a landslide victory: Churchill was voted out. He was probably the greatest and most inspirational British prime minister of the twentieth century.

Above: Churchill relaxing in his library.

switches to night bombing

Oct 1 to Nov 1, 1940 Each night (excl 6th) London suffers a bombing raid by an average of 150 aircraft. There are also sweeps across Britain. Losses: Luftwaffe 297, RAF 152

Oct 15, 1940 Over 400 bombers hit London

End Oct, 1940 Poor weather hampers operations and the Battle of Britain is over. Raids on Britain's cities continue into spring 1941, building to a climax in May before Luftwaffe units are transfered east for the invasion of the USSR

Mid-Nov, 1940 Luftwaffe temporarily switches to attacking British provincial cities including Birmingham, Bristol, Coventry, Southampton, Liverpool, Plymouth

Nov 14/15, 1940 Luftwaffe inflicts massive destruction on central Coventry

Dec 29, 1940 Devastating incendiary raid on London

Initially attacks on London are intended to destroy the docks and power and supply sources for the city. After realising that the Battle of Britain has been lost, the Luftwaffe aims to terrorise London and then other cities to destroy British morale

Sept 7, 1940 to May 12, 1941 Luftwaffe launches 71 major bombing raids on London, dropping over 18,000 tons of high-explosive. The 'Blitz' costs 43,000 British civilian lives, plus 139,000 injured. Luftwaffe losses are c.600 bombers

May 10/11, 1941 Heaviest raid hits London, making a third of Greater London's streets impassable. But this is the last of the 'Blitz' raids and Luftwaffe units are moved east preparatory to the invasion of Russia

Western Theater General Events

Sept 3, 1940 Vienna Award: Germany forces Roumania to cede Transylvania to Hungary. The Roumanian government col-lapses and King Carol II abdicates. Power is seized by pro-Nazi General Ion Antonescu

Sept 6, 1940 First 8 Lend–Lease

THE ITALIAN ARMY

At the start of hostilities the Italian Army had 72 divisions, mostly unmechanized infantry. The majority were poorly trained and poorly equipped. There were only three armored divisions and these also were badly equipped. A great many Italian tanks were of the two-man tankette variety and were no match for the British armor.

Italy entered the war in June 1940, invaded France, which was on the verge of collapse, and declared war on Britain.

The Italian leader, Benito Mussolini, had a large Italian Army based in Libya, of several hundred thousand troops. In neighbouring Egypt the British Army had but 36,000 men guarding the Suez Canal. On September 13,

Above: *Italian Mechanized Unit*
Below: *Italian troops, North Africa, late 1940*

Opposite page: *Italian trenches defending Tobruk*

1940, Marshal Graziani, with five Italian divisions, advanced into Egypt but stopped in front of the main British defenses at Mersa Matruh. The British mounted a counter-offensive on December 9, 1940 and inflicted heavy casualties on the Italians, who were thrown out of Egypt and back more than 300 miles into Libya. It was only with the aid of the German Afrika Korps that the Italian Army avoided losing Libya.

In the meantime, in October 1940, Mussolini also declared war on the Greeks, but the Italian Army's attempts to invade Greece ended in total failure.

The Italian Army also sent many thousands of men to fight in the Russian campaign in support of Germany.

When Allied forces invaded Sicily and then Italy in the summer of 1943, there were only some 12 divisions available for home defense. They were soon defeated.

destroyers handed by USA to Britain

Sept 7, 1940 Britain is on highest alert ('Cromwell') for invasion; it lasts 12 days

Sept 13, 1940 Italians invade Egypt

Sept 16, 1940 Italians take Sidi Barrani and fortify

Sept 23/4, 1940 Berlin bombed

Sept 23–5, 1940 A naval force ignominiously fails to persuade the French West African colony to renounce its loyalty to Vichy

Sept 24, 1940 Major reinforcements arrive in Egypt from Britain

Sept 27, 1940 Tripartite pact between Germany, Italy and Japan: the Axis powers will support one another in the event of attack

Oct 27, 1940 German pocket battleship *Admiral Scheer* begins anti-commerce cruise

Oct 28, 1940 Italians invade Greece

November, 1940 Italian submarines join U-boats in France for the Battle of the Atlantic

Nov 4, 1940 Greeks counterattack and expel the Italians from Greece within days, advancing into Albania until halted by bad weather

Nov 5, 1940 British armed merchant cruiser *Jervis Bay*, escorting convoy HX84, is sunk by *Admiral Scheer* while the convoy scatters losing just 5 of 37 merchantmen

Nov 7, 1940 Roosevelt re-elected as President of the United States for a record third term

Nov 11/12, 1940 *Taranto Raid.* Aircraft from HMS *Illustrious* inflict serious damage on 3 Italian battleships in port. The Italian Fleet withdraws to the west of Italy

Nov 12–13, 1940 Hitler-Molotov discussions concerning Russo-German affairs fails to reach mutual understanding

Nov 16, 1940 Hamburg: first use of incendiaries to mark target

Nov 16/17, 1940 Large RAF raid on Mannheim initiating city centers as targets instead of industry. This is in response to German raids on British cities and begins the strategy of 'area bombing'

Left: British Mk I tanks were used during the early fighting in North Africa but they soon became outclassed.

March 28–29 1941
Cape Matapan
3 Italian heavy
cruisers sunk

July 19 1940
Italian cruiser
Bartolomeo Colleoni
sunk

CRETE

May 20 to June 1 1941
Air/sea battle around Crete
RN lose 3 cruisers
& 6 destroyers

ITALIAN SUPPLY ROUTES

BRITISH MALT

Nov 25 1941
HMS Barham
sunk

Operation 'Compass'

Rommel's 1st offensive

Benghazi

Gazala

Tobruk

Operation 'Compass'

Sidi
Barrani

Mechili

Bardia

Beda Fomm

L I B Y A

Rommel's 1st offensive

El Agheila

XXXX

ROMMEL

E G Y P

Operation 'Compass' was the first major World War II Allied military operation in the Western Desert Campaign. It resulted in British Commonwealth forces pushing across a great stretch of Libya and capturing over 100,000 Italian soldiers with very few casualties of their own.

OPERATION 'COMPASS'

	BRITISH AND COMMONWEALTH	ITALIAN
Strength	31,000	150,000
Artillery	120 guns	1,600 guns
Tanks	275 tanks & 60 armd cars	600 tanks
Casualties	500 dead 1,373 wounded	3,000 dead 115,000 captured 400 tanks 1,292 guns

This North Africa map shows events between Operation 'Compass' in December 1940 and Rommel's advance until November 1941

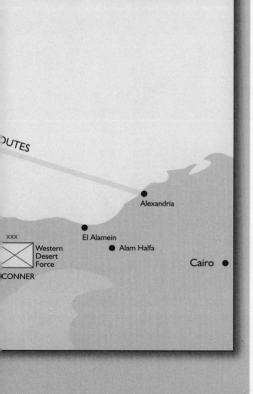

Nov 20–4, 1940 Hungary, Roumania and Slovakia join the Axis
Nov 27, 1940 Battle of Cape Teulada: Italians intercept British rendezvous off Sardinia of forces from Gibraltar and Alexandria but withdraw after damage to a cruiser and 2 destroyers
Dec 13, 1940 Hitler's directive for the conquest of the Balkans
Dec 18, 1940 Hitler's Directive for the invasion of Russia
Dec 25 1940 German raider *Admiral Hipper* repulsed by British troop convoy in North Atlantic; sinking just 1 ship, she returns to Brest

NORTH AFRICA: The 'Compass' Offensive
Dec 9, 1940 British Western Desert Force, commanded by General O'Connor, opens offensive in North Africa after a 60-mile approach march
Dec 11, 1940 British take Sidi Barrani and nearby Italian positions
Jan 5, 1941 6th Australian Div takes Bardia
Jan 7, 1941 British besiege Tobruk
Jan 22, 1941 British capture Tobruk
Feb 6, 1941 Australians take Benghazi
Feb 6–7, 1941 Battle of Beda Fomm: 20,000 Italians are cut off and surrender

Western Theater General Events
Jan to March, 1941 Luftwaffe gradually redeploys east to Bulgaria and Roumania in readiness for the opening of the Eastern Front
Jan 10, 1941 German Fliegerkorps X, now deployed to the Mediterranean, begins attacks on British ships, damaging battleship *Warspite* and carrier *Illustrious*
Jan 10, 1941 Russo-German treaty concerning spheres of influence
Jan 10–11, 1941 British convoy 'Excess' from Gibraltar to Malta and Greece
Jan 11, 1941 Hitler's Directive No. 22 sets out plans to aid the Italian war effort
Jan, 19, 1941 Mussolini visits Hitler and accepts German military assistance in North

THE ITALIAN AIR FORCE

When entering the war, the Regia Aeronautica thought that there was still a place for highly maneuverable biplane fighters, and the Fiat CR.42 Falco was the world's last and possibly the best, but it was soon outclassed by modern monoplane designs.

Italian wartime aircraft were generally no more than mediocre and always deficient in gun armament and bomb load. Some types could only be described, operationally speaking, as complete failures.

However the Macchi MC.200 was an admirable fighter with great agility and superb handling qualities, comparable with the British Hurricane. The graceful MC.202 Folgore was also a good fighter, but the armament proved insufficient when compared to its combat foes. The best Italian fighter of the war was the

Above: S.M.79 Sparviero bomber.

Below: A Macchi MC.200 Saetta fighter shown here being rearmed

MC.205 Veltro, which could meet the North American P-51D Mustang on equal terms.

Italian bombers were generally poor and outdated; Italy's best and most important bomber of WW2 was the Savoia-Marchetti S.M.79 Sparviero. It was a rugged aircraft, and proved to be an outstanding torpedo-bomber, sinking numerous Allied warships and taking a heavy toll of merchant ships.

MC.200 Saetta fighter

MC.202 Folgore fighter

Africa

Jan 20, 1941 German Wannsee Conference: Heydricht coordinates plans for the Holocaust

Jan 24, 1941 Italians counterattack in Albania

EAST AFRICA: The Allied Reconquest
Jan, 19, 1941 British General Platt's forces invade Abyssinia from Sudan

Jan 24, 1941 From Kenya, General Cunningham invades southern Abyssinia and Italian Somaliland

Jan 31, 1941 9th Indian Brigade takes Metemma

Feb 3–12, 1941 First phase of battles for Keren

Feb 25, 1941 Mogadishu taken

March 15–27, 1941 Final phase of battles for Keren

March 16, 1941 British forces cross from Aden to Berbera

April 6, 1941 Addis Ababa captured

April 8, 1941 Capture of Massawa completes the conquest of Eritrea

April 16, 1941 Capital of Eritrea, Asmara, surrenders

May 5, 1941 Haile Selassi enters Addis Abbaba

May 22, 1941 Capture of Soddu in southern Abyssinia

May 27, 1941 Fall of Gondar in the north completes the elimination of the Italian Empire in East Africa

Western Theater General Events
January to April, 1941 Luftwaffe intensifies bombing of Malta

Jan 29 to March 29, 1941 British-US staff conference decides on 'Germany first' policy in the event of the USA joining hostilities

Feb 1, 1941 USA organizes the navy into three fleets: Atlantic, Pacific and Asiatic

Feb 4, 1941 German Condor long-range bombers deployed for Battle of the Atlantic

Feb 6, 1941 Rommel given command of German troops in Libya

HITLER'S ALLIES

Roumania had two of its provinces, Bessarabia and Northern Bukovina, forcibly annexed by the Soviet Union in June 1940, but the Roumanians' obsolete army could do nothing about this so they began to reorganise and modernise with the aid of 18,000 German military advisors. This modernisation was not completed when the Germans invaded the USSR in June 1941. Even so, and always poorly equipped, the Roumanians joined with the Germans, retaking their lost provinces and advancing east. They became heavily involved in the Battle of Stalingrad, where their casualties were enormous. In August 1944 there was a coup in Roumania and the new government changed sides and joined the Allies against Germany. During the war casualties were in the region of 350,000 soldiers killed.

Hungary began acquiring territory from its neighbours in October 1939, firstly from Slovakia and then, in 1940, from Roumania. Allied with Germany, she participated in the invasion of Yugoslavia, occupying one of its regions. Hungary's generally poorly equipped army again joined with the Germans and declared war on Russia in 1941. As the war progressed the Hungarian forces were gradually to become less involved in the fighting. Eventually the Soviets occupied Budapest on October 15, 1944, after a cease-fire had been agreed. Estimates of casualties vary, but possibly as many as 150,000 died.

Bulgaria was officially at war only with Great Britain and then the USA. Following the Balkans campaign in 1941, Bulgaria occupied parts of Greece. She also aided the Germans during their occupation of parts of Yugoslavia.

Below: Hungarian troops with their German-pattern helmets.

As the Soviet Army began to approach the Bulgarian frontier there was a military coup and Bulgaria made peace with the Allies and changed sides. During the last nine months of the war the Bulgarians lost over 6,500 soldiers killed and nearly 22,000 wounded while fighting the Germans.

With the fall of France, the Germans allowed a collaborationist French State to exist in the southern provinces of the country, with its capital at Vichy, headed by Marshal Pétain. Vichy French forces fought against the Allies in French North Africa, French West Africa, Madagascar and Syria.

Men from the occupied countries who bore sympathies for Germany and the Nazi movement joined volunteer units fighting alongside the German forces against the allies.

Above: Arthur Quist, second in commander of the Norwegian SS volunteer Legion.

Feb 6, 1941 Hitler tries again to involve Spain in the war, but on 26th Franco declares support for Germany and Italy but declines to enter the conflict

Feb 9, 1941 British Force H from Gibraltar bombards Genoa and Livorno

Feb 10/11, 1941 Stirling 4-engined heavy bombers make debut raid against oil tanks in Rotterdam

Feb 12, 1941 British Foreign Secretary Eden tours Balkans but fails to organize anti-Axis treaty. Only Greece agrees

Feb 12, 1941 Rommel arrives at Tripoli

Feb 14, 1941 Advance elements of German 5th Light Div arrive Tripoli

Feb, 19 to May 12, 1941 Luftwaffe raids mainly against British ports

Feb 23, 1941 Greece agrees to accept British reinforcements. This forces Wavell to divert troops from Libya

Feb 23, 1941 British monitor *Terror* sunk by Luftwaffe off Tobruk

Feb 24/5, 1941 Manchester heavy bombers, precursor of the Lancaster, make debut raid against Brest

Feb 25, 1941 British submarine *Upholder* sinks an Italian cruiser

March 1, 1941 Bulgaria, under pressure, joins the Axis leaving only Yugoslavia and Greece outside the Italo-German alliance

March 4, 1941 British troops begin redeployment to Greece

March 4, 1941 British Commandos raid Lofoten Islands and capture German 'Heimisch' ciphers

March 5, 1941 Royal Navy escorted convoys begin moving British troops from Egypt to Greece

March 6, 1941 Luftwaffe blocks Suez Canal with mines for 3 weeks

March 7, 1941 First elements of British forces arrive in Greece

March 7/8 and 17, 1941 Three U-boat aces are lost – Prien (killed aboard *U-47*), Kretschmer (*U-99*) and Schepke (killed aboard *U-99*) – to British destroyers

March 8, 1941 US-UK Lend–Lease ratified

THE BALKANS

The Greek armed forces suffered from a shortage of modern weapons. When the Italians invaded in October 1940 the Army totalled 18 divisions and numbered 430,000 men. The mountainous terrain along the Greek/Albanian frontier was well suited to the Greek defense, and the outnumbered Greeks were able to contain the invading Italian forces and then force them back into Albania from where they came. With only 120 aircraft, the outnumbered Greek Air Force put up a brave and stubborn resistance against overwhelming numbers of Italian aircraft. By the time of the German invasion in April 1941 only 41 Greek aircraft were operational. Less than six months later the Greek Army and British forces sent to aid them were totally overwhelmed by the Germans on April 6, 1941. The country capitulated on April 20.

The Yugoslavian Army, including reserves, had a strength on paper of nearly 1,200,000 troops. It had only 110 obsolescent light tanks and the Army moved at a walking pace. When the German attack came on April 6, 1941 the front crumbled, and when the Italian and Hungarian forces joined the assault two days later any organised resistance quickly began to fail; by April 17 it had totally collapsed.

The Yugoslavian Air Force had approximately 500 aircraft, but when pitted against the might of the Luftwaffe it stood little chance and by the end of the first week of fighting had almost ceased to exist.

The invasion of the Balkans forced Hitler to postpone his invasion of Russia by six vital weeks and the German Army was anxious to redeploy in preparation for that task.

Therefore, the task of rounding up and disarming defeated Yugoslavian soldiers was not carried out effectively and perhaps as many as 300,000 managed to retain their arms. Many of these joined the resistance under such leaders as Tito and fought on in the mountains.

Below: Greek machine-gunners. **Above right:** *Yugoslavian troops.*

Left: General Metaxas, the Prime Minister of Greece, died in January 1941.

Below: King George II of the Hellenes.

Left: King Peter II of Yugoslavia while in exile in England during the war.

by US Congress

March 10/11, 1941 Le Havre, first operation by Halifaxes

March, 19, 1941 Battle of the Atlantic Committee set up by Churchill to direct operations, as losses to the U-boats rise

March 25, 1941 Yugoslavia is forced to join the Axis

March 27, 1941 Anti-Nazi coup d'état in Yugoslavia: Prince Paul ousted in favor of his heir, Prince Peter, with General Simovic as head of government

March 26, 1941 British cruiser *York* badly damaged by Italian explosive craft in Suda Bay, Crete

March 28, 1941 Battle of Cape Matapan. The British and Italian Fleets meet off Crete/Greece. The Italians are chased back to port with the loss of 3 cruisers and 2 destroyers

March 31/April 1, 1941 Emden, first RAF use of 4,000lb bomb

NORTH AFRICA

Feb–March 1941 German Deutsches Afrika Korps arrives in North Africa under command of Erwin Rommel

March 24, 1941 Rommel attacks El Agheila; British troops there withdraw

March 31, 1941 Rommel attacks Agedabia and expels the British 2nd Armoured Division

April 4, 1941 Rommel takes Benghazi

April 7/8, 1941 Germans capture British General O'Connor

April 11, 1941 Rommel attacks Tobruk, which holds out

April 11, 1941 Germans advance to the Halfaya Pass on the Egyptian frontier

GERMAN CONQUEST OF THE BALKANS

April 6, 1941 Germany invades Yugoslavia and Greece

April 9, 1941 Germans take Salonika

April 10, 1941 Germans take Zagreb

April 11, 1941 Italians advance from Albania up the Dalmatian coast

Hungary, Roumania and Bulgaria were by the spring of 1941 within the Tripartite Pact and ready as a launching ground for Hitler's planned assault on the USSR. To the south-west, however, the Italians had been humiliated by the Greeks, their invasion of October 28 1940 having been repulsed by November 4. Subsequently they had been pushed back into Albania.

Hitler forced Yugoslavia to sign the Tripartite Pact on March 25, 1941, but two days later an anti-Nazi coup took place in Belgrade. Hitler reacted in fury, postponing the Russian operation and rapidly deploying his forces south. On April 6, 1941, Axis forces thrust into Yugoslavia from Austria (now part of Greater Germany), Hungary, Roumania and Bulgaria, while from Bulgaria and Albania columns advanced into Greece – all preceded by heavy air attacks.

Yugoslavian forces rapidly fell to pieces. By 13th Belgrade, little more than fifty miles from the Roumanian border, had fallen; on 16th Sarajevo was taken; and meanwhile Italy cleared the Adriatic coast from north and south. Next day, Yugoslavia surrendered.

BALKAN ARMED FORCES

Forces	BULGARIA	HUNGARY	ROUMANIA	YUGOSLAVIA		GREECE
Troops	650,000	700,000	1,700,000	1,400,000		500,000
Aircraft	100	1,000	1,000	800		120

Churchill had offered Greece military assistance, reluctantly accepted, but it was a diversion of troops that would stretch Britain's forces in North Africa to breaking point. The British Expeditionary Force, Force W, had hardly landed and begun its march to take up position on the Aliakmon Line, designed to protect Macedonia, when the blow fell. The main strength of the Greek army still faced the Italians in Albania, but the weight of the German onslaught came from Bulgaria and via southern Yugoslavia.

From Yugoslavia, the Greek Metaxas Line, protecting Macedonia, could be outflanked, and German columns advancing rapidly south took Salonika on 9th, trapping the Greek Second Army. An outer encircling move via Skopje and through the Monastir gap between the mountains and the Aliakmon Line forced the British to start falling back on 10th. On 18th the Germans penetrated the Aliakmon Line and two days later Greek First Army on the Albanian Front capitulated. The British, their left flank exposed by this surrender, were destined for yet another evacuation, which was agreed with the Greeks on 19th. Via rearguard positions at Mount Olympus and Thermopylae, they began to take ship on 22nd, completing on 28th, the day after the Germans drove into Athens.

One further objective now beckoned Hitler – Crete, an invaluable forward base for air operations against the British in the eastern Mediterranean. Crete was held by the 30,000 British troops evacuated from Greece, seriously lacking in equipment (almost all that arrived in Greece was destroyed before evacuation), plus some 10,000 Greeks. British command of the sea was inadequate to protect the island in the face of overwhelming air power. The Germans came by plane in a revolutionary mass deployment of paratroops on May 20. Uninspired British generalship conceded control of the airfields first at Maleme, then the three others, enabling the German Ju 52s to fly in ever more troops. British forces left Crete between May 28 and June 1, a hazardous operation in itself, given the Luftwaffe's command of the air, which cost the Royal navy three cruisers and six destroyers. But losses among the German parachute troops had been high, and the Fallschirmjäger would not be used on such a scale again.

April 13, 1941 Germans take Belgrade
April 17, 1941 Yugoslavia capitulates. Prince Peter is flown to London and sets up a government in exile
April 22–8, 1941 British troops evacuate Greece
April 23, 1941 Greece surrenders

IRAQ
April 1, 1941 Pro-German Rashid Ali seizes power in Iraq
May 9, 1941 British 'Habforce' brigade enters Iraq from Palestine
April 18, 1941 10th Indian Div, diverted from sailing to Malaya, begins landing in the Persian Gulf
April 29, 1941 British air base at Habbaniyah besieged by Rashid Ali
May 18, 1941 'Habforce' relieves Habbaniyah
May 27, 1941 Basra secured by 10th Indian Div
May 30, 1941 British enter Baghdad, Rashid Ali having fled the previous day

Western Theater General Events
April 1, 1941 German pocket battleship *Admiral Scheer* returns to Bergen from a commerce-raiding cruise, having sunk 16 merchantmen
April 2, 1941 'Death ride of the Italian Red Sea Squadron' – sent on 'do or die' missions, the 7 destroyers are sunk, captured or run aground
April 6, 1941 British ammunition ship *Clan Fraser* explodes in Piraeus after being bombed
April 11, 1941 Pan-American neutrality zone extended to 26°W
April 12, 1941 Greenland garrisoned by US troops
May 5–12, 1941 Convoy 'Tiger' reaches Alexandria with armor and aircraft, having passed through the Mediterranean
May 7, 1941 British capture German weathership *München* with vital cipher codes

SINKING THE BISMARCK

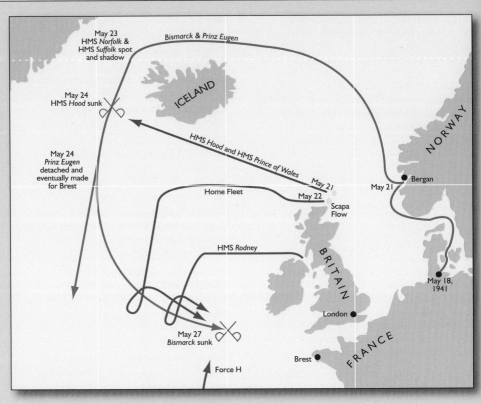

- May 23
HMS *Norfolk* &
HMS *Suffolk* spot
and shadow
- Bismarck & Prinz Eugen
- ICELAND
- May 24
HMS *Hood* sunk
- May 24
Prinz Eugen
detached and
eventually made
for Brest
- HMS Hood and HMS Prince of Wales
- May 21
- Home Fleet
- May 22
- Scapa
Flow
- HMS *Rodney*
- NORWAY
- May 21
- Bergan
- BRITAIN
- May 18,
1941
- London
- May 27
Bismarck sunk
- Brest
- FRANCE
- Force H

Above: *HMS* Hood *and (below)* Bismarck.

Surface Raiders

The German Navy (Kriegsmarine) was far inferior in numbers to the Royal Navy but possessed a number of powerful ships that sortied into the Atlantic to attack the shipping lanes. Most famous of these was the pocket battleship *Graf Spee*, which after a successful cruise in the South Atlantic was trapped after the Battle of the River Plate and scuttled. The other pocket battleships, battlecruisers and cruisers also sortied in 1939 and 1940, such activities in the Atlantic virtually ceasing after the sinking of *Bismarck* in May 1941. Surface ships accounted for only 6.1% of shipping sunk by the Germans during the war, as against 13.4% by aircraft and 70% by submarines.

Above: German auxiliary cruiser Atlantis *was armed with six 5.9inch guns, torpedo tubes as well as two floatplanes.*

Above: The pocket battleship Admiral Scheer seen here just before the war. She was one of the more successful of the surface raiders.

May 8, 1941 Capture of German Enigma code machine aboard *U-110* by HMS *Bulldog*; this helps British codebreakers penetrate enemy signals and locate U-boat groups

May 10, 1941 Rudolf Hess flies to Britain, where he is imprisoned. Half a century on, his mission remains a mystery

May 14, 1941 British air strikes on airfields in Vichy-controlled Syria

End May Rommel reinforced by 15th Panzer Division

May 21, 1941 British cruiser *Ajax* damaged and a destroyer sunk off Crete as the Royal Navy interdicts German seaborne reinforcements to their airborne-held bridgeheads

May 22, 1941 2 British cruisers and 4 destroyers sunk off Crete

NORTH AFRICA: Operation 'Brevity'

May 15, 1941 British 'Brevity' offensive into Libya repulsed

CRETE

May 20, 1941 Operation 'Mercury', German airborne invasion of Crete, begins. Fallschirmjäger capture Maleme

May 28 to June 1, 1941 British evacuation of Crete

THE BISMARCK SORTIE

May 18, 1941 North Atlantic sortie of German battleship *Bismarck* and heavy cruiser *Prinz Eugen* begins

May 24, 1941 British warships intercept *Bismarck* and *Prinz Eugen* in the Denmark Strait, and *Bismarck* sinks the battlecruiser *Hood*

May 26, 1941 *Bismarck* damaged by torpedo aircraft from carrier *Ark Royal* as British warships concentrate to destroy her

May 27, 1941 *Bismarck* sunk; *Prinz Eugen* meanwhile escapes to Brest

SYRIA

June 8, 1941 British and Free French invade Vichy Syria and Lebanon

June 21, 1941 Free French take Damascus

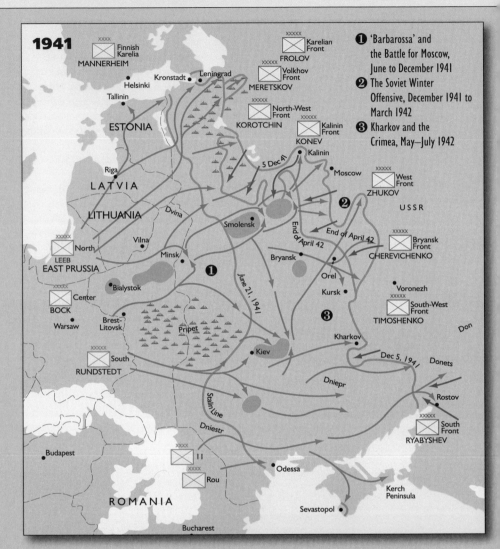

1941

Finnish Karelia
MANNERHEIM

Kronstadt • Leningrad
Helsinki •
Tallinn •

Karelian Front
FROLOV

Volkhov Front
MERETSKOV

North-West Front
KOROTCHIN

Kalinin Front
KONEV

❶ 'Barbarossa' and the Battle for Moscow, June to December 1941

❷ The Soviet Winter Offensive, December 1941 to March 1942

❸ Kharkov and the Crimea, May–July 1942

ESTONIA

Riga •

LATVIA

LITHUANIA

Dvina

Smolensk

5 Dec 41

• Kalinin

• Moscow

West Front
ZHUKOV

USSR

North
LEEB
EAST PRUSSIA

Vilna
Minsk •

End of April 42
End of April 42

Bryansk Front
CHEREVICHENKO

Center
BOCK

• Bialystok

June 21, 1941

Bryansk •

Orel •

Kursk •

• Voronezh

South-West Front
TIMOSHENKO

Warsaw •
Brest-Litovsk •

Pripet

Don

South
RUNDSTEDT

Stalin Line

• Kiev

Kharkov •

Dniepr

Dec 5, 1941

Donets

Rostov •

Dniestr

South Front
RYABYSHEV

• Budapest

II

Rou

• Odessa

Kerch Peninsula

ROMANIA

Sevastopol •

Bucharest •

At the end of September 1939, Nazi Germany and Soviet Russia agreed on spheres of influence in Eastern Europe, including the dismemberment of Poland. This latter duly accomplished, Germany set about military conquests in Western Europe while the USSR bullied concessions from the Baltic States and defeated Finland to wrest strategic territory.

At the very beginning of the war, however, Hitler had set out his plans to invade Russia, and these intentions became increasingly evident to Stalin. Russia, although a vast and populous country, was in poor condition to confront an invasion. During the 1930s, Stalin had purged his Red Army officer corps, and the resultant inadequacies of his armed forces were all too evident in the Russo–Finnish War of winter 1939/40. Secretly, Stalin did all he could to appease and cooperate with Hitler.

Despite Germany's failure to attain air superiority over Great Britain in 1940 (a necessary prerequisite for invasion) or to bomb the British into surrender, Luftwaffe units began redeployment east early in 1941. The

Above: A German soldier in Russia, 1941, about to throw a stick grenade.

conquests of Yugoslavia and Greece in April and May were merely diversions from the great plan – Operation 'Barbarossa', the largest military operation ever mounted. On June 22 the panzers drove east.

'Barbarossa' and the Battle for Moscow, June to December 1941

Three German army groups thrust into the USSR. Army Group North aimed to take Leningrad and the naval base of Kronstadt; Army Group Center attacked toward Moscow; Army Group South (south of the strategic barrier of the Pripet Marshes) struck out for Kiev. Nineteen panzer divisions with more than 3,600 tanks led the attacks. Blitzkrieg pincer moves aimed at encircling the Russians netted many thousands of prisoners but failed to destroy the Red Army on the borders. Instead, the Germans were drawn east over vast distances, ever deeper into the USSR. By September, wear and tear, and sheer logistics, began to take a toll. Leningrad was blockaded on September 4; Kiev fell on September 19. Then came the Russian weather. At the end of October, rain and mud slowed the advance; renewed offensives brought the Germans to within nineteen miles of Moscow when a sudden freeze brought operations to a halt on December 5.

July 15, 1941 Syria secured by the Allies
NORTH AFRICA: Operation 'Battleaxe'
June 15–17, 1941 British 'Battleaxe' offensive in North Africa repulsed by Rommel

GERMAN INVASION OF RUSSIA:
Operation 'Barbarossa'
The Germans adopt a multiple pincer strategy, enveloping the Soviets and creating 'pockets' of resistance; they then force the surrender of the cut-off troops
June 22, 1941 Germany invades USSR
June 23, 1941 German forces mask Brest-Litovsk and advance fifty miles
June 29, 1941 Finland attacks in the Karelian isthmus
July 1, 1941 Germans take Riga
July 2, 1941 Germans breach Stalin Line into Latvia
July 3, 1941 290,000 Soviet troops surrender in the Bialystok pocket, with 2,500 tanks
July 9, 1941 Germans take Vitebsk
July 12, 1941 Anglo-Soviet mutual assistance pact signed
July 15, 1941 Germans create Smolensk encirclement
July 15, 1941 Germans create Uman/Kiev/Odessa encirclement
July, 19, 1941 Hitler diverts his troops from the capture of Moscow in favor of thrusts against Leningrad and Ukraine
July 22, 1941 Germans begin bombing of Moscow
July 27, 1941 Germans capture Estonian capital Tallinn
July 31, 1941 Germans reach Lake Ilmen
Aug 5, 1941 310,000 Soviet troops surrender in the Smolensk pocket
Aug 8, 1941 100,000 Soviet troops surrender in the Uman pocket
Aug 17, 1941 Germans besiege Odessa
Sept 4, 1941 Germans and Finns blockade Leningrad. The siege will last some 900 days
Sept 5, 1941 Hitler reverts to his original plan, aiming for Moscow
Sept, 19, 1941 Germans take Kiev and

THE GERMAN ARMY

The Field Army was organized into army groups, then armies and army corps. In 1944 there were 11 army groups controlling 26 armies with the division being the basic unit. In 1939 a division was approximately 17,500 strong although by 1944 the established strength had been reduced to just over 12,500. 304 divisions had been formed, of which 31 had been Panzer divisions. During the war the German Army mobilised 12½ million men; over three million of these were killed and seven million wounded.

In September 1939 Germany invaded Poland with 60 out of a total of 106 divisions – nearly 1½ million men. When invading the West in 1940, the Army deployed 2½ million men with 2,500 tanks in 135 divisions. Three million men were deployed in June 1941 for the invasion of Russia, comprising 160 divisions and

Right and below: German troops and armour during the advance into Russia, Operation 'Barbarossa'.

nearly 4,000 tanks. After June 1941 never less than 60% of the German Army's strength was deployed on the Russian Front.

Employing revolutionary Blitzkrieg tactics, the German Army cut a swathe across Europe and within the first twelve months of hostilities had the greater part of western Europe under its control. 1941 then saw the conquest of the Balkans as well as General Rommel's Afrika Korps slicing through the British Army in North Africa.

The June 1941 invasion of Russia opened with a whole series of German victories until halted by the atrocious weather of the Russian winter. The Army had not been equipped with the appropriate winter gear, having anticipated that the Russian Army would be beaten before the winter arrived. In 1942, with the return of warmer weather, the successes continued until halted by the battle for Stalingrad during the winter of 1942/43. After the German defeat at the Battle of Kursk, in the summer of 1943, Soviet forces always held the initiative.

On June 6, 1944 – D-Day – the Allied forces from England landed in Normandy. The German Army deployed 58 divisions in the West, ten being Panzer divisions, to counter this. They were now having to contend with a war being fought on two fronts. There were some counter-offensives – such as that at the Battle of the Bulge, but the eventual outcome was inevitable.

The German soldier was very professional and well trained, aggressive in attack and stubborn in defense. He was always adaptable, particularly in the later years of the war, when shortages of equipment were being felt.

Even though not part of the regular Army, Waffen-SS divisions fought alongside it. By May 1945, 38 divisions had been recruited, having enlisted 800,000 men, although, of these, only a half a dozen were fully fledged combat units. These divisions often received the best equipment, especially tanks. Used as a type of combat 'fire brigade', they were often able to stabilise a battlefield crisis. The Waffen-SS played a critical role on all the fronts, apart from that in North Africa. They achieved a considerable reputation for their endurance in battle and were looked upon as an élite force. This reputation was only matched by that for cruelty, and many war crimes and atrocities were committed. Some units were recruited from the peoples of conquered countries. Altogether nearly one in four of their number would die in battle.

600,000 prisoners plus 2,500 tanks

Sept 25, 1941 Germans invade Crimea

Sept 27, 1941 Autumn rains begin

Sept 30, 1941 Germans launch drive on Moscow, Operation 'Typhoon'

Oct 10, 1941 Stalin puts Zhukov in command of the Soviet West Front defending Moscow

Oct 14, 1941 50,000 Soviet troops surrender in the Bryansk pocket

Oct 16, 1941 Muscovites panic. Stalin remains there but much of the government moves beyond the Urals

Oct 16, 1941 Germans take Odessa

Oct 17, 1941 Germans take Taganrog

Oct 18, 1941 Germans are now just 80 miles west of Moscow

Oct 24, 1941 Germans take Kharkov

End Oct, 1941 Rain, mud and cold weather force the exhausted Germans to slow the offensive

Oct 27, 1941 Germans secure the Crimea excluding Sevastopol and Kerch

Nov 15, 1941 Germans launch a new offensive toward Moscow, which has now been heavily reinforced

Nov 16, 1941 Germans capture Kerch

Nov 20, 1941 Germans take Rostov

Nov 23, 1941 Germans are within 30 miles of Moscow

Nov 29, 1941 Soviet counterattack on Rostov forces von Rundstedt to pull back to the Mius River; Hitler sacks him

Dec 5, 1941 Sudden freeze halts German offensive 19 miles from Moscow

Dec 5, 1941 Soviet counterattack by the Kalinin Front north-west of Moscow regains 20 miles, aiming for Klin

Dec 5, 1941 Britain declares war on Finland, Roumania and Hungary

Dec 6, 1941 Soviet counterattack by the West Front (immediately west of Moscow) launched to eliminate the Germans' northern pincer around the capital

Dec 7, 1941 Soviet counterattack by West Front south of Moscow

Dec 13, 1941 Soviet counterattack south

ADOLF HITLER

A veteran of World War I, Austrian born Adolf Hitler joined the German Workers' Party in 1919, later renaming it the National Socialist German Workers Party (Nazi Party). By 1921 he was its leader and in 1923 he led an unsuccessful putsch to overthrow the German Weimar Republic, for which he served a very short prison sentence. The Nazi party steadily grew and as a result of the election of 1933 Hitler was made Chancellor of Germany. Within eighteen months he had suspended the constitution and suppressed all political opposition, giving himself total dictatorial powers. He transformed the German economy to meet the needs of war. His very aggressive foreign policy led to the annexation of Austria and Czechoslovakia before the war and then invasion of Poland, which started World War II. His racial policies were brutal, concentration camps being built to house those he considered racially impure as well as any political opponents. He achieved remarkable military success early in the war and he increasingly believed in his own invincibility, but by 1942 the tide was turning. His dream of Lebensraum (living space) for the German people was the reasoning for the invasion of the USSR which was ultimately responsible for his downfall. His decisions led to the destruction of the German forces at Stalingrad: his refusal to allow them to retreat regardless of cost proved disastrous. As the war progressed his health began to

HITLER	
Dates	1889–1945
Background	Austrian; Failed artist, World War I soldier
Offices	The Leader of the Nazi Party; Chanceller of Germany; Führer

Below: Adolf Hitler at a Nazi rally during the mid-1930s, in the uniform of the SA (Sturm Abteilung), or Brownshirts, the paramilitary section of the Nazi Party, whose purpose incuded protecting Hitler and disrupting the meetings of political opponents. The SA numbered more than four million men by 1934 and played a key role in Hitler's rise to power.

deteriorate. He became increasingly unrealistic with regard to the military forces available to Germany, at the end deploying units which existed only on paper. There was an unsuccessful assassination attempt by Army officers in July 1944. At the end, Hitler committed suicide along with his mistress Eva Braun in April 1945 in his bunker in Berlin as the Russian were battling for the city.

Above: *After the fall of France in June 1940, the Führer poses before the Eiffel Tower in Paris.*

of Moscow by the South-West Front aiming to hit the right flank of the Germans' southern pincer around Moscow

Dec 14–19, 1941 German High Command crisis: von Brauchitsch (CinC) orders a strategic withdrawal; this Hitler countermands and takes personal command. Subsequent command changes reflect Hitler's obsession to avoid withdrawals at any cost. In fact the German offensive has been halted mainly by the onset of harsh winter conditions for which they are unprepared

Dec 15, 1941 Soviets retake Klin

Dec 29, 1941 Soviet amphibious attack on the Crimea fails to achieve decisive results

January, 1942 The Soviet offensive plan is an attempted double envelopment of the German Army Group Center

Jan–Feb, 1942 Intense fighting west of Moscow as the Soviet thrusts attempt encirclement about Vyazma

Feb 8, 1942 90,000 Germans encircled at Demyansk

March, 19, 1942 Soviet Second Shock Army, part of the thrust to relieve Leningrad, cut off north of Novgorod

End March, 1942 Soviet counterattacks stall, having failed to achieve significant success but having pushed the Germans back before Moscow

NORTH AFRICA:
The 'Crusader' Offensive
Nov 18, 1941 to Jan 6, 1942 British 'Crusader' offensive

Nov 17/18, 1941 First, unsuccessful, raid by SAS

Nov 24, 1941 Rommel counterattacks towards the Egyptian border ('dash to the wire') but by 26th has to turn back to avoid being cut off

Dec 7, 1941 British attack Rommel at Gazala

Dec 7, 1941 Tobruk relieved

By Jan 6, 1942 British have forced Rommel

ERWIN ROMMEL

Rommel, who saw military service during World War I, was perceived by the Allies as an honourable opponent of great ability. Personally brave and audacious, he espoused Guderian's Blitzkrieg philosophy and was one of the most successful exponents of tank warfare. The 1940 Campaign in the West, saw his 7th 'Ghost' Panzer Division as one of the spearheads of the German advance. An adventurous leader of German and Italian forces in North Africa, defeating British formations of far greater strength, he often surprised his enemy by his tactics, reacting quickly to events and attaining the initiative even when attacked. The Battle of Gazala was a masterpiece of daring tank warfare, but at Alam Halfa and First Alamein his resources were insufficient to achieve the decisive victory he sought. Defeat at Alamein was due largely to his inferiority in numbers and matériel, but he conducted masterly defensive battles in Tunisia. He strengthened the Atlantic defences, but was unable to persuade Hitler to allow him deploy armored formations forward which he hoped would defeat the Allies on the beaches. Injured by air attack and then implicated in the July Bomb Plot on Hitler's life, he was forced to take his own life.

ERWIN ROMMEL	
Rank attained	Generalfeldmarschall (1942)
Dates	1891–1944
Background	Career soldier; Berlin Military Academy; awarded *Pour le Mérite* in World War I; wrote *Infantry Attacks!* treatise on infantry tactics 1927
Commands	Hitler's personal bodyguard 1933–37; 7th Panzer Division during Campaign in the West; Afrika Korps (later Panzerarmee Afrika) 1941–43; advisory command Italy 1943–44; command of troops on Western Front (France/Belgium) 1944
Campaigns	West 1940; Africa 1941–44; Normandy 1944
Battles	Two successful offensives in the Western Desert 1941–42; Gazala 1942; took Tobruk 1942; Alam Halfa and two Battles of El Alamein 1942; Kasserine Pass 1943; Mareth Line 1943; Tunisia 1943; Normandy 1944

Below: Rommel's Afrika Korps Mk IV tanks pass a knocked-out British Bren Gun Carrier.

Above: General Rommel with the 15th Panzer Division between Tobruk and Sidi Oma, Libya, early 1941.

Below: Field Marshal Rommel with his aides during 1942

back out of Cyrenaica

Western Theater General Events

June 12–14, 1941 German cruiser *Lützow* damaged by British aerial torpedoes

June 17, 1941 Finland begins secretly to mobilize. Allied with Germany, Finland will attack toward Leningrad

July 4, 1941 Tito calls the Yugoslavs to arms against the Germans and Italians

July 5, 1941 Wavell replaced by Auchinleck as Middle East commander

July 7, 1941 US troops replace British garrison in Iceland

July 8, 1941 Wilhelmshaven, first RAF B-17 raid

July 15, 1941 Argentia, Newfoundland, air base established for US flights to Britain

July 22–5, 1941 Aircraft from British carriers *Victorious* and *Furious* raid Petsamo and Kirkenes

July 25/6, 1941 Italian 10th MAS Flotilla attacks Valletta Harbour, Malta, with explosive motor boats and human torpedoes, but is detected in advance and destroyed

August, 1941 British Admiralty forbids raids to capture Enigma codes, fearful that the Germans will realize how far their codes are being penetrated

Aug 2, 1941 US-Soviet Lend-Lease begins. Iran willl become an important route for the supplies to reach Russia

Aug 9–12 Churchill and Roosevelt confer at Placentia Bay, Newfoundland

Aug 11/12, 1941 Mönchengladbach, first RAF use of Gee navigational aid

Aug, 19–29, 1941 Polish troops take over from Australian garrison of Tobruk

Aug 25/6, 1941 Emden, last RAF B-17 operation

Aug 29/30, 1941 Frankfurt, first raid by Australian squadrons in Bomber Command

IRAN

Aug 25, 1941 Iran invaded by British and Soviet forces

Aug 29, 1941 Cease-fire in Iran. British troops have meanwhile secured the Abadan

THE ITALIAN NAVY

The handsome and well-designed ships of the Italian Navy joined the war in June 1940. It had six battleships, two of them very modern ships (later joined by two more), 22 cruisers, 59 large fleet destroyers and 67 small escort destroyers, and 113 submarines. This fleet outnumbered the British Mediterranean Fleet, but it was handicapped by a lack of technical expertise with radar and asdic (sonar), plus the absence of any aircraft carriers.

The four modern battleships of the Vittorio Veneto class compared well with foreign designs. One of them was among the three battleships disabled during the attack on Taranto harbour by Royal Navy Swordfish torpedo bombers during November 1940. Another was sunk by German bombers using radio-guided bombs, after Italy surrendered to the Allies.

Italy lost twelve of its cruisers. The largest single loss was at the Battle of Matapan in

Top: Zara *class cruiser* Fiume.
Center: Navigatori *class destroyer* Da Noli.
Below: Vittorio Veneto *class battleship* Littorio.

March 1941 when three of the four heavy *Zara* class ships (plus two destroyers) were sunk by British warships.

Italy's fleet destroyers were large, well-armed ships and the smaller escort destroyers of the anti-submarine arm were acknowledged as being very efficient. Nevertheless the total losses were high: 70% of the destroyers that entered service were sunk.

Above: *The battleship* Roma *fitting out in 1942, showing her forward triple 15-inch gun turrets.*

oilfields
Sept 17, 1941 Britain and Russia occupy Tehran. The Shah abdicates

Western Theater General Events
Axis logistics supply routes to North Africa are now practically severed by the British
Sept 14–25, 1941 Rommel, now reinforced by 21st Panzer Div and 90th Light Div, raids towards Sidi Barrani
Sept 15, 1941 Atlantic Charter defines Allies' war aims
Sept 18–28, 1941 First transatlantic convoy accompanied by escort carrier, *Audacity*
Sept 21, 1941 First 'Arctic convoy' sails from Hvalfjord, Iceland, with munitions for Russia, arriving Archangel Aug 31 without loss
Sept 26, 1941 British Western Desert Force renamed Eighth Army
Sept 27, 1941 US launches first prefabricated Liberty ship at Baltimore
Sept 29, 1941 Second Arctic convoy, PQ1, leaves Iceland and arrives Archangel Oct 11 without loss
Sept 29 to Oct 1, 1941 Moscow conference discusses aid for USSR
Sept–Dec, 1941 Germans drive Tito's Yugoslav partisans from Serbia to Bosnia
Oct 17, 1941 U-boat torpedoes and damages US destroyer *Kearny*
Oct 21, 1941 British Force K (2 cruisers and 2 destroyers) deployed to Malta
Oct 31, 1941 U-boat torpedoes and sinks US destroyer *Reuben James*
Nov 7/8, 1941 RAF large-scale raids on Berlin, Mannheim and the Ruhr suffer big losses
Nov 13/14, 1941 British carrier *Ark Royal* sunk in Mediterranean by *U-81*
Nov 18/19, 1941 Alexandria raid by Italian frogmen cripples British battleships *Queen Elizabeth* and *Valiant*
Nov, 19, 1941 German auxiliary cruiser *Kormoran* sinks after action with HMAS *Sydney*, which also sinks
Nov 22, 1941 German raider *Atlantis* scut-

FRANKLIN D. ROOSEVELT

One of the greatest of the American presidents, Franklin Delano Roosevelt was elected four times to the office. When Hitler attacked Poland, he tried to make American military aid available to Britain and France as well as taking measures to build up the US armed forces, even though there was strong isolationist opposition to this. After the fall of France the draft for military service was introduced. Roosevelt signed the 'Lend-Lease' bill in March 1941 so that the US could provide aid to Great Britain, Roosevelt seeing the United States as the 'arsenal of democracy'. Four days after the Japanese attacked Pearl Harbor on December 7, 1941, Germany and Italy declared war on the United States. Roosevelt took an active role in choosing the top US military commanders and worked very closely with them on wartime strategy. 'The Declaration of the United Nations,' was made on January 1, 1942, whereby Roosevelt moved to create a grand alliance against the Axis powers: all nations at war with the Axis agreed not to make a separate peace and pledged themselves to what was to become the UN. In early 1944 he was given a full medical examination which found serious heart and circulatory problems. Never truly well, he had contracted poliomyelitis in 1921 and had never regained the full use of his legs. The stress and strain of the war was wearing him out and on April 12, 1945, he suffered a massive stroke, dying within a few hours without regaining consciousness. He was 63 years old. His death came within weeks of the victory in Europe and within months of that over Japan.

Below: Roosevelt seated between Stalin and Churchill at the Yalta Conference in 1945.

ROOSEVELT

Dates	1882–1945
Background	Democratic Party politician
Offices	President of the USA and Commander-in-Chief of the US Armed Forces

Right: President Franklin D. Roosevelt signing the declaration of war against Japan, December 8, 1941.

Below: Roosevelt in conference with General MacArthur, Admiral Leahy and Admiral Nimitz (standing) while on tour in Hawaiian Islands, 1944.

The strategic plan proposed by Admiral Yamamoto, CinC Japanese Combined Fleet, was colored by the British attack on Taranto in November 1940, in which a surprise attack by carrier-borne aircraft had inflicted significant damage on the Italian battle fleet. This Yamamoto proposed to imitate, but on a larger scale, as a fundamental component of what became known as Plan 'Z'. Essentially, Japan had to hit hard and fast, before the Allies could recover:
▶ Seizure of Malaya, Singapore and the Dutch East Indies, source of vital raw materials
▶ Destruction of the US fleet at Pearl Harbor, Hawaii
▶ US forces to be eliminated on the Philippines; the Philippines to be captured later
▶ Seizure of the islands of Wake and Guam to cut US communications
Then consolidation and defense against counterattack.

JAPANESE EXPANSIONISM TO 1941

Following conquests in the Russo-Japanese War and subsequently, and with an alarmingly fast-growing population, Japan becomes increasingly expansionist after World War I.
1931 Mukden Incident leads to Japanese conquest of Manchuria
1937 Marco Polo Bridge incident is pretext for Japanese invasion of China and infamous 'rape of Nanking'. Subsequent campaigns enlarge the Japanese-controlled area of China. USA supplies Chinese leader Chiang Kai-shek via the Burma Road through the southern Himalayas from Burma. American-Japanese relations worsen
1940 Japan proclaims the Greater East Asia Co-prosperity Sphere and signs Tripartite Pact with Germany and Italy
1940 US 'Magic' cryptologists break Japanese diplomatic codes
1940-1 German conquests in Europe weaken the position of the European imperial powers in the Far East. Japan coerces Vichy French to permit Japanese troops to enter Indo-China, from where Japan can interdict the Burma Road
April 13, 1941 Russo-Japanese Non-Aggression Pact following several border incidents and Russian military successes
July 26, 1941 USA freezes Japanese assets in America following unproductive negotiations. Japan plans for war: Phase I, capture the 'Southern Resources Area' (mainly the Dutch East Indies) and defensible perimeter locations around the 'Co-Prosperity Sphere'; Phase 2, consolidate and strengthen the defenses; Phase 3, defend until the USA is weary of war. Negotiations continue, but Japan is already working to a timetable for military operations
Oct 18, 1941 Tojo becomes Prime Minister of Japan, replacing the relatively moderate Prince Konoye

1941 COUNTDOWN TO WAR
▶**Dec 2** US 'Magic' intercepts read Japanese orders to destroy codes at the Japanese Embassy in Washington
▶ **Dec 4** Japanese Embassy begins leaving Washington
▶ **Dec 6** Roosevelt pleads with the Emperor of Japan to draw back from war
▶ **Dec 7** The Japanese declaration of war reaches Washington after news of Pearl Harbor
▶ **Dec 8** President Roosevelt asks Congress to declare war on Japan. He describes Dec 7 as 'a day which will live in infamy'

TOJO

Dates	1884–1948
Background	Professional soldier
Offices	Prime Minister; Minister of War; Home Minister; Foreign Minister; Commander-in-Chief of the General Staff.

Hideki Tojo held extreme right-wing views and was a supporter of Nazi Germany. He became Prime Minister of Japan in October 1941. After failing to reach agreement with the USA, he ordered the attack on Pearl Harbor on December 7, 1941. The war went went well for Japan for the first six months. Later, however, Tojo realised that Japan would not win the war, and he resigned from office when Saipan was lost in July 1944. He attempted suicide by shooting himself in the chest in order to avoid arrest by the US military in 1945. He survived and was tried as a war criminal. Hideki Tojo was executed for war crimes on December 23, 1948.

HIROHITO

Dates	1901–1989
Background	Grandson of the great reforming
Offices	Emperor from 1926

The Japanese Emperor Hirohito reluctantly supported the war against China and the invasion of Manchuria in 1937 and approved the attack on Pearl Harbor. With the loss of Okinawa in 1945, Hirohito wanted to seek a negotiated settlement with the Allies. His government refused. After the destruction of Hiroshima and Nagasaki Hirohito called a meeting of the Japanese Supreme Council. They wanted to continue the fight but Hirohito intervened. The people of Japan heard the Emperor's voice for the first time on August 15 when he announced Japan's unconditional surrender and the end of the war. Many wanted him to be tried as a war criminal but the head of the occupation forces General MacArthur, refused, believing that Japan would be easier to rule if Hirohito remained.

Above: The Japanese Emperor Hirohito.

tles during encounter with British cruiser *Devonshire* after 622-day cruise

Nov 25, 1941 British battleship *Barham* sunk in Mediterranean by *U-331*

Dec 2, 1941 Hitler's Directive to dominate the central Mediterranean. Kesselring is reinforced by Fliegerkorps II from the Russian Front

Dec 11, 1941 Germany and Italy declare war on USA

Dec 12, 1941 Vichy French ships in USA requisitioned by USA

Dec 17, 1941 First Battle of Sirte between Italians and British is indecisive

Dec 22, 1941 to Jan 13, 1942 Allied 'Arcadia' Conference, Washington

Dec 27, 1941 British Commandos raid Vaagso, Norway

FAR EASTERN THEATER: THE COUNTDOWN TO WAR

Nov 27, 1941 US Chief of Naval Operations Admiral Stark sends 'war warning' message to US commanders in Hawaii and Philippines

Nov 28, 1941 US carrier *Enterprise* sails for Wake Island to ferry aircraft there

Nov 30, 1941 Japanese reject US proposals for the solution of the Far East crisis

Dec 2, 1941 US 'Magic' intercepts read Japanese orders to destroy codes at the Japanese Embassy in Washington

Dec 4, 1941 Japanese Embassy begins leaving Washington

Dec 4, 1941 *Enterprise* delivers aircraft to Wake Island then sets course to return to Pearl Harbor

Dec 5, 1941 US carrier *Lexington* sails for Midway atoll to ferry aircraft there

Dec 6, 1941 Roosevelt pleads with the Emperor of Japan to draw back from war

PEARL HARBOR

Nov 5 Japanese Admiral Yamamoto issues Top Secret Order No. 1, setting out the plan for the Pearl Harbor attack to the Combined Fleet

PEARL HARBOR

As US–Japanese negotiations continued into November 1941, the Japanese Navy prepared for the surprise attack and, the day before Japan rejected US proposals to defuse the crisis, the striking fleet set sail from its anchorage in the Kurile Islands, north of the Japanese mainland. On December 2, Admiral Nagumo received the go-ahead from Tokyo and five days later launched one of the most infamous and successful surprise attacks in history. In two waves, torpedo-bombers, dive-bombers and high-altitude bombers struck at airfields and warships in the Hawaiian islands, destroying most US aircraft on the ground.

Japanese casualties were light – less than 100 – against those of the Americans: 2,403 dead, 1,178 wounded, and 169 US aircraft were destroyed for the loss of 29 of the attackers. Four Japanese midget submarines were lost. Most disastrous for the US was the damage inflicted on the fleet. All the battleships were hit. *Oklahoma* capsized; *West Virginia* was half-sunk; *Arizona* was half-sunk, the explosion of her forward magazine causing heavy

Left: The USS Arizona burning and sinking after the attack by the Japanese carriers on Pearl Harbor.

Below: USS Shaw exploding during the Japanese raid.

casualties; *California* was sunk at her berth; *Nevada*, with six bomb hits and one torpedo strike, managed to get under way and was beached.

The Japanese victory was flawed, however. As the Japanese themselves were demonstrating, air power now outweighed big guns at sea, and the three US carriers were not at Pearl Harbor – *Enterprise* and *Lexington* were ferrying aircraft to the forward islands, *Saratoga* was about to depart San Diego. (*Enterprise* was in fact nearing Oahu as the Japanese attack went in.) The damage to the US battlefleet gave Japan time, as planned; the failure to eliminate the carriers would be decisive in the battles to come.

Nov 26 Japanese strike force leaves Hitokappu Bay in the Kurile Islands, beginning the 3,400-mile voyage to Hawaii
Dec 2 Nagumo receives confirmation orders for the Pearl Harbor attack
Dec 3 The Japanese fleet makes rendezvous with supply ships and refuels
Dec 7 Pearl Harbor attacked by 363 aircraft in two waves, striking airfields and warships. Japanese midget submarines make a simultaneous attack but to little effect. Practically all US aircraft on the ground are destroyed. US warships sent to the bottom include 5 battleships and 2 cruisers

Far Eastern Theater General Events
Dec 7, 1941 The Japanese declaration of war reaches Washington after news of Pearl Harbor
Dec 8, 1941 President Roosevelt asks Congress to declare war on Japan. He describes Dec 7 as 'a day which will live in infamy'
Dec 8, 1941 Japanese bombard Midway island
Dec 8, 1941 Japanese 25th Army lands in northern Malaya at Kota Bharu and in southern Thailand at Singora and Patani
Dec 8, 1941 British battleship *Prince of Wales* and battlecruiser *Repulse* (Force Z) sail from Singapore to intercept Japanese invasion of Malaya
Dec 8, 1941 Japanese bomb Hong Kong and Singapore
Dec 9, 1941 Japanese take two islands in the Gilberts: Tarawa and Makin
Dec 8–9, 1941 Japanese bomb British airfields in northern Malaya, destroying many aircraft on the ground
Dec 9, 1941 Japanese Fifteenth Army enters Bangkok
Dec 10, 1941 Japanese take Guam
Dec 10, 1941 *Prince of Wales* and *Repulse* sunk by land-based Japanese aircraft
Dec 11, 1941 Japanese invasion of Wake Island repulsed
Dec 13, 1941 US relief force for Wake

PEARL HARBOR

Left: *The smoke rising from Hickam Field.*

Below: *A Japanese photo-graph taken during the attack on Pearl Harbor, December 7, 1941. In the distance, the smoke rises from Hickam Field.*

Right: USS Arizona *burning after the Japanese attack.*

Centre right: USS West Virginia *aflame.*

Bottom right: *Wrecked USS* Downes *at left and* USS Cassin *at right. In the rear is* USS Pennsylvania, *33,100-ton flagship of the Pacific Fleet, which suffered only light damage.*

MALAYA AND SINGAPORE

As tensions in the Far East mounted, two British capital ships, the battleship *Prince of Wales* and the battlecruiser *Repulse*, had been despatched to Singapore, their presence intended to deter the Japanese. But aircraft were in woefully short supply and when the two ships, as Force 'Z', put to sea in search of the Japanese invasion fleet, they did so with inadequate air cover. Attacked by Japanese aircraft, they were rapidly sent to the bottom, the first great shock of the campaign.

On December 8 the Japanese 25th Army began making landings on the north-east coast of Malaya and on the Kra Isthmus in the south of Thailand. Following the defense plan drawn up by General Percival before the war, British Imperial troops advanced into Thailand to deny the Japanese the use of airfields there (Operation 'Matador') but were rapidly thrown back. Then, in a campaign notable for the poor generalship of the defenders, characterized by a lack of initiative and adaptability, the Japanese advanced down the Malayan peninsula, outflanking and infiltrating British defensive positions one by one. The jungle that had been deemed impenetrable by the British presented little problem to the Japanese, whose fighting capabilities had been seriously underestimated. By the end of January General Yamashita's 35,000 troops were facing Singapore Island, where Percival had four divisions. On February 8 and 9 the Japanese crossed and quickly pushed toward the city. A determined counter-attack with the superior numbers at Percival's command could have repulsed the Japanese, now at the end of overstretched lines of com-

munication. Instead, on 15th, General Percival surrendered – one of the most shameful episodes in British military history. Singapore had been seen as the bastion of the British Empire in the Far East and an impregnable fortress. Its loss sent a shock wave throughout the world.

Above: *One of Singapore's 15-inch coastal defence guns elevated for firing, 8 December 1941.*

Below: *The battlecruiser HMS* Repulse, *which was sunk with the battleship HMS* Prince of Wales, *on 10 December 1941.*

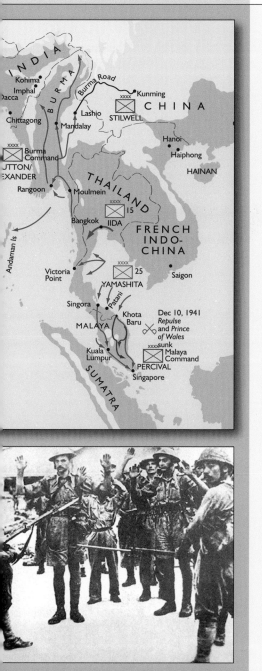

Map labels:
INDIA · BURMA · CHINA · THAILAND · FRENCH INDO-CHINA · MALAYA · SUMATRA

Kohima · Imphal · Dacca · Chittagong · Burma Road · Kunming · Lashio · Mandalay · STILWELL · Hanoi · Haiphong · HAINAN · Burma Command · JTTON/ EXANDER · Rangoon · Moulmein · Bangkok · IIDA · 15 · Victoria Point · YAMASHITA · Patani · Saigon · 25 · Singora · Khota Baru · Kuala Lumpur · PERCIVAL · Singapore · Andaman Is

Dec 10, 1941 *Repulse* and *Prince of Wales* sunk

sunk Malaya Command

Above: British troops of the Suffolk Regiment surrender to Japanese infantry at Singapore.

under Admiral Fletcher sets sail from Pearl Harbor but will not arrive in time. Wake falls on 23rd

Dec 15, 1941 Japanese enter Thailand in the southern Kra Isthmus

Dec 16, 1941 British forces destroy the airfield and oilfield respectively before the Japanese land at Kuching, Sarawak, and Seria, Brunei

Dec 23, 1941 Japanese bomb Rangoon

Dec 28, 1941 General Wavell, late of British Middle East Command, becomes commander of British forces in the Far East

Dec 31, 1941 Admiral Nimitz becomes commander of the US Asiatic Fleet

HONG KONG

Dec 11, 1941 British garrison of Hong Kong withdraws to the island

Dec 18, 1941 Japanese cross to Hong Kong Island

Dec 25, 1941 Japanese take Hong Kong

MALAYA AND THE FALL OF SINGAPORE

Dec 17, 1941 British fall back on Ipoh pursued closely by the Japanese

Jan 11, 1942 Outflanking each British defense position, and making amphibious landings down the west coast, the Japanese enter Kuala Lumpur

Jan 15, 1942 Johore defense line is breached by the Japanese

Jan 22–4, 1942 Indian, British and Australian reinforcements reach Singapore

Jan 31, 1942 British forces complete withdrawal from Malaya to Singapore Island

Feb 8/9, 1942 Two Japanese divisions land on Singapore's west coast

Feb 13, 1942 Last ships leave Singapore; next day they are devastated by a Japanese air attack

Feb 15, 1942 Singapore surrenders

PHILIPPINES: The Japanese Conquest

Dec 8, 1941 Japanese surprise bombing of US Clark Field and other airfields near

THE JAPANESE CARRIER STRIKE FORCE

The Japanese aircraft carrier force conducted the spectacularly successful raid on Pearl Harbor on December 7, 1941. All eight battleships of the US Pacific Fleet were either sunk or badly damaged, plus two cruisers and two destroyers. The raid was inspired by the British Fleet Air Arm's attack on the Italian Fleet at Taranto on November 11, 1940.

The Imperial Japanese Navy carriers were the spearhead of a dramatic series of naval victories during the first six months of the Pacific war, but at the Battle of the Coral Sea they lost their first carrier. Then, one month later, the loss of four carriers at the Battle of Midway on June 4, 1942, was a real disaster, compounded by the loss of so many irreplaceable Japanese aircrew. There then followed a series of defeats and losses. Then, at the Battle of the Philippine Sea on June 19–20, 1944, Japan

Kaga	
Displacement	30,000 tons
Crew	1,340
Armament	60 aircraft
Engine	Four turbines, 91,000hp, max. speed 27.5 knots
Dimensions	Length: 782ft 6in Beam: 100ft 0in

The aircraft carrier Kaga.

received another body blow, the loss of another three carriers. Japanese carrier-borne air power was now practically non-existent. The final humiliation came at the Battle of Cape Engaño, on October 25, 1944, where the remaining carriers were used only as decoys because of their lack of trained aircrew; four more carriers were lost. Japan completed 22 aircraft carriers during the war, losing 19. One of the main Japanese failings was that they did not have an aircrew training system capable of keeping up with losses. The US Navy did, and provided for expansion.

Ryujo	
Displacement	8,000 tons
Crew	600
Armament	48 aircraft
Engine	Two turbines, 65,000hp, max. speed 29 knots
Dimensions	Length: 590ft 3in Beam: 75ft 6in

The Japanese carrier Ryujo.

Shokaku class	
Displacement	32,000 tons
Crew	1,660
Armament	84 aircraft
Engine	Four turbines, 160,000hp, max. speed 34 knots
Dimensions	Length: 844ft 10in Beam: 95ft 1in

Below: A Shokaku *class carrier.*

Above: Carrier Ryujo. Below: Japanese carrier planes prepare to take off for the Pearl Harbor attack.

YAMAMOTO

Rank attained	Admiral
Dates	1884–1943
Background	Career sailor, Etajima naval academy
Commands	C-in-C of the Combined Fleet, 1939–43

Admiral Isoroku Yamamoto was responsible for the enlargement of the Japanese Navy before the war. He was wounded in action during the Russo-Japanese War of 1904–5. He later studied in the USA and was fully aware of US industrial might. He opposed the war against the USA because he thought that Japan would eventually lose, but he planned the Pearl Harbor attack as he reasoned that a pre-emptive strike was Japan's only option. Yamamoto then tried to wipe out the US carriers at the Battle of Midway but ended up being heavily defeated. On 18 April 1943 US fighters intercepted the aircraft in which he was a passenger, shot it down and killed him. Well regarded, Yamamoto was an early proponent of naval air power and

Nagumo

Yamamoto

Kurita

NAGUMO

Rank attained	Vice-Admiral
Dates	1887–1944
Background	Career sailor
Commands	C-in-C of the Combined Fleet's Carrier Strike Force, 1941–44

understood the influence it would have on naval warfare.

Vice-Admiral Chuichi Nagumo was in command of the élite First Carrier Strike Force (Kido Butai) that attacked Pearl Harbor. Not being an aviation specialist, he was overcautious and decided not to make a third attack which could have proved decisive. Again he proved to be hesitant during the Battle of Midway, paying the price by losing four aircraft carriers. He lost two more sea battles, at the Eastern Solomons and in the Santa Cruz Islands. He was then relieved of his command. Organising the defence of Saipan, when all was

KURITA

Rank attained	Vice-Admiral
Dates	1889–1977
Background	Career sailor
Commands	C-in-C 7th Cruiser Squadron, 1941; Close Support Force, 1942; First Striking Force, 1944

lost to the Americans, he committed suicide.

Vice-Admiral Takeo Kurita spent a large proportion of his naval career afloat. He commanded the Cruiser Squadron covering the invasion fleet that invaded Malaya and then the Dutch East Indies. He was at the battles of Midway and Leyte Gulf. At Leyte he led the First Strike Force, consisting of battleships, cruisers and destroyers. These vessels inflicted the most damage on the US ships, sinking an escort carrier and three destroyers. However, when things were getting desperate for the Americans, Kurita pulled back, his warships short of fuel.

Manila eliminates US Far East Air Force

Dec 9, 1941 Japanese bomb and destroy Cavite Navy Yard in Manila bay

Dec 10, 1941 Japanese land on the north coast of Luzon

Dec 12, 1941 Japanese land on the south coast of Luzon

Dec 22, 1941 Japanese make large-scale landings in Lingayen Gulf and begin to advance south toward Manila

Dec 24, 1941 Japanese land on east coast of Luzon at Lamon Bay and advance north-west on Manila

Dec 26, 1941 Manila is declared an open city as US/Filipino forces withdraw to the Bataan Peninsula

Jan 2, 1942 Japanese enter Manila

Jan 5, 1942 US withdrawal to Bataan completed

Jan 9, 1942 Japanese begin attacking the 15-mile wide Bataan defense line

Jan 22, 1942 As the Japanese advance through the defenses based on Mounts Santa Rosa and Natib, MacArthur begins withdrawal to the final line, Bagac–Orion

March 11, 1942 Under orders from President Roosevelt, MacArthur leaves the Philippines for Australia to take up command of all Allied forces in the Pacific

March 24, 1942 Japanese intensify bombing of Allied forces in Bataan and on the island of Corregidor

April 3, 1942 Japanese begin all-out attack on the Allied perimeter

April 9, 1942 Allied forces in Bataan – 78,000 men – surrender

May 5, 1942 Japanese land on Corregidor

May 7, 1942 General Wainwright surrenders the 15,000 Allied troops on Corregidor

May 10, 1942 Surrender of the remaining Allied forces in the Philippines

DUTCH EAST INDIES

Jan 11, 1942 Japanese landings on north of Celebes

Jan 25, 1942 Japanese landings at Lae on

Above: *Eighth Army Matilda tanks advance across the desert.*

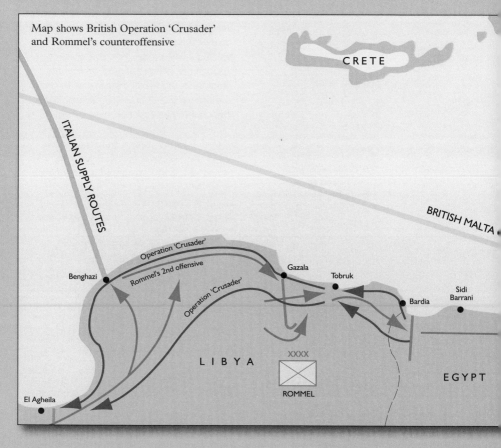

Map shows British Operation 'Crusader' and Rommel's counteroffensive

CRETE

ITALIAN SUPPLY ROUTES

BRITISH MALTA

Operation 'Crusader'

Rommel's 2nd offensive

Operation 'Crusader'

Benghazi

Gazala

Tobruk

Sidi Barrani

Bardia

LIBYA

XXXX

ROMMEL

EGYPT

El Agheila

Above: General Auchinleck, C-in-C Middle East with Lieutenant-General Ritchie.

Rommel's Second Offensive, January– February, 1942

Reinforced with more tanks, and with shorter lines of supply, Rommel struck back sooner than expected, on January 21, catching the dispersed British off balance and capturing much matériel as he advanced. By the end of January he had retaken Benghazi, but was now overstretched and forced to pause before the British Gazala Line, west of Tobruk.

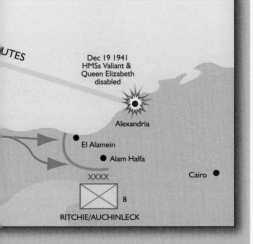

New Guinea
Jan 30, 1942 Japanese take Amboina on Ceram
Feb 14, 1942 Japanese airborne landings on Sumatra at Palembang
Feb 15, 1942 Japanese airborne landings on Sumatra at Muntok
Feb, 19, 1942 Japanese land on Timor
March 9, 1942 Dutch East Indies surrenders

Far Eastern Theater General Events
Jan 4, 1942 Japanese begin bombing Rabaul in the Bismarck Archipelago
Jan 7, 1942 Japanese secure Sarawak
Jan 11, 1942 Japanese landings on north-east coast of Borneo
Jan, 19, 1942 Japanese secure north Borneo
Jan 21, 1942 Japanese begin bombing New Guinea
Jan 23, 1942 Japanese landings at Rabaul and New Ireland
Jan 24, 1942 Japanese landings on east coast of Borneo at Balikpapan
Jan 24, 1942 Battle of the Macassar Strait. US destroyers and submarines attack Japanese invasion force bound for Borneo

NORTH AFRICA: Rommel's Second Offensive
Jan 17, 1942 Bardia surrenders to Eighth Army
Jan 21, 1942 Rommel, reinforced with 45 new tanks, attacks
Jan 22, 1942 Germans take Agedabia
Jan 22, 1942 DAK becomes Panzerarmee Afrika
Jan 29, 1942 Rommel takes Benghazi
Feb 4, 1942 Rommel halts west of Tobruk at the British Gazala Line

Western Theater General Events
January, 1942 There are 262 air raids on Malta
January to March German drive against Tito's Yugoslav partisans in Bosnia is joined by rival Cetnik partisans
Jan 13, 1942 U-boats deployed against US

One of the most important developments of the war was radar (radio detection and ranging), which uses radio waves to detect the presence of distant objects. From 1934 it had been developed by most of the world's powers and was immediately seen as a way of detecting aircraft and providing early warning of an air attack. It proved particularly useful during the Battle of Britain in 1940, the British having established, pre-war, a chain of radar stations known as Chain Home, and indeed was critical in winning that battle for the British. As the war progressed radar was increasingly fitted to ships and aircraft, proving very important during the Battle of the Atlantic. During the Allied combined bombing campaign of Germany, countermeasures had to be taken by the Allies to disrupt and confuse the German radar. One method was to drop large amounts of thin strips of tin foil ('Window'), which reflected the radar beams, saturating the German radar stations with huge numbers of false targets.

Radio navigation systems were used by both sides to assist bombers in locating targets. An early German system named 'Knickebein' utilized two transmitting stations: the bomber crews flew along the steady 'note lane' from the first radio transmitter, releasing their bombs when they passed through the steady 'note lane' from a second transmitter as it crossed the first. The British used similar systems employing ground stations, such as Gee and Oboe, and the US Shoran.

The Enigma cipher machine was used by the Germans to encode their military signals, each German military unit needing a machine to encipher and decipher coded messages. It was an electro-mechanical device relying on a series of rotating wheels to scramble messages into incoherent ciphertext. Both the transmitting and receiving Enigmas were set to the same code: if you knew how the rotors were set you got the message – if not, just a stream of indecipherable and random letters. The machine could be set to many millions of combinations, each one generating a completely different ciphertext message. In 1940 British codebreakers stationed at Bletchley Park managed to crack the Enigma code resulting in the 'Ultra' codebreakers. By the summer of 1944 they were using the world's first electronic computer to speed the process.

Above: *A German Enigma coding machine.*

Below: *A German Ju 88 nightfighter showing the radar antennae on its nose.*

Above: *The Chain Home radar towers provided radar coverage around the east and south coasts of England. (See page 43.)*

Below: *The Bruneval Raid was a successful British Combined Operations airborne landing to capture components of a German Würzburg radar set at Bruneval, France, on 27/28 February, 1942. British scientists needed to find out more about Würzburg radar so that they could come up with countermeasures in their ongoing 'battle of the beams' with German scientists.*

GERMAN WARSHIPS

In December 1939 the 'pocket battleship' *Admiral Graf Spee* was scuttled after the famous Battle of the River Plate action with British cruisers. Along with her two sister ships, *Lützow* (ex *Deutschland*) and *Admiral Scheer*, she made up a revolutionary class of small battleships. Ideal for long-range commerce raiding, they sank or captured some 30 Allied merchant ships.

The *Scharnhorst* and *Gneisenau* were superbly equipped battlecruisers. They were fast, well armed and well armored. Between them they sank a British aircraft carrier, two destroyers, an armed merchant cruiser and 22 Allied merchant ships.

The *Scharnhorst* was eventually brought to bay and sunk by Royal Navy warships at the Battle of the North Cape in December 1943.

The mighty sisters *Bismarck* and *Tirpitz* were the most formidable German battleships of World War II. After the *Bismarck* had sunk HMS *Hood*, the pride of the British Fleet, she was hunted down and then pounded into submission by British battleships' guns and sunk

Top: *The 'Pocket battleship'* Admiral Scheer.
Center: *The light cruiser* Nürnberg.
Below: *The battlecruiser* Gneisenau.

in the Atlantic in May 1941. *Tirpitz* was targeted and sunk by RAF Lancaster bombers using 5.5-ton 'Tallboy' high-penetration bombs.

Two heavy cruisers took part in the battle for Norway in 1940, the *Admiral Hipper* and the *Blücher*, where *Blücher* was sunk. *Prinz Eugen* accompanied *Bismarck* on her fateful sortie and survived. The *Admiral Hipper* had a successful career during the course of which she was responsible for sinking two British destroyers, a corvette, a minesweeper and eight merchant ships.

The light cruisers served the Kriegsmarine with mixed success but they did provide useful support in many operations. Two were lost during the Norwegian campaign, the *Königsberg* to Royal Navy Skua dive bombers and the *Karlsruhe* to the British submarine HMS *Truant*. The *Köln* was sunk by US bombers two months before the war ended.

Also during the Norwegian campaign, at the battles for Narvik, the Kriegsmarine lost ten destroyers to warships of the Royal Navy.

Above: *A flotilla of German destroyers in line ahead.*

coastal shipping

Jan 14, 1942 German battleship *Tirpitz* arrives Trondheim, Norway, to threaten Allied Arctic convoys to Russia

Jan 20, 1942 Wannsee conference. Heydrich plans the 'Final Solution', the extermination of the Jews

Jan 26, 1942 First contingent of US troops arrive in Britain

Jan 29/30, 1942 Unsuccessful RAF raid on *Tirpitz*

February, 1942 There are 236 air raids on Malta

February to March, 1942 Rommel pleads with Hitler for reinforcements, believing he can reach the Suez Canal. Meanwhile Churchill urges Auchinleck to launch a counterattack

Feb 1, 1942 U-boats move to a new code, foxing Allied codebreakers for a year

Feb 10, 1942 Pacific War Council established

Feb 11–13, 1942 The 'Channel Dash'. German raiders *Scharnhorst*, *Gneisenau* and *Prinz Eugen* return to German ports from Brest to avoid constant bombing by the RAF. They audaciously transit the English Channel sustaining hardly any damage

Feb 23, 1942 'Bomber' Harris takes charge of RAF Bomber Command

Feb 23, 1942 German cruiser *Prinz Eugen* damaged by torpedo from British submarine *Trident*

Feb 26/7, 1942 German battlecruiser *Gneisenau* seriously damaged by RAF bombing in Kiel

Feb 27/8, 1942 British raid captures Würzburg radar at Bruneval, France

BURMA: The Allied Retreat

Jan 15, 1942 Japanese advance up the Kra Isthmus

Jan 20, 1942 Japanese General Iida's Fifteenth Army invades Burma from central Thailand

Feb 23, 1942 Retreating across the Sittang River, a bridge is blown prematurely, trapping part of the 17th Indian Division

THE JAPANESE ARMY

The Japanese soldier could be fanatical in combat, being instilled with the samurai code of *Bushido* and absolute loyalty to the Japanese Emperor. Death before surrender was the accepted norm.

In 1941 the Japanese Army had 51 divisions and numbered 1,700,000 men. It was mostly stationed in China and Manchuria. The Japanese had occupied Manchuria in 1931 and then attacked China in 1937. In China they were engaged by both the Nationalist Chinese forces and the Communists. At the beginning of 1942 the various Japanese Armies began to go on the offensive in the Pacific, conquering Hong Kong, the Philippines, Thailand, Burma, the Dutch East Indies and Malaya. The Japanese Army performed superbly in the early stages of the Pacific conflict and had gained control over a huge geographical area that extended from the borders of India in the west to New Guinea in the south, all within six months.

The turning point in the Pacific War came in the summer of 1942 as the US went on the offensive. As the war progressed, the Japanese Army suffered heavily in losses of matériel, territory and men. But every piece of territory that they defended exacted a price paid on both sides, and it was always high in the terms of the lives of the soldiers fighting. Notable among the battles were those for Iwo Jima and Okinawa.

Below: Japanese troops in the field.

By 1945 there were 5.5 million men in the Japanese Army. If the two atomic bombs had not been dropped and if the Japanese government had not surrendered, the Allies would have had to invade the Japanese home islands, possibly in November 1945. The dedication shown by the Japanese soldier in defense of lands other than his own would have been as nothing compared to the ferocity he would have undoubtedly have shown in the defense of his homeland.

Below: Banzai!

Above: Heavily laden Japanese infantrymen.

Below: Type 89 medium tank. Japanese tank design was inferior to those of the other main protagonists of the war.

March 7, 1942 British evacuate Rangoon

March 12, 1942 US General Stilwell leads Chinese Fifth and Sixth Armies down the Burma Road to hold the left flank against the Japanese

March 8, 1942 Japanese enter Rangoon

March 13–20, 1942 General Alexander, now in command of British forces in Burma, establishes a defensive frontline from Prome to Toungoo

March 24, 1942 Japanese attack the Chinese at Toungoo

March 29, 1942 The Chinese, almost encircled by the Japanese at Toungoo, escape north

March 30, 1942 Chinese retreat from Toungoo, exposing Burcorps' left flank which withdraws north from the Prome area

March 30/1, 1942 Japanese attack Prome

April 2, 1942 British retreat from Prome

April 12, 1942 Japanese take Myanaung, turning Burcorps' right flank

April 15, 1942 British begin destruction of Ynangyaung oilwells and pull back north

April 18, 1942 Japanese attack Chinese and overwhelm them

April 29, 1942 Japanese take Lashio, cutting communications between Mandalay and China

May 1, 1942 Japanese take Mandalay and Monywa, the latter development threatening the Burcorps' retreat

May 4, 1942 British evacuate Akyab on the coast

May 8, 1942 Japanese take Myitkyina in north of Burma

May 11, 1942 Slim fights rearguard action at Kalewa

May 15, 1942 Stilwell enters Assam

May 20, 1942 Burcorps crosses into India

Far Eastern Theater General Events

Feb 19, 1942 Japanese bomb Darwin, north Australia

Feb 19, 1942 Battle of Lumbok Strait. Japanese invasion fleet for Bali repulses

Japanese Navy aircraft bore the brunt of the air fighting of the Pacific Campaign and among them were some excellent designs. In particular, the 'Zero' fighter outclassed all the Allied fighters facing it in terms of range, agility and speed during 1941/42. Dive- and torpedo-bombers were similarly well advanced at that stage of the war. These aircraft were blessed with a particularly long range, as was necessary when flying over the Pacific Ocean, but at the expense of protection for fuel tanks and sufficient armour, in order to save weight.

The Imperial Japanese Army Air Force was also equipped with some good aircraft. Notable fighters were the Kawasaki Hien 'Tony' and the Nakajima Hayate 'Frank'. The latter was the JAAF's finest fighter of the Pacific War. Entering service in August 1944, and though fighting against overwhelming odds, it acquitted itself very well.

Japanese bombers were all good, long-range aircraft but had limited bomb-carrying capacity and because they lacked protection were vulnerable to the Allied fighters' fire power. Japan even had its own rocket-powered fighter based on the German Me 163, but it never entered service before the war ended.

The Yokosuka MXY-7 'Ohka' (Cherry Blossom) was a purpose-built, rocket powered kamikaze aircraft employed by Japan towards the end of World War II. The United States gave the aircraft the name *Baka* (Japanese for 'idiot'). It was a manned cruise missile that was carried underneath a bomber to within range of its target; on release, the pilot would first glide toward the target and when close enough he would fire the Ohka's rocket engine and guide the missile towards the ship that he intended to sink. They did not prove to be successful in combat as most of the aircraft carrying them were shot down before reaching the launch point.

'Kate' level/torpedo bomber

Nakajima B5N 'Kate'	
Weight	9,000lb
Crew	Three
Armament	One 7.7mm machine-gun and 1,764lb bomb-load/torpedo
Range	1,200 miles
Engine	Nakajima, 1,000hp, max. speed 235mph
Dimensions	Length: 33ft 9in. Wing span: 50ft 11in Height: 12ft 1in
Production	1,149

Mitsubishi G4M 'Betty'	
Weight	27,500lb
Crew	Seven
Armament	One 20mm cannon and four 7.7mm machine-guns, 2,200lb bomb-load
Range	3,700 miles (max.)
Engine	2 Mitsubishi, 1,800hp, max. speed 272mph
Dimensions	Length: 65ft 7in. Wing span: 82ft 0in Height: 19ft 8in
Production	2,446 (all marks)

Below: Mitsubishi G4M 'Betty' bomber.

'Zero' fighter

Mitsubishi A6M 'Zero'	
Weight	6,000lb
Crew	One
Armament	Two 20mm cannon and two 7.7mm machine-guns
Range	1,200 miles
Engine	Nakajima, 1,130hp, max. speed 350mph
Dimensions	Length: 29ft 11in. Wing span: 39ft 4in Height: 11ft 6in
Production	11,283 (all marks)

Yokosuka 'Ohka' Model 11	
Weight	4.720lb
Crew	One
Armament	2,650lb warhead
Range	35 miles
Engine	Three rocket motors, max. speed 390mph
Dimensions	Length: 20ft 0in. Wing span: 16ft 8in Height: 3ft 11in
Production	750

Yokosuka 'Ohka'

Allied squadron

Feb 27, 1942 Battle of the Java Sea. Allied squadron intercepting Japanese invasion of Java destroyed

March 1, 1942 Battle of the Sunda Strait. Surviving Allied ships attempting escape to Australia intercepted by Japanese force who sink 2 cruisers and 4 destroyers

Late February–March 1942 Chennault's American volunteers, the 'Flying Tigers', fight defensive air battles over Rangoon

March 1942 US Tenth Air Force deploys to India

March 8, 1942 Japanese land at Salamaua and Lae in New Guinea

March 10, 1942 Japanese bomb Port Moresby, Papua

March 10, 1942 Salamau and Lae bombed by aircraft from US carriers *Lexington* and *Yorktown*

March 10, 1942 Japanese land at Finschhafen in New Guinea

March 12, 1942 US forces occupy New Caledonia

March 19, 1942 General Slim takes command of I Burma Corps (effectively field command of all British and Indian troops in Burma)

March 21, 1942 Major Japanese air raid destroys most remaining Allied aircraft on the ground at Magwe

March 22, 1942 Japanese bomb Darwin

March 23, 1942 Japanese bomb Port Moresby

March 27, 1942 Admiral King replaces Admiral Stark and becomes CinC US Fleet and Chief of Naval Operations

March 30, 1942 Allied Command Pacific reorganized: South-West Pacific Command: General MacArthur, Pacific Ocean Zone: Admiral Nimitz

March 30, 1942 Pacific War Council established in Washington to plan strategy in the theater. Nations involved are the USA, Britain, Canada, Australia, New Zealand, The Netherlands and China

March 30, 1942 Japanese occupy

ROYAL NAVY SHIPS

A total of 86 cruisers saw service with the Royal Navy during the course of hostilities, and during the six years 27 were lost and 29 new ships completed. They were heavily engaged in all the major fleet actions involving the RN, and also hunted down commerce raiders and undertook convoy escort and protection. Typical were the Town class. They were well balanced, well armed and good fighting ships.

Nearly 380 destroyers saw British service, including the 50 old US destroyers handed over to the British as part of 'Lend–Lease'. Over 100 ships were lost. The destroyers were the RN's workhorses, accounting for scores of U-boats and enemy aircraft as well as some major enemy warships. They were ships called upon for escorting and fighting through even the smallest and hard-pressed of convoys, as well as escorting the most prestigious capital ships.

Right: *The Tribal class destroyer HMS Maori.*

Tribal Class Destroyers

Displacement	2,000 tons
Crew	190
Armament	8 x 4.7in guns, 4 x 21in torpedo tubes
Engine	Two turbines, 44,000hp, max. speed 36 knots
Dimensions	Length: 377ft 6in Beam 36ft 6in

Town Class Cruisers

Displacement	11,000tons
Crew	850
Armament	12 x 6in, 8 x 4in guns
Armor	Max: 114mm. Min: 25mm
Engine	Four turbines 75,000hp max. speed 32 knots
Dimensions	Length: 591ft 6in Beam 61ft 8in

Flower Class Corvettes

Displacement	925 tons
Crew	85
Armament	1 x 4in & 1 x 2pdr AA guns plus depth charges
Engine	Four cylinder 2,750hp engine, max. speed 16 knots
Dimensions	Length: 190ft 0in Beam 33ft 0in

Flower class corvette

Below: *The Town class cruiser HMS Gloucester.*

But the RN's unsung heroes of the war were the slow sloops, frigates and corvettes, which numbered well over a thousand. They performed the grueling and tedious duty of ocean as well as coastal convoy escort and often more efficiently than the more glamorous destroyer.

Above: A 0.5 inch machine-gun quadruple anti-aircraft mount.

Above: The fo'c'sle and open bridge of the cruiser HMS Sheffield.

Christmas Island
April 3, 1942 Japanese bomb Mandalay
April 6, 1942 Japanese land on Manus in the Bismarck Archipelago
April 18, 1942 Doolittle raid on Tokyo: 16 B-25s from carrier *Hornet* with escorts from *Enterprise* make symbolic strike on the Japanese homeland
April 22, 1942 Japanese First Air Fleet returns to Japan

Western Theater General Events
March, 1942 Allied Arctic convoys begin to come under heavy German attack
March, 1942 British aircraft reinforcements deployed to Malta in face of Axis interdiction
March 3/4, 1942 Billancourt Renault factory, precision raid
March 3/4, 1942 Minelaying mission marks first RAF use of Lancasters
March 6, 1942 German battleship *Tirpitz* sorties without success against Allied Arctic convoy PQ12, which is the last to reach Russia intact
March 10/11, 1942 Essen, first use of Lancasters for bombing
March 22, 1942 2nd Battle of Sirte Gulf. Italian warships intercept Alexandria–Malta convoy but are repulsed
March 27, 1942 *Tirpitz* attacked by RAF in Trondheim
March 27/8, 1942 British amphibious attack cripples strategically important dry dock at St-Nazaire
March 28/9, 1942 Lübeck, trial incendiary attack
March 30/1, 1942 Unsuccessful RAF raid on *Tirpitz*
March to April, 1942 Twice the tonnage of bombs dropped on London during the Blitz fall on Malta
April 1, 1942 US begin 'Bucket brigade' daytime convoy system along US coast
April 5, 1942 Hitler's Directive No. 41 outlines a new strategy: a drive to the Caucasus oilfields and the industrial areas of

THE JAPANESE NAVY

When Japan attacked Pearl Harbor she had ten battleships, ten aircraft carriers, 38 cruisers, 112 destroyers and 65 submarines – a very well trained and formidable Navy. Of the 451 warships Japan eventually commissioned during the war, 332 were sunk. Japan always lagged behind the Allies with regard to vital technological advances such as radar and asdic but made up for this with superior combat skills, such as night gunnery and the use of very long range torpedoes. For the first six months of the fighting the Japanese Navy swept all before it until the defeat at the Battle of Midway.

The mighty *Yamato* and *Musashi* were the largest battleships ever built, but they eventually fell foul of US Navy warplanes and were sunk by them. Three other battleships were sunk in the same way, another three by US warships, another by a combination of aircraft and warships and one by submarine.

Japan's powerful cruisers had some striking successes during the early part of the conflict, the heavy cruisers being particularly formidable, but by the war's end 41 of their number had been sunk and only two remained afloat.

The same can be said for the destroyer force which was equipped with some very potent ships. It was in the thick of the fighting, but eventually it succumbed to the US Navy, lossing 106 of the 126 that eventually entered service.

Takao Class Cruisers	
Displacement	15,000 tons
Crew	773
Armament	10 x 8in, 4 x 4.7in guns
Armor	Max: 127mm. Min: 13mm
Engine	Four turbines, 130,000hp, max. speed 27 knots
Dimensions	Length: 668ft 6in Beam 59ft 2in

Cruiser Takao

Kagero Class Destroyers	
Displacement	2,500 tons
Crew	240
Armament	6 x 5in guns & 8 x 24in torpedo tubes
Engine	Two turbines, 52,000hp, max. speed 35 knots
Dimensions	Length: 388ft 9in Beam 35ft 5in

Right: Kagero *class Destroyer.*

Yamato Class Battleships	
Displacement	70,000 tons
Crew	2,500
Armament	9 x 18.1in, 12 x 6.1in guns
Armor	Max: 545mm. Min: 200mm
Engine	Four turbines, 150,000hp, max. speed 27 knots
Dimensions	Length: 862ft 11in Beam 121ft 1in

Below: The battleship Yamato.

Left: Japanese seaman wearing 'Blues'.

Right: Japanese seaman wearing 'Whites'.

Above: The light Cruiser Kinu.

the south

April 10/11, 1942 Essen, first RAF use of 8,000lb bomb

April 16, 1942 British Singleton Enquiry into strategic bombing

April 16, 1942 Malta awarded George Cross by King George VI. But by now Axis minefields have compromised Malta as a naval base and on May 11 Kesselring declares Malta neutralized. From January to July there is only one 24-hour period without an air raid on the island

April 17, 1942 Augsburg, daylight raid

April 18, 1942 US east coast night-time blackout begins

April 24, 1942 Exeter bombed

April 23–7, 1942 Rostock bombed

April 27/8, 1942 Another unsuccessful RAF raid on *Tirpitz*

April to June, 1942 Baedeker Raids: Luftwaffe attacks on British cities of Bath, Norwich, Exeter, Canterbury and York, all three-star cities in the famous tourist guidebook, in retaliation for RAF area bombing of Lübeck and Rostock

April to June, 1942 Germans drive Tito's Yugoslav partisans in Bosnia farther west

INDIAN OCEAN: The Japanese Incursion

March 12, 1942 British evacuate Andaman Islands

March 23, 1942 Japanese occupy Andaman Islands

March 25, 1942 Japanese First Air Fleet enters the Indian Ocean with 5 carriers, 4 battleships, plus cruisers and destroyers

April 5, 1942 Japanese carrier aircraft attack Colombo. British cruisers *Dorsetshire* and *Cornwall* are sunk

April 6, 1942 Japanese raid British/Indian shipping in the Indian Ocean

April 9, 1942 Japanese raid Trincomalee and sink British carrier *Hermes*

RUSSIA: Operations in the Crimea

May 8–16, 1942 The Germans attack and capture Kerch

Small arms had not changed a great deal from those used in World War I but in the second war a greater use was made of light machine-guns and submachine-guns. As the war progressed, new semi-automatic rifles such as the American M1 Garand, the German Gew 43 and the Soviet Tokarev SVT38 made their mark. The German MG34 and 42 saw the advent of the general purpose machine-gun, which could be configured for use in the light as well as the medium role.

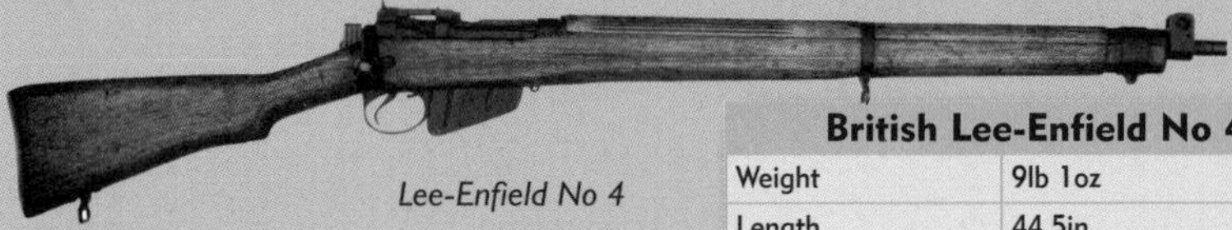

Lee-Enfield No 4

British Lee-Enfield No 4 Rifle

Weight	9lb 1oz
Length	44.5in
Capacity	10-round magazine
Rate of fire	Single-shot, bolt action
Muzzle velocity	2,400ft/sec
Calibre	.303in

British Bren Light Machine-gun

Weight	22lb 5oz
Length	45.25in
Capacity	30-round magazine
Rate of fire	500 rpm
Muzzle velocity	2,400ft/sec
Calibre	.303in

Bren light machine-gun

MP40 Submachine-gun

US 1919A4 Machine-gun

Weight	31lb 0oz
Length	41in
Capacity	250-round belt
Rate of fire	500 rpm
Muzzle velocity	2,800ft/sec
Calibre	.30in

German MP40 Submachine-gun

Weight	8lb 12oz
Length	32.75in
Capacity	32-round magazine
Rate of fire	500 rpm
Muzzle velocity	1,250ft/sec
Calibre	9mm

1919A4 Medium machine-gun

Above: *A US Marine wearing a World War II Marine Corps uniform, holding a .30 caliber M1 Garand rifle. There were 5.4 million Garands built. It weighs 9.5 lb to 10.2lb. A length of 43.6 in, with a barrel length of 24in. A rate of fire of 16–24 rounds/min. Muzzle velocity of 2750-2800 ft/s and an effective range of 500yds with a magazine capacity of one 8-round clip. The M1 Garand was the first semi-automatic rifle to be generally issued to troops of any of the combatant nations.*

June 7, 1942 Germans assault Sevastopol after 5 days of heavy bombardment
July 3, 1942 Sevastopol falls to the Germans

CORAL SEA
May 1, 1942 US carriers *Yorktown* and *Lexington*, plus escorts, rendezvous in the south-east Coral Sea to form Task Force 17 under Admiral Fletcher. Their mission is to frustrate the Japanese invasion of Port Moresby, revealed by 'Magic' intercepts
May 4, 1942 TF17 attacks the Japanese force that has just invaded Tulagi
May 5, 1942 Japanese force covering Port Moresby landing enters the Coral Sea
May 7–8, 1942 Battle of the Coral Sea. First naval battle in which the opposing surface ships never sight each other directly. Air strikes are exchanged: *Lexington* is crippled and later abandoned and scuttled; Japanese carrier *Shokaku* is disabled. In terms of destruction, this is a Japanese victory; but the Japanese Port Moresby invasion is postponed

Far Eastern Theater General Events
May 2, 1942 Australians evacuate Tulagi in the Solomons
May 3, 1942 Japanese occupy Tulagi
May 5, 1942 British land on Madagascar, which is run by Vichy French
May 5, 1942 Yamamoto's orders for Operation 'Mi', the capture of Midway island and the Aleutian Operation 'AL'
May 11, 1942 Japanese offensive in China to deny US use of airfields in Chekiang
June 10, 1942 Americans discover that there are Japanese garrisons on Attu and Kiska in the Aleutians

RUSSIA: Kharkov Counter-Offensive
May 12, 1942 Soviets surprise the Germans near Kharkov
May 18, 1942 German offensive 'Fridericus' eliminates the salient gained by the Soviets at Isyum
May 22, 1942 Germans encircle

BATTLE OF MIDWAY

The destruction meted out by the Japanese carriers at Pearl Harbor left the Americans with no serviceable battleships in the Pacific, but America's three big fleet carriers remained. Now Admiral Yamamoto planned an operation that would draw these into battle and destroy them, while at the same time seizing Midway island, a valuable

air base just 1,000 miles from Tokyo. Simultaneously a fleet was sent north to take two islands in the Aleutians and to bombard Dutch Harbor in Alaska, an American air and submarine base.

By May 28, the fleets were at sea – Hosogaya's Northern Force with two carriers and four battleships heading for the Aleutians, Nagumo's First Carrier Striking Force setting course for Midway, with four carriers and support from three battleships, plus cruisers and destroyers. In the support group was Yamamoto himself, aboard *Yamato*, the biggest battleship in the world. An invasion fleet sailed from Saipan.

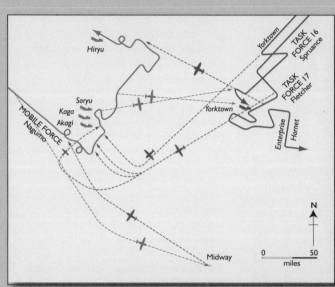

Below: Douglas Devastator torpedo bombers – aboard the USS Enterprise before the Battle of Midway. Only four of the aircraft shown here were destined to return from attacking the Japanese Fleet.

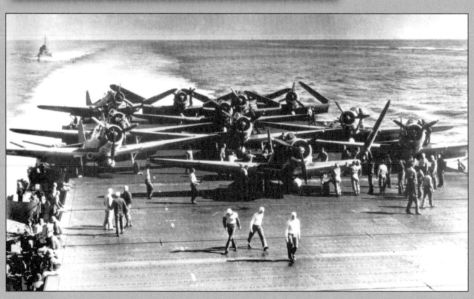

Above: *The burning Japanese aircraft carrier* Hiryu, *photographed after sunrise on 5 June 1942. Hiryu sank a few hours later. Note collapsed flight deck over the forward hangar.*

MIDWAY – OPPOSING FORCES

	Carriers	Battleships	Cruisers	Destroyers
JAPAN				
Nagumo	4	2	3	12
Hosogaya	2	—	4	10
Yamamoto	1	3	1	9
Kondo	1	2	1	8
USA				
Spruance	2	—	6	9
Fletcher	1	—	2	5

Kostenko's South-West front
May 29, 1942 Germans eliminate the Kharkov pocket, taking 214,000 prisoners and 1,200 tanks

MIDWAY
May 26, 1942 Having been warned in advance by 'Magic' intercepts about the Midway attack, US air and marine reinforcements reach Midway Island
May 27–8, 1942 Japanese forces depart Japan for the Aleutians and Midway operations
May 30, 1942 Nimitz sends his three carriers, with cruiser and destroyer support, to rendezvous off Midway: Task Force 16 (Spruance) with *Enterprise* and *Hornet* and Task Force 17 (Fletcher) with *Yorktown*
June 2, 1942 US TFs 16 and 17 meet 350 miles north-east of Midway
June 3, 1942 US B-17s from Midway attack the Japanese invasion force 600 miles northwest without success
June 4, 1942 The fleets exchange a series of air attacks, US aircraft from Midway joining them. Japanese carriers *Soryu* and *Kaga* sink. US carrier *Yorktown* is crippled
June 5, 1942 Japanese heavy cruisers *Mogami* and *Mikuma* collide and sustain damage while manoeuvering to avoid submarine attack. *Mikuma* is then sunk by air attack
June 5, 1942 Two more Japanese carriers are lost: *Akagi* ia scuttled; *Hiryu* sinks after damage the previous day
June 6, 1942 Japanese withdraw. The damaged US carrier *Yorktown* is torpedoed by Japanese submarine *I-168* but remains afloat
June 7, 1942 *Yorktown* sinks

Western Theater General Events
May 30/1, 1942 Cologne, first '1000-bomber' raid; first RAF use of Mosquito
June 1/2, 1942 Essen '1000-bomber' raid
June 25/6, 1942 Bremen '1000-bomber' raid
May 26, 1942 Anglo-Soviet treaty covering

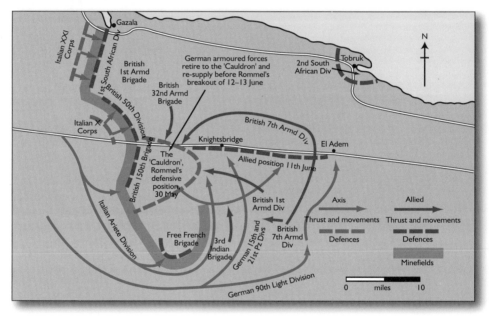

Labels on map:

Gazala

Italian XXI Corps

British 1st Armd Brigade

1st South African Div

British 50th Division

British 32nd Armd Brigade

German armoured forces retire to the 'Cauldron' and re-supply before Rommel's breakout of 12–13 June

2nd South African Div

Tobruk

N

Italian X Corps

British 150th Brigade

British 7th Armd Div

Knightsbridge

El Adem

The 'Cauldron', Rommel's defensive position 30 May

Allied position 11th June

Italian Ariete Division

British 1st Armd Div

Free French Brigade

3rd Indian Brigade

German 15th and 21st Pz Divs

British 7th Armd Div

German 90th Light Division

Axis
Thrust and movements
Defences

Allied
Thrust and movements
Defences

Minefields

0   miles   10

GAZALA – OPPOSING FORCES

	AXIS	BRITISH/COMONWEALTH
Troops	90,000	100,000
Tanks	560; 332 German 228 Italian	849
Aircraft	704; 312 German, 392 Italian; 497 in service	320; 190 in service

Left: A Schwerer Panzerspahwägen Sd Kfz 231 eight-wheeled armored car of the Afrika Korps in the Western Desert.

Gazala and Tobruk, May–June, 1942

Rommel's attack on the Gazala Line was an epic of maneuver and the epitome of armored warfare in the desert. Rommel deployed 560 tanks, including 242 PzKpfw IIIs against 849 British, which included 167 Grants with 75mm guns. Attempting to outflank and roll up the British position, Rommel's tanks outfought the British at the Battles of the Cauldron and Knightsbridge. The British fell back in disarray and on June 18 Rommel was once more before Tobruk. The port fell three days later, sending a shock wave through the British command. More to the point, it furnished Rommel with invaluable supplies of fuel, food, ammunition and vehicles.

Below: A 25-pounder field gun in the Western Desert, a very effective gun and the backbone of the British artillery.

hostilities with Germany

May 27, 1942 Himmler's deputy, Reinhard Heydrich, mortally wounded by Czech assassins from London

June 12–16, 1942 Convoys 'Harpoon' and 'Vigorous' from Gibraltar and Alexandria to Malta attacked by Italian warships and Luftwaffe. 'Vigorous' is forced to turn back; only 2 of 17 merchantmen in 'Harpoon' get through

June 18, 1942 Churchill confers with Roosevelt in Washington

June 25, 1942 Eisenhower appointed commander US forces in the European Theater (ETO)

NORTH AFRICA: Gazala and Tobruk
May 26–9, 1942 Rommel, attacks the Gazala Line

May 26 to June 13, 1942 Battle of Gazala

June 2–10, 1942 Battle of the Cauldron: Rommel drives around the south of the Gazala Line. British counterattacks fail

June 11, 1942 Bir Hacheim, with a Free French garrison cut off at the south of the Gazala Line, falls to Rommel

June 11–13, 1942 Battle of Knightsbridge: Rommel destroys much of the British armor, and British units begin to withdraw

June 18, 1942 Tobruk besieged

June 21, 1942 Tobruk captured by Rommel

June 30, 1942 Eighth Army consolidates at El Alamein

With Rommel seemingly poised to take the Suez Canal and with the panzers of Army Group South racing for the Caucasus, there appears the possibility of Germany wresting the Middle East, with its oilfields, from Allied control

Far Eastern Theater General Events
July, 1942 General Chennault assumes command of American Air Force in China
Late June/Early July, 1942 Japanese land on Guadalcanal to survey the site for an airfield. Construction begins near Lunga Point
July, 1942 US establish China-Burma-India

BERNARD MONTGOMERY

After being wounded in World War I in 1914, Montgomery served as a staff officer. An ascetic man, he was a master of detail. He commanded the 3rd Division during the Battle of France in 1940. For the next two years he concentrated on army training. In the late summer of 1942 he was appointed to command the Eighth Army in North Africa. His victory at the Battle of El Alamein in October 1942 was one of the turning points of the war, although, during the follow-up to the battle, he was accused by some of letting the remainder of the Axis forces slip away after the battle. Cornered between Montgomery with the Eighth Army and Allied forces from the 'Torch' landings in the west, the Axis forces surrendered in May 1943. He then commanded the British forces during the invasion of Sicily and the landings in southern Italy and was transferred back to the UK in December 1943 to help plan for the landings in Normandy. His influence and organisational skills came to the fore in this crucial planning stage, contributing in no small measure to the success of the landings. After commanding the landings of June 6, 1944 he commanded the British and Canadian forces in their drive across Belgium and Holland and north-west Germany, taking the final surrender there on 4 May 1945. Montgomery was an egocentric and conceited man, and many found it difficult to work with him, but he was able to communicate with the soldiers under his command, instilling them with his own self-confidence.

Below: *Montgomery (left) with HM King George VI.*

MONTGOMERY	
Rank attained	Field Marshal
Dates	1887–1976
Background	Career soldier; Sandhurst Military Academy; wounded in 1914
Commands	3th Division during Campaign in France, 1940; UK 5th and then 12th Corps, 1940–41; South-Eastern Command 1941–42; Eighth Army 1942–43; 21st Army Group 1944–45
Campaigns	France, 1940; North Africa 1942–43; Sicily 1943; Italy 1943; North- West Europe, 1944–45
Battles	2nd El Alamein 1942; Mareth Line, 1943; Normandy, 1944, Arnhem, 1944; Rhine, 1945

Above: *Montgomery posing in the turret of a Sherman tank.*

First Alamein, July, 1942

Two days after the capture of Tobruk, Rommel resumed his pursuit of the British to Mersa Matruh (26/7 June) and then to prepared positions at El Alamein, just 60 miles from Alexandria. Now at the end of a very long supply line, Rommel attempted to 'bounce' the British position, but the First Battle of Alamein (July 1–27) became a series of attacks and counterattacks, ending in stalemate.

Alam Halfa, August–September, 1942

During August, Churchill visited Egypt to assess the situation for himself, and the result was a change of leadership, General Bernard Montgomery taking command of the Eighth Army with General Harold Alexander as Commander Middle East. Hitler meanwhile promoted Rommel to Field Marshal, but the 'Desert Fox' suffered increasingly from ill health. On August 30 the Axis army made a flanking attack on the British line but was repulsed at Alam Halfa ridge. Limited by fuel shortages and harassed by British bombing, the panzers fell back. This was, effectively, the Axis 'high tide' in North Africa.

**Second Battle of El Alamein,
October 23 to November 4, 1942**
After a heavy bombardment, on October 23 Montgomery launched his attack. The battle became one of attrition, as the Eighth Army advanced through the Axis minefields. On November 4 the Allies achieved breakthrough; Rommel began to retreat, and the decisive battle of the desert war had been won. By the third week of January 1943 Rommel was in Tunisia, pursued with lengthening lines of communication by the Eighth Army.

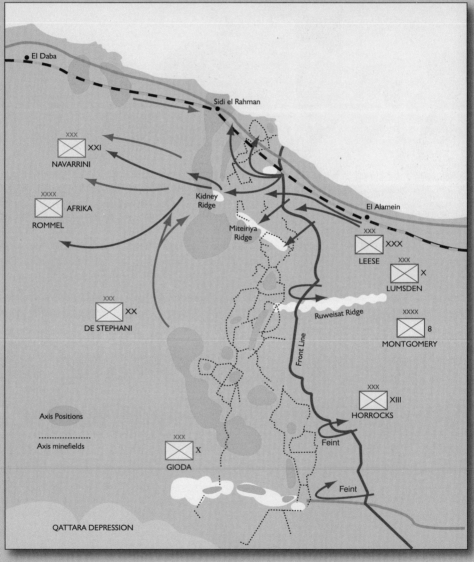

Opposite page:
Top: *An Eighth Army Bren gunner ready to open fire as his companion digs in.*
Bottom: *A knocked-out German Panzer IV being inspected by an Eighth Army soldier.*

EL ALAMEIN – OPPOSING FORCES

	AXIS	BRITISH/COMONWEALTH
Troops	104,000; 50,000 German, 54,000 Italian	195,000
Tanks	489; 211 German, 278 Italian	1,029
Artillery	1,219 guns; 475 Field & medium, 744 anti-tank	2,311 guns; 908 Field & medium, 1,403 anti-tank
Aircraft	675; 275 German, 400 Italian; 350 in service	750; 530 in service

Command under General Stilwell to work with Chinese leader Chiang Kai-shek. Construction of the Japanese Burma–Thailand railway begins, initially by the slave labor of 3,000 prisoners of war from Changi Jail in Singapore

July 2, 1942 US directive for the recapture of the Solomon Islands: to take Santa Cruz, Tulagi and Guadalcanal, then Rabaul

July 22, 1942 US Guadalcanal invasion force sails from New Zealand for the Solomons

NORTH AFRICA: First Battle of El Alamein
June 26–9, 1942 Germans attack and take Mersa Matruh

July 1–27, 1942 1st Battle of Alamein. Rommel attacks but is repulsed

Aug 3, 1942 Churchill visits Cairo and reorganizes the local command

Aug 18, 1942 Montgomery takes command of the Eighth Army. Alexander becomes overall commander Middle East

Sept 13/14, 1942 British land and sea raids, on Tobruk, Benghazi and Barce fail with the loss of 3 destroyers

Aug 30 to Sept 2, 1942 Battle of Alam Halfa. Rommel swings around the southern edge of the Alamein line and attacks Alam Halfa Ridge but is repulsed and falls back. Both sides begin to reinforce and regroup

Sept 23, 1942 Rommel returns to Europe for medical care, leaving Stumme in command of Panzerarmee Afrika

Second Battle of El Alamein
Oct 23/4, 1942 Artillery bombardment precedes XXX Corps attack in the north (Operation 'Lightfoot') while XIII Corps feints in the south

Oct 23 to Nov 4, 1942 Battle of El Alamein

Oct 25, 1942 Rommel returns, Stumme having been killed by a mine the day before

Oct 26, 1942 Montgomery orders a pause in the attack, which has secured Miteiriya and Kidney Ridges but is now making slow

The German Drive to the Caucasus, June–September 1942

The second major German offensive on the Eastern Front opened on June 28, a massive thrust to the south-east that surprised the Russians – having captured a copy of the German plan, Stalin believed this was but a feint, while the main blow would be directed at Moscow. On July 7, Voronezh fell, and by the end of July the Germans were across the Don and Donetz Rivers. But again, Hitler kept altering the axes of attack and switching unit deployments, fatally compromising both the thrust on Stalingrad and on the Caucasus oilfields. Commanders who disagreed were dismissed. On August 10, German forces reached the suburbs of Stalingrad; five days later the southern spearheads arrived at the foothills of the Caucasus mountains, this offensive losing impetus and stopping by the beginning of November.

Red Army infantry, with an anti-tank rifle.

ZHUKOV

Rank attained	Marshal
Dates	1896–1974
Background	Career soldier, NCO in Tsarist Army; Red Army, 1918
Commands	Leningrad Front, 1941; West Front, 1941–42; West Theatre, 1942–45
Campaigns/ Battles	Mongolia, 1939; Leningrad, 1941; Moscow, 1941–42; Stalingrad, 1942–43; Kursk, 1943; Poland, 1944; Berlin, 1945

Georgi Zhukov was the son of a peasant, serving in the Imperial Russian Army during World War I before joining the Red Army. When commanding the Soviet forces in Mongolia he defeated the Japanese Kwantung Army. In 1941 he became the Soviet Chief of the General Staff. In July 1941 he was posted to the armies east of Moscow. He was ordered to take command at Leningrad. He then returned to Moscow, counterattacking the Germans on December 6, 1941. Named Deputy Supreme Commander, he played a part in defeating the Germans at Stalingrad. The victory at Kursk merged into the Soviet Summer Offensive, when he co-ordinated the First and Second Ukrainian Fronts in the drive west. Zhukov personally took command of the First Ukrainian Front when its commander was wounded in February 1944. He helped to co-ordinate Operation 'Bagration', the summer offensive in 1944, in which the Soviets destroyed the Germans' Army Group Centre. In November he was put in command of the First Belorussian Front, which had the most direct approach to Berlin. With the fall of Berlin he became the most celebrated of all the Soviet marshals.

progress
Oct 27, 1942 Rommel counterattacks unsuccessfully
Nov 2, 1942 Montgomery renewes the attack, Operation 'Supercharge', which achieves breakthrough by 4th
Nov 6–7, 1942 British pursuit of the retreating Germans hampered by heavy rain
Nov 13, 1942 British retake Tobruk
Nov 20, 1942 British retake Benghazi
Nov 24, 1942 Rommel halts at El Agheila, the start-point for his two offensives, while the British bring up supplies via Benghazi
Dec 13, 1942 Rommel withdraws for Tunisia despite Hitler's insistance that he make a stand at El Agheila
Dec 26, 1942 Rommel halts at Buerat, ordered by Mussolini to make a stand here
Jan 13, 1943 Rommel withdraws from Buerat as Montgomery prepares to attack

RUSSIA: German Drive to the Caucasus and the Battle for Stalingrad
June 1, 1942 Hitler visits Army Group South's HQ at Poltava to confirm plans for the impending offensive
June, 19, 1942 Soviets capture a copy of the German plan
June 22–6, 1942 Germans take Kupyansk
June 28, 1942 German Second Army launches offensive from the Kursk area towards Voronezh
June 30, 1942 German Sixth Army attacks south-west from the Kharkov area
July 5, 1942 German Army Group B reaches the Don River
July 7, 1942 Germans take the offensive to cross the Donets River
July 7, 1942 Germans take Voronezh
July 13–18, 1942 Hitler switches the emphasis of attack from Stalingrad to the Donets and back again. The result will be to weaken the forces thrusting for Stalingrad
July 23, 1942 Hitler makes further changes to the axes of the offensive, diverting more forces from the Stalingrad thrust to the

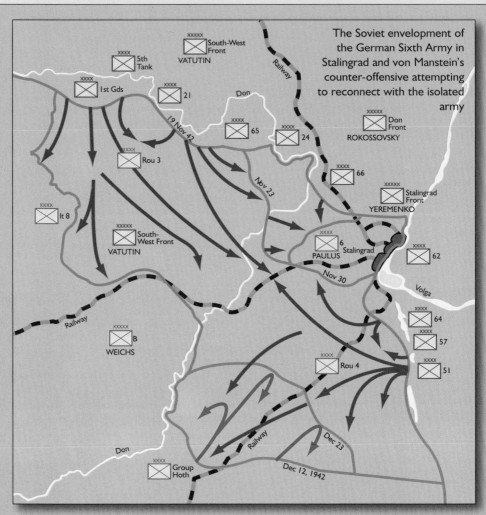

The Soviet envelopment of the German Sixth Army in Stalingrad and von Manstein's counter-offensive attempting to reconnect with the isolated army

Left and right:
German infantry at Stalingrad, Autumn 1942. The right hand photo shows them being supported by a Panzer IV tank.

Stalingrad,
September 1942 to February 1943

Stalingrad, symbolic as an industrial city built under communism, was a key rail and river junction. Stalin declared that it must not fall and Soviet troops poured into its defence. The battle became one of attrition amongst the rubble of a city pounded to destruction. Then on November 19 Soviet offensives to north and south struck the flanks of the German salient, and four days later the pincers closed, trapping Paulus's Sixth Army battling in the city. Between December 12 and 28, Manstein's 'Winter Storm' counterattack failed to relieve Stalingrad, and attempts to supply the Germans by air proved totally inadequate. By February 2, the German remnant of some 90,000 men was forced to surrender. Stalingrad had cost Hitler more than 200,000 men and was the turning-point of the war on the Eastern Front.

Caucasus

Aug 5, 1942 Germans take Voroshilovsk

Aug 9, 1942 Germans secure Maikop oil-fields

Aug 10, 1942 German Sixth Army (Paulus) crosses the lower Don River and reaches the outskirts of Stalingrad

Aug 15, 1942 Germans reach the foothills of the Caucasus mountains

Aug, 19 to end Sept, 1942 Soviet attempts to relieve Leningrad fail

Aug, 19, 1942 The Battle of Stalingrad begins as Paulus attacks the city

Aug 24, 1942 Stalin orders that Stalingrad must not fall

Sept 6, 1942 Germans take Novorossisk

Sept–Oct, 1942 Soviets plan a strategic envelopment of German forces in Stalingrad, with pincers from the north (South-West Front) and south (Stalingrad Front)

Sept 20, 1942 Fighting decreases in intensity at Stalingrad as Paulus calls for reinforcements. The Soviet defenders are now penned into a 10x4-mile area along the west bank of the Volga River

Sept 28, 1942 Germans renew the battle for Stalingrad, but the struggle for the city has reached stalemate

Nov 2, 1942 German southernmost thrust in the Caucasus halts as winter, increasing Soviet resistance and logistics problems take their toll

Nov 11, 1942 Renewed Soviet counter-attacks in Stalingrad to pin the Germans

Nov, 19, 1942 Soviet offensive 'Uranus', to cut off Stalingrad, begins

Nov 23, 1942 The Soviet pincers close, trapping German Sixth and part of Fourth Panzer Army, some 330,000 men

Nov 24, 1942 The Luftwaffe plans to resupply Paulus's trapped forces by air: but capacity falls far short of need – 750 tons per day are required; the average delivered is 90

Nov 25/6 Greeks, with British agents, destroy Gorgopotamus viaduct on Athens–

GERMAN LEADERS

GÖRING

Dates	1893–1946
Background	World War I fighter pilot
Offices	Reich Marshal; C-in-C Luftwaffe; Prussian Minister of Interior

A World War I fighter ace, **Hermann Göring** became an early member of the Nazi party and when Hitler came to power he was made German Air Minister and Prime Minister of Prussia. He created, and until 1936, was the head of, the Gestapo, and he also created and led the Luftwaffe. In 1939 Hitler designated him as his successor. He was responsible for the air war waged by Germany but failed to prevent the Dunkirk evacuation, failed to win the Battle of Britain and failed to sustain Sixth Army trapped in Stalingrad. Hitler deprived him of all formal authority in 1943 and then dismissed him shortly before the war ended. He surrendered to American forces and was a chief defendant at the Nuremberg trials. He defended himself with dignity but was convicted and sentenced to death. However, he committed suicide by taking a poison capsule hidden within a false tooth two hours before his scheduled hanging.

GOEBBELS

Dates	1897–1945
Background	Doctorate of Philosophy
Offices	Minister of Propaganda and Public Enlightenment

Joseph Goebbels could not serve during World War I as he was disabled with a club foot. He joined the Nazi Party in 1924 and by 1929 he was in overall charge of the Nazi propaganda machine – a position in which he excelled. When Hitler came to power Goebbels was appointed Minister of Enlightenment and Propaganda: he controlled all aspects of communication, the Press, radio, publishing, cinema and theatre. The great Nazi rallies at Nuremberg, even by today's standards of complexity and size, were major organisational achievements. During World War II, when it seemed that all was going Germany's way, it was easy for Goebbels to persuade the public that things were fine. However, after the

Göring *Goebbels*

defeat at the Battle of Stalingrad this was becoming increasingly difficult. In 1944 he was appointed Reich Commissioner for Total Mobilisation, conscripting women and cutting back on education and entertainment. He was the only senior Nazi leader to stay with Hitler to the end in his bunker as the Battle for Berlin raged above them in April/May 1945. On May 1 he poisoned his six children, shot his wife and then himself.

HIMMLER

Rank attained	Reichsführer-SS
Dates	1900–1945
Background	*Freikorps*, poultry farmer
Commands	SS, 1929; Army Group Vistula, 1945

The son of a schoolteacher, **Heinrich Himmler** trained as an officer at the end of World War I but saw no active service. He then became a poultry farmer. In 1925 he joined the Nazi party and became deputy leader of the SS in 1927 (then only 280 strong). He became its leader in January 1929. Under his leadership the SS expanded, and by January 1933 it numbered over 50,000. After the Nazi party came to power he organised the very efficient liquidation of the leadership of the rival SA, which then became subordinated in power to the SS. He established dominance over state security in every sphere, including the police. He established the first concentration camps. Obsessed with racial purity, he wanted the SS to be at the forefront of the Aryan ideal. He oversaw the 'Final Solution', the exter-

Himmler

Heydrich

mination of the Jews. He was looked upon as the natural successor to Hitler as the Führer, but when he made tentative overtures to the Allies regarding peace Hitler dismissed him from all posts and ordered his arrest. He tried to escape the Allies in disguise but was captured by the British and committed suicide.

HEYDRICH

Rank attained	Obergruppenführer
Dates	1904–1942
Background	*Freikorps.* Cashiered from the German Navy
Commands	Deputy leader SS, 1934; Deputy Reichsprotektor of Bohemia and Moravia, 1942

The son of a music teacher, **Reinhard Heydrich** joined the German Navy in 1922 but was forced to resign after a scandalous affair with an influential industrialist's daughter in 1931. He then joined the SS. Himmler saw his potential and promoted him to be his deputy. In 1934 he took command of the Gestapo in Berlin and eventually the Gestapo nationwide. Many high-ranking individuals within the Nazi party were frightened of him, aware of his total lack of humanity and his very ambitious nature. He had a hand in drafting the 'Final Solution' and in the systematic murder of the Jews in the death camps. Shortly after being created Reichs-protektor of Bohemia-Moravia (occupied Czechoslovakia), on June 4, 1942, he was assassinated in Prague by a team of Free Czech agents parachuted from Britain. The village of Lidice was destroyed and the adults murdered in reprisal.

Salonika railway

Nov 27, 1942 German Army Group Don, under von Manstein, formed to relieve Stalingrad

Dec 2–7, 1942 Soviets make failed attempt to cut off part of the German pocket at Gumrak

Dec 12, 1942 German counterattack to relieve Paulus ('Winter Storm') launched The Soviet counter to the German relief attempt is aimed at the flanks of von Manstein's line, held by Italians in the north and Roumanians in the south

Dec 16, 1942 Soviets destroy Italian Eighth Army on the north of von Manstein's line

Dec, 19–23, 1942 Germans attempt to break the Myshkova Line but make no progress

Dec 28, 1942 The German relief attempt has failed. Hitler agrees to a withdrawal, which will leave Stalingrad isolated 125 miles behind the Soviet lines

Jan 10, 1943 Soviet offensive to destroy German Sixth Army cut off in Stalingrad

Jan 12–18, 1943 Soviet offensive lifts the blockade of Leningrad

Jan 16, 1943 Milch joins von Manstein to command Luftwaffe resupply of Stalingrad; but only 40 tons a day are getting through. He manages to increase this by 50% but it is still far too little

Jan 22, 1943 Terminal phase of the Soviet assault on Stalingrad: the vital airfield of Gumrak is captured and the German defenders split

Jan 23, 1943 From now on only parachute supply is possible for the Germans

Jan 24, 1943 Hitler forbids attempts to break out and still will not countenance surrender

Jan 31, 1943 Paulus, despite promotion to field marshal (a German field marshal has never surrendered) surrenders the German southern pocket

Feb 2, 1943 The German northern pocket surrenders. 91,000 are prisoners. Stalingrad is the turning-point on the

GUDERIAN

Rank attained	General
Dates	1888–1954
Background	Career soldier; Metz War School; wrote *Achtung Panzer!* treatise on tank tactics, 1937
Commands	XIX Panzer Corps, 1939–40; 2nd Panzer Group, 1941; Chief of Panzer Command, 1943; Chief of Army General Staff; 1944
Campaigns	Poland, 1939; West, 1940; Russia, 1941

Guderian   *Manstein*

In the 1930s **Heinz Guderian** proposed the revolutionary theory that tanks were the primary weapon, then published a book on the subject. He laid the foundations for the first three Panzer divisions in 1935. The Polish and Western Campaigns of 1939 and 1940 proved the theory of Blitzkrieg that he espoused. His ideas worked well in Russia in 1941, where his force, 2nd Panzer Group, captured huge numbers of Soviet soldiers, but his criticism of Hitler's military tactics led to his dismissal in December 1941. For over a year he was not given an appointment, but he was recalled as Inspector of Armoured Troops, making him the chief of the Panzer Command. He was invited to join the July Bomb Plot to kill Hitler, but declined. He was made Chief of the General Staff, but he continued to fall out with Hitler and was forced to take sick leave just a month or so before the end of the war.

The son of a Prussian aristocrat, **Erich von Manstein** is considered as one of the ablest of the German generals during World War II. After he was wounded in World War I he served as a staff officer. He was von Rundstedt's Chief of Staff during the Polish Campaign in 1939. His inspired ideas for the campaign in the West were adopted by Hitler, even though opposed by Field Marshal von Brauchitsch, the Commander-in-Chief and General Halder, the Chief of Staff. The ensuing conquest of France was a military triumph during which Manstein commanded XXXVIII Corps. In Russia his Eleventh Army defeated the Soviets in the Crimea. During the Battle of Stalingrad he almost managed to relieve the Sixth Army trapped there. Then, commanding Army Group South in a counteroffensive, he won a major victory at Kharkov. After the German defeat at the Battle of Kursk in 1943 he led his forces through a series of defensive battles as the Germans were pushed back by the Soviets. By March 1944 he had fallen out of favor with Hitler, and as a result he was dismissed and never held another command.

VON MANSTEIN

Rank attained	Field Marshal
Dates	1887–1973
Background	Career soldier
Commands	XXXVIII Corps, 1940; LVI Panzer Corps, 1941; Eleventh Army, 1941; Army Group Don, 1942; Army Group South,1943
Campaigns	West, 1940; Russia 1941–44

Albert Kesselring served as a army staff officer during World War I. In 1936 he transferred to the Luftwaffe. He commanded Luftflotte I (First Air Fleet) during the Polish campaign and Luftflotte II during the 1940 campaign in the West. His air fleet participated in the Battle of Britain. Luftflotte II was then transferred east for the invasion of Russia. He was appointed C-in-C South in 1941 to establish Axis air dominance over the Mediterranean and was involved with the campaign in the North African desert. He conducted a brilliant defense in Sicily and Italy, always without adequate reserves of men and equipment. In March 1945 Hitler transferred him to take over command in the West but

KESSELRING

Rank attained	Field Marshal
Dates	1889–1960
Background	Career soldier, then service with Luftwaffe
Commands	Luftflotte I, 1939; Luftflotte II, 1940; C-in-C South, 1941–45; C-in-C West, 1945
Campaigns	Poland, 1939; Belgium/France, 1940; Battle of Britain, 1940; Russia, 1941; Mediterranean, 1941–45; C-in-C West, 1945

VON RUNDSTEDT

Rank attained	Field Marshal
Dates	1875–1953
Background	Career soldier, Kriegsakademie, Berlin
Commands	Army Group South, 1939; C-in-C South, 1939; Army Group South, 1939; C-in-C West, 1940; Army Group South, 1941; C-in-C West; 1942
Campaigns	Poland, 1939; France, 1940; Russia, 1941; The West, 1942–44

Germany was about to collapse and he negotiated surrender with the Americans. He was found guilty of war crimes but his death sentence was commuted to one of life imprisonment and in 1953 he was released on grounds of ill health.

The aristocratic Prussian, **Gerd von Rundstedt** served as a staff officer during World War I. He retired in 1938 but was brought back to help plan the invasion of Poland. He commanded Army Group A that led the attack in the West and the fall of France. Promoted to Field Marshal in July 1940, he was to command the aborted invasion of Great Britain. He then commanded Army Group South during the invasion of Russia. He was dismissed by Hitler in November 1941 for withdrawing against orders. He was recalled for active service in March 1942, becoming C-in-C West. He clashed with Rommel over how to defeat the expected invasion. He conducted a skilled defense in the West and is considered one of the outstanding German commanders of the war. Hitler dismissed him again in March 1945. He was to be put on trial for war crimes but ill health saved him.

Kesselring talks with Rommel

Kesselring

von Rundstedt

123

On November 6, 1942, General MacArthur moved his headquarters to Port Moresby, capital of Papua. During the previous four months his men had fought across the Owen Stanley Mountains to his north, tasked with ejecting the Japanese from the Buna–Gona area on the north coast.

On July 2 the US Joint Chiefs of Staff had ordered him to begin to clear Papua-New Guinea of Japanese troops who had established themselves at several points including Gona. From here an advance party during July ascended the Kokoda Trail toward Port Moresby over the Owen Stanley Mountains. These rise to some 13,000 feet, and the 100-mile trail was narrow, muddy and often near-vertical. An Australian-Papuan unit, Maroubra Force, was already at Kokoda, at the peak of the mountain ridge, and on July 23 the Japanese attacked them. Forced back, Maroubra Force was joined on August 21 by a

brigade of the 7th Australian Division, just returned from service in the Middle East. However, the Japanese were simultaneously reinforced, and by the middle of September pushed the Australians back down the Trail to Imita Ridge, the last viable defensive position before Port Moresby.

At the south-eastern tip of Papua, meanwhile, a Japanese landing had been repulsed during the first week of September, and, with insecure lines of communication across the mountains, the Kokoda force pulled back to consolidate before renewing the offensive. The Allied force, now reinforced with American troops, followed up the Trail, taking Kokoda on November 2 and continued the advance towards Buna and Gona, where they arrived by 19th.

The area was strongly defended, more Japanese having landed, and the Allied troops were tired and demoralized after the hardships of the Kokoda Trail, where they had been supplied

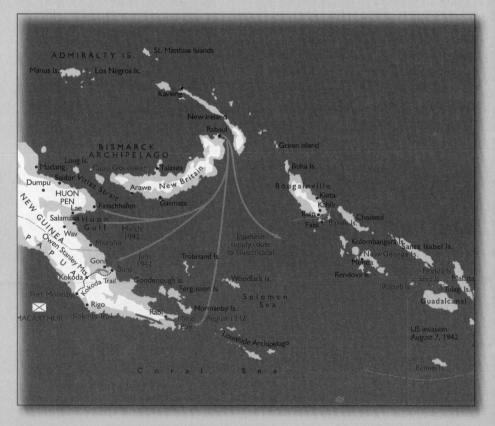

Above: Australian troops on the Kokoda Trail.

inadequately by air drops. Malaria was rife – there would be more than 16,000 cases by the end of the campaign. Mud, swamps, jungle and the rigors of the terrain had taken a terrible toll. For the Allies, this had been a badly prepared campaign, with insufficient logistic planning. To put new life into the troops, MacArthur called in General Eichelberger, and he set about bringing the campaign to an end. On December 8, Gona was taken; on the 14th Buna village; and the Mission there fell on January 2. The hardships of the Kokoda Trail were shared by both sides: of the 20,000 Japanese troops deployed there, some 12,000 perished.

Above: A US C-47 transport plane dropping supplies to the Australian troops.

Russian Front

PAPUA-NEW GUINEA:

Buna-Gona and the Kokoda Trail

July 2, 1942 General MacArthur is ordered to begin clearing Japanese from Papua-New Guinea

July 7, 1942 Maroubra Force ascends the arduous Kokoda Trail at the center of the Owen Stanley Mountains

July 15, 1942 Maroubra Force reaches Kokoda

July 21, 1942 Japanese advance force lands at Gona and advances up the Kokoda Trail

July 23, 1942 Japanese eject Maroubra Force from Kokoda

Mid–Aug, 1942 Australian 7th Division's 1st brigade (returned from the Middle East) arrives at Port Moresby

Aug 8, 1942 Kokoda temporarily retaken by Maroubra Force

Aug 18–21, 1942 Japanese land at Buna in force

Aug 21, 1942 Australian 7th Division links up with Maroubra Force

Aug 25–9, 1942 Japanese land in Milne Bay at the south-eastern tip of Papua, but 'Magic' intelligence has forewarned the Allies who deploy forces to meet them

Aug 28, 1942 Australians attack Japanese at Milne Bay

Aug 29, 1942 Japanese push Australians on the Kokoda Trail back to Myola

Sept 4, 1942 Australians retire from Myola

Sept 4–6, 1942 Japanese forced to evacuate Milne Bay

Sept 8, 1942 Australians forced back from Efogi

Sept 14–17, 1942 Australian reinforcements counterattack on the Kokoda Trail but are repulsed and forced back to Imita Ridge

Sept 24, 1942 Failure at Milne Bay and over-extended lines of communication constantly under aerial attack lead the Japanese to pull back on the Kokoda Trail

Sept 15, 1942 US reinforcements arrive at Port Moresby

ARTILLERY

During World War II artillery needed to be very mobile, in contrast to the demands of the previous conflict, which had generally been characterised by static trench warfare. As the war progressed, an increasing number of guns of all calibres were mounted on tracked vehicles as, for example, self-propelled guns and tank destroyers. Some German guns remained horse-drawn throughout the war.

The most numerous type of artillery were field guns and howitzers, e.g., the 105mm guns of Germany and the USA and the British 25pdr. Next most numerous were heavy guns such as the 155mm and 8in calibre weapons. Free-flight rockets were used en masse, particularly by the Russian Army.

USA 155mm 'Long Tom' SP Gun	
Weight	58,000lb
Length	12ft 3in
Range	25,000yds
Shell weight	95lb
Muzzle velocity	2,800ft/sec
Calibre	6in

US 155mm 'Long Tom' self-propelled gun

Below: German 88mm gun and the half-track for towing it.

German 88mm Flak 18	
Weight	4,985lb
Length	16ft 2in
Range	16,000yds
Shell weight	21lb
Muzzle velocity	2,690ft/sec
Calibre	3.46in

The Germans soon realised that their 88mm anti-aircraft gun was easily adaptable for use against tanks − its high-velocity shells could pierce Allied armor at very long range.

Anti-aircraft artillery saw the first use of proximity-fused shells, which with the aid of shell-mounted sensors, would explode near the target, thus causing lethal damage even without making a direct hit.

British 25pdr Field Gun	
Weight	3,960lb
Length	8ft 11in
Range	13,400yds
Shell weight	25lb
Muzzle velocity	2,000ft/sec
Calibre	3.45in

British 25pdr field gun

Oct 6, 1942 US force advances along the Kapa Kapa Track to outflank Kokoda, while other forces land at Pongani, south of Buna
Oct 21–8, 1942 Allies attack Japanese rearguard at Eora Creek
Nov 2, 1942 Allies take Kokoda
Nov 5–10, 1942 Allies push Japanese from Ovi
Nov 15, 1942 Allies advance on Gona
Nov 16, 1942 Allies begin attacking Gona
Nov 17, 1942 More Japanese arrive at Buna
Nov 18–19, 1942 Allies arrive before Buna-Gona, where the Japanese are strongly entrenched
The Kokoda/Buna-Gona campaign is fought during bad weather in mountainous terrain, imposing a terrible strain on the soldiers of both sides

Far Eastern Theater General Events
Aug 17–18, 1942 US decoy raid by Carlson's Raiders on Makin in the Gilbert Islands, while the Guadalcanal operation is beginning. Some 200 Marines are landed by two submarines and destroy the Japanese garrison before returning to the submarines. This prompts the Japanese to reinforce the island group
Aug 26, 1942 Chinese Army in India training center opened at Ramgarh
Aug 27, 1942 In the Aleutians, Japanese begin transferring the Attu garrison to Kiska
Aug 30, 1942 US occupy Adak in the Aleutians
Sept 21, 1942 Boeing B-29 bomber makes its first flight
Sept 25, 1942 American atomic bomb development allotted to the Army, as the 'Manhattan Project'. Dr Robert Oppenheimer leads team at Los Alamos, New Mexico, and Oak Ridge, Tennessee
Mid–Sept, 1942 British conceive the 'Anakim' Plan for the capture of Rangoon and Moulmein by amphibious landings in late 1943 or 1944
Oct 18, 1942 Ghormley replaced by Halsey

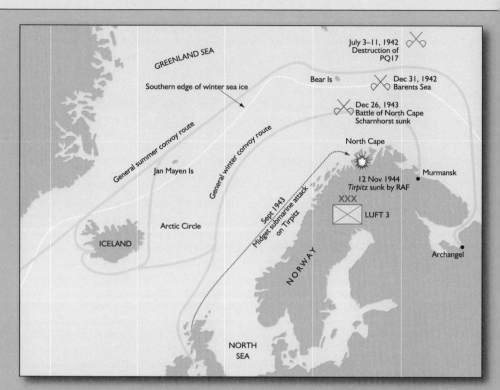

July 3–11, 1942
Destruction of
PQ17

GREENLAND SEA

Bear Is

Dec 31, 1942
Barents Sea

Southern edge of winter sea ice

Dec 26, 1943
Battle of North Cape
Scharnhorst sunk

General summer convoy route

General winter convoy route

North Cape

Jan Mayen Is

Murmansk

12 Nov 1944
Tirpitz sunk by RAF

Sept 1943
Midget submarine attack
on Tirpitz

XXX

LUFT 3

Arctic Circle

ICELAND

NORWAY

Archangel

NORTH
SEA

M ore dangerous even than the Atlantic
convoys were those to Russia, their
destinations Archangel, Molotovsk and the ice-
free port of Murmansk. Convoys had to navigate
around the long coastline of Norway from where
the menace of U-boats was joined by that of
surface warships and aircraft. The loss rate was
thus higher than that for other convoy routes. In
the case of PQ17 (June–July 1942), the most

disastrous of the convoy battles, Allied losses of
tanks, vehicles and aircraft were the equivalent of
a major land battle.

The first convoy sailed from Scapa Flow on
August 21, 1941; the last on April 16, 1945.
More than 4,400,000 tons of *matériel* was sent,
joining some four times that amount sent via
the slower overland route via Persia and the air
route across the Bering Strait.

Above: *Convoy – life-blood of the Allied war effort. Churchill subsequently remarked that the Battle of the Atlantic worried him more than any other campaign.*

Above: Depth charge fuzes being set aboard an Allied escort vessel.

Above: An escort vessel's depth-charge thrower.

in command of Allied South Pacific forces

Oct 29, 1942 Japanese reoccupy Attu in the Aleutians

Nov 6, 1942 MacArthur establishes his HQ at Port Moresby

Mid–Nov, 1942 Japanese land and build airfield at Munda Point on New Georgia

Western Theater General Events

June 27 to July 11, 1942 Battle of Arctic convoy PQ17. Menaced by *Tirpitz*, *Admiral Scheer* and *Admiral Hipper*, the convoy scatters on 4th and is practically destroyed in detail by U-boats and aircraft. Only 10 of 34 ships get through. 430 tanks, 3,350 vehicles, 210 aircraft and 153 seamen are lost. Arctic convoys are suspended until September

July 1/2, 1942 Churchill's government defeats Vote of No Confidence in British House of Commons

August Start of troop transport from USA to England aboard fast passenger liners including *Queen Mary* and *Queen Elizabeth*

Aug 10–15, 1942 Gibraltar-Malta convoy 'Pedestal': 5 of 14 ships including vital tanker *Ohio* get through. The convoy saves the Maltese from starvation. On 11th aircraft carrier *Eagle* is sunk

Aug 11, 1942 RAF Pathfinder Force established

Aug 12, 1942 Churchill confers with Stalin in Moscow

Aug 17, 1942 Rouen, first European raid by US Eighth AF heavy bombers

Aug 18/19, 1942 Flensburg, first RAF Pathfinder raid

Aug, 19, 1942 Canadian and British amphibious raid on Dieppe fails disastrously. The operation remains controversial to this day

August/September, 1942 US interlocking convoy system begins along the eastern coast of North America, halting the heavy losses to U-boats

Sept 12, 1942 British AMC *Laconia* torpedoed in S Atlantic. Realizing that women, children and 1,800 Italian PoWs are

Below: The Type VIIC was the mainstay of the U-boat force. This drawing shows an early configuration.

Type VIIC	
Displacement	865 tons
Crew	44
Armament	4 x 21in torpedo tubes forward, one aft. 1 x 88mm gun and 1 x 20mm AA gun
Range	8,500 miles surfaced
Engine/motor	3,200hp surfaced, 750hp submerged, max. speed: surfaced 17.5 knots, submerged 7 knots
Dimensions	Length: 218ft 3in Beam 20ft 3in
Production	705

Type IXC	
Displacement	1,250 tons
Crew	49
Armament	4 x 21in torpedo tubes forward, 2 aft. 1 x 105mm gun, 1 x 37mm AA and 1 x 20mm AA gun
Range	13,500 miles surfaced
Engine/motor	4,400hp surfaced, 1,000hp submerged, max. speed: surfaced 18.2 knots, submerged 7.7 knots
Dimensions	Length: 252ft 3in Beam 22ft 9in
Production	163

Type XXI	
Displacement	1,650 tons
Crew	57
Armament	6 x 21in torpedo tubes forward, 4 x 30mm AA guns or 4 x 20mm AA guns
Range	15,500 miles surfaced
Engine/motor	4,800hp surfaced, 226hp submerged, max. speed: surfaced 17.5 knots, submerged 16 knots
Dimensions	Length: 251ft 9in Beam 21ft 9in
Production	118 (1,300 planned)

Raeder   Dönitz

Below: A later-war Type VIIC, with main gun removed and additional anti-aircraft guns aft of the conning-tower, reflecting the changed operating parameters – less chance of sinking merchantmen by surface action in convoys guarded by increased numbers of escorts, and with greater risk of detection and attack from the air.

During the war 1,170 U-boats were built, of which 1,000 went on operations. Of these 781 were lost – a loss rate of nearly 80%.

The workhorse of the German submarine fleet was the Type VII. A good design, it underwent many updates and improvements, the main model being the Type VIIC.

U-boats only dived when necessary: they were designed for a good surface speed and a long range on diesel engines. While they were submerged they could only operate on battery-powered electric motors, and these had a very limited endurance – one hour at 9 knots or four days at 2 knots, though after one day the air would become fouled. They tended to make attacks at night, on the surface, using their high speed and low silhouette in order to avoid detection.

In the latter part of the war schnorkels began to be fitted, giving the U-boats the means to run their powerful diesel engines while submerged, as these needed oxygen to operate.

The new Type XXI boats began to enter service as the war was drawing to a close. They had a greatly increased battery capacity and a much better top speed when operating on either diesel engines or electric motors.

RAEDER

Rank attained	Grand Admiral
Dates	1876–1960
Background	Career sailor
Commands	C-in-C German Navy, 1939–43

Admiral Erich Raeder saw service in World War I and naval action during the Battle of Jutland. He developed the idea of the 'pocket' battleship. Hitler appointed him C-in-C of the German Navy. He was in overall command of the planning of the successful seaborne invasion of Norway, but he thought that the projected invasion of Great Britain in 1940 far too ambitious. Hitler and he always clashed with regard to the use of the German surface fleet. After the failure of German ships during the Battle of the Barents Sea, Hitler threatened to scrap the surface fleet and deploy only U-boats. He then had Raeder dismissed and replaced him

with Dönitz. Raeder was sentenced to ten years' imprisonment for war crimes at Nuremberg.

Karl Dönitz also saw service during World War I, including the command of a U-boat. In 1939 he published a monograph *Die U-bootswaffe* (The U-Boat Arm). He developed the tactical concept of the submarine 'wolf pack' wherein a number of submarines would simultaneously attack a convoy at night, on the surface, using their superior surface speed and low silhouette to avoid the escorts. When he received command of the U-Boat Arm he established firm control over the technical aspects of submarine design as well as their tactical use. He started the war with just 57 boats, and even though initially there were problems with German torpedo design the U-boat Arm had some spectacular successes, such as the sinking of the British battleship HMS *Royal Oak* within the confines of the British naval base at Scapa Flow. Between May and December 1940, a period that the U-boat Arm called 'Die Glückliche Zeit' (The Happy Time), the U-boats operated with a high degree of success considering how few in number they were. A second 'Happy Time' lasted from January to August 1942 with U-boats attacking unprotected US shipping off the east coast of the United States. By 1943 Dönitz had more that 200 U-boats in commission but by then the Allies had got the better of them. It was not impossible that Dönitz could have forced Britain to surrender had he been given sufficient numbers of U-boats earlier in the war. Hitler always held Dönitz in high regard and named him as his successor: he became Head of State on April 30, 1945, negotiating the capitulation. A well-respected leader and highly regarded by both his foes and those that served with him, he was sentenced to ten years' imprisonment at the Nuremberg Trials.

DÖNITZ

Rank attained	Grand Admiral
Dates	1891–1980
Background	Career sailor
Commands	Flag Officer Commanding U-Boats, 1935; C-in-C German Navy, 1943

Above: *Aerial view of Henderson Field on Guadalcanal, late August 1942. The view looks north-west with the Lunga River and Lunga Point at the top of the image.*

The Allies now sought to halt the Japanese advance in the Solomons, which threatened to cut lines of communication between the United States and Australia. On August 7 began one of the toughest battles of the Pacific War, fought in swamp, jungle, grassland, in the skies and at sea. The initial landings were problem-free, and the airfield under construction near Lunga Point was captured and renamed Henderson Field (in honor of a Marine pilot killed at Midway).

The Japanese were not slow to react, reinforcing and engaging with the Marines in a series of fierce battles, culminating in the Battle of 'Bloody Ridge' on September 12–14, where they were repulsed in an all-out attempt to retake the airfield.

Above: U.S. Marines rest in the field on Guadalcanal, circa August–December 1942.

Above: Japanese dead, killed while trying to outflank Marines on Guadalcanal.

aboard, the U-boat organizes rescue but, by misunderstanding, is subsequently attacked. The result is the German 'Laconia Order' to U-boats forbidding rescue of sunken ships

Sept 12–18, 1942 Arctic convoys restart with PQ18, which loses 13 ships

Oct 17, 1942 Le Creusot, longest-distance USAAF air raid thus far

Oct 22/3, 1942 Genoa, first large-scale raid on the city

Oct 24, 1942 Milan bombed

Oct 23, 1942 Western Task Force, bound for Morocco, leaves USA

Nov 11, 1942 Germans occupy Vichy France

Dec 6, 1942 Eindhoven bombed

Dec 20/1, 1942 Lutterade, first RAF use of Oboe navigational aid

Dec 31, 1942 Battle of the Barents Sea: *Lützow*, *Admiral Hipper* and 6 destroyers attack Arctic convoy JW51B but are repulsed

MADAGASCAR: The Allied Takeover

Sept 10, 1942 British amphibious landing at Majunga on Madagascar

Sept 18, 1942 British amphibious landing at Tamatave on Madagascar

Nov 5, 1942 British finally secure Madagascar

GUADALCANAL: The Turning-Point Campaign

Aug 7, 1942 US landings on Guadalcanal, Tulagi, Gavutu and surrounding islands. Tulagi and Gavutu are opposed; Guadalcanal is not

Aug 9, 1942 Battle of Savo Island. Japanese squadron under Admiral Mikawa surprises a US force. The Americans lose four cruisers sunk and one damaged. Both sides withdraw, leaving the Marines on shore unsupported

Aug 8, 1942 US troops seize Japanese airfield and name it Henderson Field

Aug 19, 1942 First Battle of the Matanikau: US destroy a small Japanese garrison

Aug 21, 1942 Battle of the Tenaru. US

US MARINE CORPS

The strength of the Marine Corps at the time of the Japanese attack on Pearl Harbor was 65,000, but by the end of the war it had risen to 450,000, incorporating six combat divisions. The Corps suffered over 90,000 casualties, of which 20,000 were killed.

The US Marines are a separate service within the US Navy, being the latter's land combat troops as well as having an autonomous amphibious operations role. It also had its own aviation with 10 squadrons at the start of the war and 132 squadrons at the end, flying bombing, fighter and tactical air support missions. The top-scoring USMC fighter ace was Gregory 'Pappy' Boyington, with 24 kills to his credit.

The esprit de corps of the US Marines is legendary. One of the USA's toughest military services, they were in continuous combat in the Pacific from the battle for Wake Island in December 1941 to Okinawa in June 1945. The Marines experienced some of the most gruelling battles of the entire conflict.

The Marine Corps began its development of modern amphibious warfare techniques working closely with the Navy. With the increasing experience of the amphibious assaults in the Pacific, the Marines became ever more proficient and the developing tactics were given ample chance to prove themselves during the assaults on Guadalcanal, Bougainville, Tarawa,

Roi-Namur, Eniwetok, New Britain, Tinian, Guam, Peleliu, Iwo Jima and Okinawa.

The Iwo Jima battle cost the Marines about 20,000 casualties, the highest number suffered by the Corps in a single engagement. It epitomised the fighting spirit of the Corps. A very small Pacific island 650 miles south of Japan, it had strategic significance due to its proximity to the Japanese homeland. The Japanese turned the entire volcanic island into a labyrinth of large tunnels and fortifications. The battle was hard and the determination of the Japanese defenders implacable, only a handful of whom survived. When the Marines reached the summit of Mount Suribachi on February 23 the American flag was raised.

Right: *The famous image of US Marines raising the Stars and Stripes on Mount Suribachi.*

Below: *US Marines fighting on Bougainville.*

Above: Portrait of a Marine on the island of Guam, July 1944.

Above: A Marine dashes through Japanese machine-gun fire while crossing a draw called Death Valley by the men fighting there, Okinawa, May 10, 1945.

Marines defeat a Japanese attack

Aug 24, 1942 Battle of the Eastern Solomons. Indecisive Japanese attempt to reinforce Guadalcanal, but the Japanese light carrier *Ryujo* is sunk and 90 aircraft lost. US carrier *Enterprise* is badly damaged

Aug 27, 1942 Second Battle of the Matanikau: US attack repulsed

Sept 8, 1942 Tasimboko Raid. US raiders and parachutists destroy Japanese supplies

Sept 12–14, 1942 Battle of 'Bloody Ridge'. Japanese make a three-pronged attack to retake Henderson Field. The attacks are disjointed and unsuccessful

Sept 23 to Oct 9, 1942 General Vandegrift initiates three operations to expand the Lunga Perimeter by attempting to push the Japanese from Matanikau, but the Japanese hold on and prove too strong

Oct 11, 1942 Battle of Cape Esperance. Both sides land reinforcements and the Japanese bombard Henderson Field

Oct 23–26, 1942 Battle for Henderson Field. Major Japanese air/land/sea offensive defeated

Oct 26, 1942 Battle of the Santa Cruz Islands, east of the Solomons. US carrier *Hornet* is sunk, leaving the US with just one serviceable carrier

Nov 1–4, 1942 American western offensive. US Marines cross the Matanikau and pass Point Cruz

Nov 2–3, 1942 American eastern offensive. US Marines push the Japanese from the Koli Point area

Nov 5 to Dec 4, 1942 US 2nd Raider Battalion ('Carlson's Raiders') patrols from Aola to Mount Austen

Nov 12–13, 1942 First Naval Battle of Guadalcanal. US ships land reinforcements and come under fire from a Japanese force including two battleships en route to bombard Henderson Field. Japanese battleship *Hiei* is sunk and both commanding admirals are killed

Nov 14–15, 1942 Second Naval Battle for Guadalcanal. A Japanese bombardment

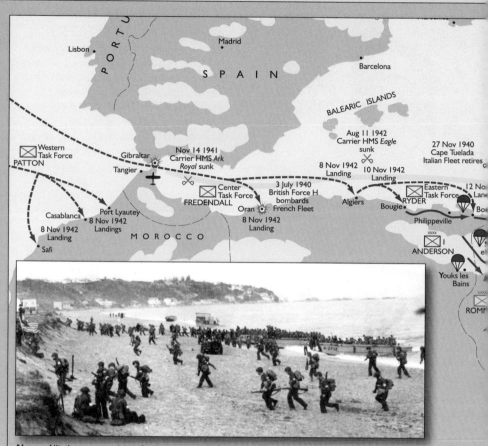

Above: Allied troops coming ashore, unopposed, during the 'Torch' landings.

The 'Torch' Landings, November, 1942

Intended to open up a second front against the Axis, and thereby relieve pressure on the Russians, the Allied invasion of Vichy French Morocco and Algeria involved major US troop involvement in theater for the first time. Convoys from Scotland and direct from the USA made landings around Casablanca, at Oran and Algiers. The French put up a fight until the 10th. As a result, a suspicious Hitler sent forces to occupy Vichy France and to seize the remnant of the French fleet at Toulon. Meanwhile German troops were deployed to Tunisia.

A week after the landings, Allied forces entered Tunisia from the west, but the German build-up of troops there was accelerating. The Allied advance, delayed by rain and directed unimpressively, met an aggressive resistance led by some of Hitler's élite paratroops. A quick conquest of Tunisia was frustrated, and the campaign dragged on through the spring of 1943. German counterattacks in the Eastern Dorsals led to a surprise stroke by Rommel against First Army at Kasserine, while his spoiling attack on Eighth Army at Medenine was blunted by a lack of surprise owing to Allied 'Ultra' decrypts. Eighth Army finally cracked Rommel's Mareth Line defenses by the end of March and joined the First Army frontline within fifty miles of Tunis by April 21. Tunisia fell on May 7 and four days later Tunisia was in Allied hands, together with nearly a quarter of a million prisoners.

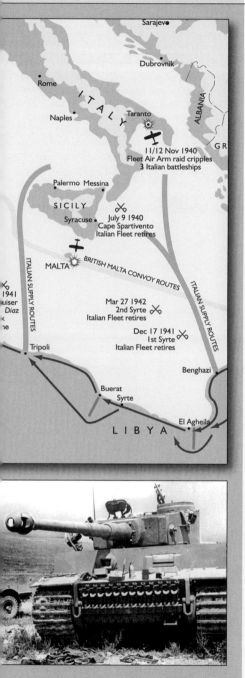

On the map:

Sarajevo

Dubrovnik

Rome

I T A L Y

Naples

Taranto

ALBANIA

11/12 Nov 1940
Fleet Air Arm raid cripples
3 Italian battleships

G R

Palermo Messina

SICILY

Syracuse July 9 1940
Cape Spartivento
Italian Fleet retires

MALTA BRITISH MALTA CONVOY ROUTES

ITALIAN SUPPLY ROUTES

ITALIAN SUPPLY ROUTES

1941
uiser
Diaz
ne

Mar 27 1942
2nd Syrte
Italian Fleet retires

Dec 17 1941
1st Syrte
Italian Fleet retires

Tripoli

Benghazi

Buerat
Syrte

El Agheila

L I B Y A

Above: A German Tiger tank knocked-out during the fighting in Tunisia.

force is turned back by the US force, which includes two battleships. *South Dakota* is badly damaged, but *Washington* sinks Japanese battleship *Kirishima*. This is the last major attempt by the Japanese to land reinforcements

NORTH AFRICA: 'Torch' Landings/Tunisia
Escorting the invasion fleet for 'Torch' are US battleships *Massachusetts*, *Texas* and *New York* plus other units. These subsequently augment Allied naval strength in the Mediterranean

Oct 26, 1942 Center and Eastern Task Forces, bound for Algeria, leave Scotland
Nov 8, 1942 'Torch' Landings in Morocco and Algeria meet Vichy French resistance
Nov 9, 1942 Paratroops from Sicily spearhead German deployment to Tunisia
Nov 10, 1942 Admiral Darlan, Vichy High Commissioner in Algeria, orders ceasefire
Nov 11, 1942 Allied 36 Bde makes amphibious landing at Bougie
Nov 11, 1942 Armistice between Allies and French in Morocco and Algeria
Nov 12, 1942 Allied paratroops and commandos make air/sea landings at Bône
Nov 15–16, 1942 Allied forces advance into Tunisia but make slow progress, hampered by rain. Meanwhile the Germans become stronger as more troops arrive
Nov 24, 1942 Allied forces resume their attack
Nov 27, 1942 At Toulon the French scuttle their fleet to prevent its capture by the Germans
Nov 27 to Dec 28, 1942 Allied forces meet stiffer resistance in northern Tunisia. Battles at Bald, Green and Longstop Hills and attempts to outflank the German line fail
Dec 3, 1942 Allies seize Faid Pass in central Tunisia
Dec 24, 1942 Darlan assassinated in Algiers
Jan 23, 1943 Rommel enters Tunisia while Eighth Army enters Tripoli. Rommel fortifies the Mareth Line against Eighth Army while

BRITISH ARMY

The British Army had a strength of less than 900,000 Regular and Territorial soldiers when war was declared in September 1939.

The British Expeditionary Force (BEF) began to cross to France that same month. It was initially composed of four infantry divisions with 50 light tanks, but by May 1940 six more divisions had arrived and it now totalled over 390,000 men. Tank strength had grown to 300. On May 14, 1940 the Germans attacked and the BEF quickly became almost surrounded. It withdrew to Dunkirk and was evacuated across the Channel, back to Britain, with over 338,000 men, including 53,000 French. Another 136,000 were evacuated from other ports. They left 64,000 vital military vehicles and nearly 2,500 artillery pieces behind in France.

The Eighth Army was formed in September 1941, from the Western Desert Force that had defeated the Italians in North Africa. It included many units from the Empire. After losing ground against the Afrika Korps it won the Second Battle of El Alamein in November 1942 and eventually participated in the ejection of the Axis forces from North Africa. It then participated in the Italian campaign, fighting its way eventually into Austria. It had distinguished itself fighting in the difficult conditions of North Africa and Italy.

The Second Army was formed in 1943 and after the landings in Normandy in 1944 it fought through France, Belgium, the Netherlands and into Germany.

The worst defeat suffered by the British during the war was at Singapore where

Below: A mortar team prepares to open fire.

Sten gun.

130,000 British and colonial troops surrendered to the Japanese in February 1942.

The Fourteenth and then the Twelfth Armies fought during the long campaign and reconquest of Burma.

In terms of its military structure, each British army was divided into corps, a unit of approximately 30,000 troops and composed of two or more divisions. The division consisted of 10,000–15,000 soldiers of several different brigades, each with a strength ranging between 1,500 and 3,500. The brigade consisted of three or more battalion-size units.

The first half of the war taught the British Army some very harsh lessons in modern warfare and a series of sobering defeats were suffered, but after the victory in North Africa the majority of British battles led to victory.

Shortfalls in British equipment were made up with the huge quantities of American equipment that became available. British innovations, however, included the Sten submachine-gun, which was particularly cheap and simple to manufacture and was produced in large numbers.

At its peak the British Army had 11 armored divisions, 34 infantry divisions and two airborne divisions. Over 3½ million men and women had enlisted, of whom 144,000 were killed, 240,000 were wounded and 152,000 made prisoners of war. A great many colonial troops fought within the British Army's structure.

Above: *Eighth Army anti-tank gunners with a 6-pounder (57mm) anti-tank gun.*

redeploying north-west to bolster defense of the southern Eastern Dorsals against Allied First Army

Jan 18, 1943 Axis offensive in central Tunisia secures all the passes in the Eastern Dorsal mountains

Jan 23, 1943 Ambrosio becomes Supreme Commander Axis forces in Tunisia with Arnim's Fifth Panzer Army in the north, Rommel's First Italian Army (ex-Panzerarmee Afrika) in the south

Feb 14–22, 1943 Von Arnim and Rommel launch pincer attack across the Eastern Dorsals

Feb, 19, 1943 Rommel takes Kasserine Pass but makes little further progress

Feb 23, 1943 Axis reorganization consolidates Tunisia forces as Army Group Afrika, with Rommel in overall command

Feb 26 to March, 19, 1943 Allied offensive in the north fails to break through

March 6, 1943 Battle of Medenine: Rommel's pre-emptive strike against Eighth Army repulsed, Montgomery warned by 'Ultra' intercepts

March 17–31, 1943 Patton's II Corps thrusts in the southern Eastern Dorsals taking Gafsa and Maknassy pass

March 20–8, 1943 Eighth Army attacks and breaks through the Mareth Line. Germans fall back north to Enfidaville

April, 19–21, 1943 Eighth Army fails to break through at Enfidaville

May 6, 1943 Final Allied assault on the Axis perimeter

May 7, 1943 Allies take Tunis and Bizerta

May 11, 1943 Allies finally secure Tunisia

BURMA: First Arakan Campaign

Dec 17, 1942 British 14th Division advances down the coast from Cox's Bazaar toward Akyab

Dec 22, 1942 Japanese pull back from Maungdaw as the British approach

Dec 28, 1942 Japanese repulse attempts to take Rathedaung

Jan 7, 1943 British repulsed from Donbaik

GUADALCANAL

A significant aspect of the battle was reinforcement, as each side sought to build up troops on the island and to keep them resupplied. This led to a series of air/sea battles centering on New Georgia Sound, between Guadalcanal and the Florida Islands to the north, which became known as 'the Slot' and the Japanese reinforcement missions as the 'Tokyo Express'. Japanese warships and aircraft also pounded Henderson Field, which was under constant repair.

Such were the naval losses that the waterway was also dubbed 'Ironbottom Sound'. During seven naval battles – of Savo Island, the Eastern Solomons, Cape Esperance, the Santa Cruz Islands, First and Second Guadalcanal and Tassafaronga – the Japanese lost a light carrier, 2 battleships, 4 cruisers and 11 destroyers. The Americans lost the fleet carrier *Hornet* – leaving the badly damaged *Enterprise* the only US carrier in the Pacific – 10 cruisers and 14 destroyers. The two naval Battles of Guadalcanal were crucial, with battleship-to-battleship action, and saw the last major Japanese attempt at reinforcement.

After the air and sea battle for Henderson Field the US troops expanded their area of operations during late September. Against stubborn opposition, the Americans pushed west along the coast, finally forcing the Japanese to withdraw their surviving forces during the first days of February.

The grueling six-month battle for Guadalcanal was a major turning-point in the Pacific. The Japanese advance had been stopped, and the Allies would now begin to take the offensive.

Below: The Battle of Santa Cruz, October 26, 1942. The sky is full of bursting flak explosions. Japanese bomb splashes can just be seen astern of the carrier USS Enterprise.

Above: *The Japanese battleship* Kirishima *was sunk on November 15, 1942.*

GUADALCANAL NAVAL BATTLES LOSSES

	ALLIES	JAPANESE
Savo Island, August 8/9 1942	4 cruisers	nil
Eastern Solomons, August 23, 1942	nil	1 aircraft carrier 1 destroyer
Cape Esperance, October 11/12, 1942	1 destroyer	1 cruiser 1 destroyer
Santa Cruz, October 24–26, 1942	1 aircraft carrier	nil
Guadalcanal, November 12–15, 1942	2 cruisers, 7 destroyers	2 battleships, 1 cruiser, 3 destroyers
Tassafaronga, November 30, 1942	1 cruiser	1 destroyers

Feb 1–3, 1943 Further British attacks repulsed north of Akyab

March 7, 1943 Japanese attack on the east bank of the Mayu River

April 3, 1943 Japanese cut off and capture British brigade at Indin

April 15, 1943 General Slim takes command of British troops in the Arakan area

May 4, 1943 Japanese begin encircling Maungdaw

May 14, 1943 Japanese take Maungdaw as Slim withdraws

PAPUA-NEW GUINEA

Dec 2, 1942 Japanese reinforcements arrive north of Gona

Dec 8, 1942 Australians take Gona after hard fighting

Dec 14, 1942 More Japanese arrive to defend Buna-Gona

Dec 14, 1942 Buna village falls to the Allies

Jan 2, 1943 Allies take Buna Mission. Mopping up takes another three weeks

Early Jan, 1943 Japanese Eighteenth Army reinforces Lae and Salamaua on New Guinea. They advance inland

Jan 28, 1943 Japanese reach Australian position at Wau. Rain temporarily halts operations allowing the Australians to reinforce Wau and fight off the Japanese attack

Feb 13/14, 1943 Wingate's Chindits cross the Chindwin River into Burma aiming to cut the Myitkyina-Mandalay railway

End February The Japanese have been repulsed and forced back to Mubo. They are now heavily reinforced by the remainder of Eighteenth Army

Feb 28, 1943 Ledo Road reaches Burma frontier from China, but construction is then delayed by rain

GUADALCANAL

Nov 30, 1942 Battle of Tassafaronga. A Japanese destroyer force attempting to drop off supplies is driven away by American forces

Dec 9, 1942 1st Marine Division relieved

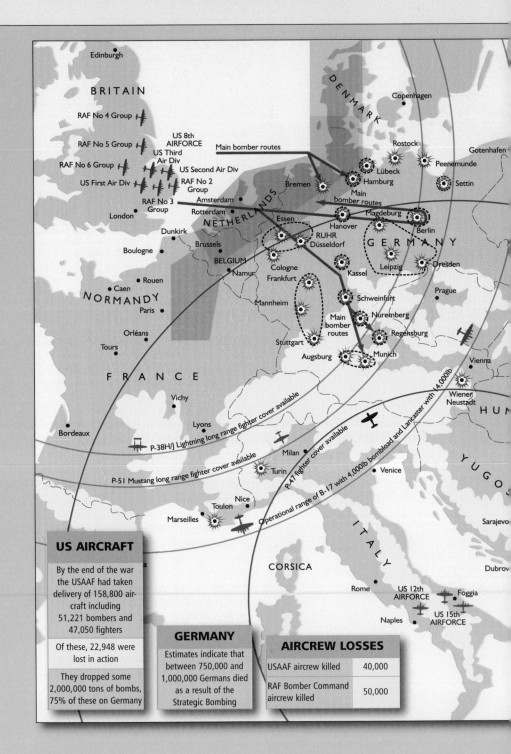

Edinburgh

BRITAIN

RAF No 4 Group

RAF No 5 Group

US 8th
AIRFORCE
US Third
Air Div

RAF No 6 Group

US Second Air Div

US First Air Div

RAF No 2
Group

RAF No 3
Group

London

Amsterdam

Rotterdam

DENMARK

Copenhagen

Rostock

Gotenhafen

Peenemunde

Lübeck

Settin

Hamburg

Bremen

Main
bomber routes

Magdeburg

Berlin

NETHERLANDS

Main bomber routes

Essen

Hanover

Dunkirk

Brussels

RUHR
Düsseldorf

GERMANY

Boulogne

BELGIUM

Namur

Cologne
Frankfurt

Kassel

Leipzig

Dresden

Caen

Rouen

NORMANDY

Paris

Mannheim

Schweinfurt

Prague

Main
bomber
routes

Nuremberg

Orléans

Stuttgart

Regensburg

Tours

Augsburg

Munich

Vienna

FRANCE

Vichy

Wiener
Neustadt

HU

Lyons

P-38H/J Lightning long range fighter cover available

Bordeaux

Milan

Venice

P-51 Mustang long range fighter cover available

Turin

P-47 fighter cover available

YUGOS

Nice

Toulon

Marseilles

Operational range of B-17 with 1,000lb bombload and Lancaster with 14,000lb

Sarajevo

CORSICA

ITALY

Dubrov

Rome

US 12th
AIRFORCE

Foggia

Naples

US 15th
AIRFORCE

US AIRCRAFT

By the end of the war the USAAF had taken delivery of 158,800 aircraft including 51,221 bombers and 47,050 fighters

Of these, 22,948 were lost in action

They dropped some 2,000,000 tons of bombs, 75% of these on Germany

GERMANY

Estimates indicate that between 750,000 and 1,000,000 Germans died as a result of the Strategic Bombing

AIRCREW LOSSES

USAAF aircrew killed	40,000
RAF Bomber Command aircrew killed	50,000

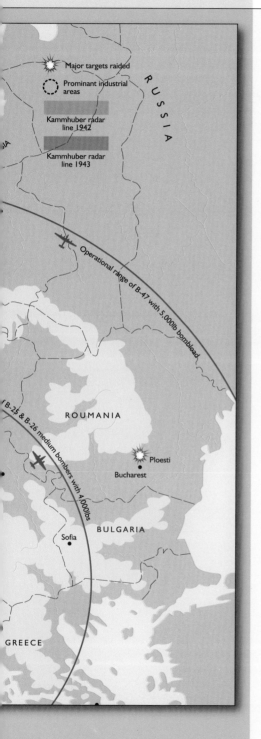

Major targets raided

Prominant industrial areas

Kammhuber radar line 1942

Kammhuber radar line 1943

R U S S I A

Operational range of B-47 with 5,000lb bombload

B-25 & B-26 medium bombers with 4,000lbs

ROUMANIA

Ploesti

Bucharest

BULGARIA

Sofia

GREECE

by XIV Corps under General Patch
Dec 15, 1942 to Jan 26, 1943 US Army offensive to drive the Japanese from Mount Austen area
Jan 13–17, 1943 US troops push the Japanese from the Point Cruz area
Jan 22–3, 1943 The westward push continues, and the Japanese are driven out of Kokumbona area
Feb 1–8, 1943 The Japanese withdraw from Doma Cove on destroyers
Feb 9, 1943 Guadalcanal is finally secured by the Americans

Western Theater General Events
Jan 1, 1943 No. 6 Group, Royal Canadian Air Force, formed; first operation Jan 3/4, Essen
Jan 30–1, 1943 Allied Casablanca conference
Jan 27, 1943 Vegesack raided (US)
Jan 30, 1943 The Battle of the Barents Sea infuriates Hitler and results in the replacement of Raeder by Dönitz as head of the Kriegsmarine
Jan 30/1, 1943 Hamburg raided, first use of H2S
Jan–March, 1943 Germans drive Tito's partisans into Montenegro
Feb 28, 1943 Vermork raid: commandos cripple German atomic research plant in Norway
Early March, 1943 U-boats sink 22% of ships in convoys attacked during a gap in 'Ultra' intelligence
Feb 23 to April 6, 1943 RAF bomb U-boat bases with limited success
March 3, 1943 RAF Mosquitoes raid Knaben molybdenum mine in Norway
March 3, 1943 Bethnal Green Tube Station accident in London: 173 people are crushed to death
March 5/6, 1943 Essen, first raid in Battle of the Ruhr
March 15–19, 1943 Battles of Atlantic convoys HX229 and SC122: 37 U-boats attack 98 merchantmen; 21 ships are sunk

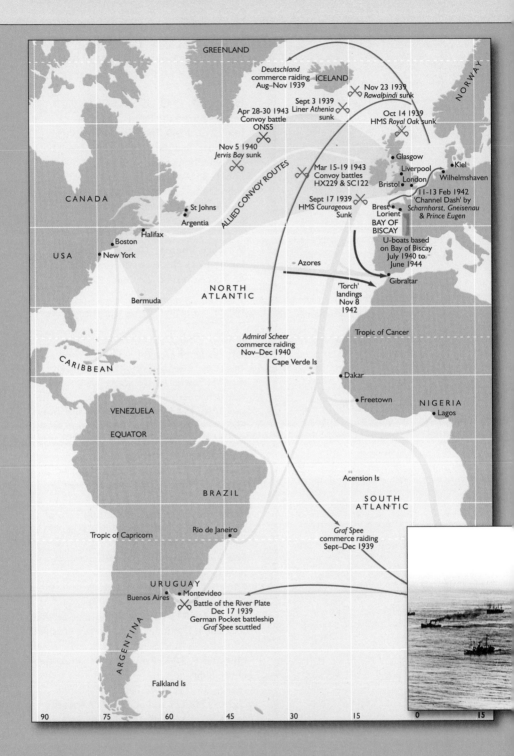

GREENLAND

Deutschland
commerce raiding   ICELAND
Aug–Nov 1939   Nov 23 1939
                           Rawalpindi sunk

                Sept 3 1939
Apr 28-30 1943 Liner *Athenia*
Convoy battle   sunk   Oct 14 1939
ONS5   HMS *Royal Oak* sunk

Nov 5 1940
Jervis Bay sunk   • Glasgow
                      Liverpool   • Kiel
                        London • Wilhelmshaven
                    Bristol •
            Mar 15-19 1943   11-13 Feb 1942
            Convoy battles   'Channel Dash' by
            HX229 & SC122   *Scharnhorst, Gneisenau*
                                  & Prince Eugen
            Sept 17 1939   Brest •
CANADA   HMS *Courageous* Lorient
            Sunk   BAY OF
                            BISCAY
        • St Johns   U-boats based
                                on Bay of Biscay
        • Argentia   July 1940 to
    • Halifax   June 1944
    • Boston
USA • New York   • Gibraltar
                    • Azores   'Torch'
                                 landings
• Bermuda   Nov 8
            NORTH   1942
            ATLANTIC

                                 Tropic of Cancer
CARIBBEAN
            Admiral Scheer
            commerce raiding
            Nov–Dec 1940
            Cape Verde Is   • Dakar

VENEZUELA   • Freetown   NIGERIA
                                              • Lagos
EQUATOR

                                 Acension Is

        BRAZIL   SOUTH
                                 ATLANTIC

Tropic of Capricorn
            • Rio de Janeiro   *Graf Spee*
                                 commerce raiding
                                 Sept–Dec 1939

URUGUAY
            • Montevideo
Buenos Aires • Battle of the River Plate
                Dec 17 1939
                German Pocket battleship
                Graf Spee scuttled

ARGENTINA

    Falkland Is

90   75   60   45   30   15   0   15

ALLIED CONVOY ROUTES

NORWAY

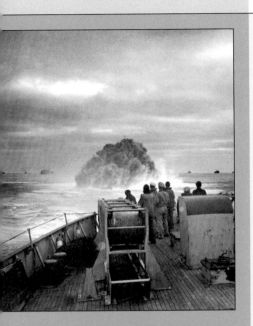

Above: A depth-charge explodes, sinking U-175 on April 17, 1943, a kill for US Coast Guard Cutter Spencer.

Below: An Allied convoy at sea. This system of protecting merchantmen from the menace of the U-boats was reintroduced in 1917 during World War I – convoys were common in the wars of earlier centuries. In 1942 it became evident that larger convoys offered better protection than smaller ones, so that convoys tended to become bigger – the biggest being one transatlantic convoy in 1944 of 187 ships.

March 26, 1943 ELAS, Communist resistance committe for liberation of Greece established

March–May, 1943 Climax of the Battle of the Atlantic. Convoys HX229 and SC122 are disastrous for the Allies. But a combination of Allied advances swings the balance decisively in their favor – including asdic, HF/DF, 10cm radar, improved depth-charges, breaking of the new 'Enigma' code, the closing of the mid-Atlantic air gap, more A/S vessels, escort carriers, and support groups independent of the convoys to hunt and sink U-boats

April 12, 1943 Eaker Plan for Combined Bomber Offensive proposes USAAF daylight bombing, RAF night attacks on German industrial infrastructure

April 13, 1943 Germans announce discovery of the mass grave marking the Katyn massacre of Polish officers, perpetrated by the Soviets in spring 1940 near Smolensk

BURMA: First Chindit Expedition
March 1, 1943 Chindits reach Pinbon
March 3–4, 1943 Chindits clash with Japanese, who are now aware of their presence
March 3, 1943 Chindits cut the railway line at Kyaiktin
March 6, 1943 Chindits destroy railway bridges near Bongyaung. Meanwhile a second body of Chindits is operating farther south as a feint. Wingate advances across the Irrawaddy River to destroy the Gokteik Gorge viaduct, which will cut the Lashio–Mandalay Road
March 24, 1943 As Japanese close in on the Chindits from three sides, Wingate is ordered to withdraw, aborting the Gokteik Gorge operation
March 28, 1943 Wingate's attempt to cross the Irrawaddy at Inywa repulsed. Chindits break up into small parties to exfiltrate
April 14–29, 1943 Chindits cross

When the the US was attacked at Pearl Harbor by the Japanese, the eight battleships of the Pacific Fleet were either sunk or badly damaged, but, apart from two, they were eventually repaired and returned to service. America had a total of 17 battleships when she started the war and 25 at the finish.

The most potent of the US Navy's battleships were the four ships of the *Iowa* class. They remained in service until the mid-1990s, two firing their guns in anger for the last time during the 1991 Gulf War.

One hundred cruisers saw service with the USN during the war years, of which ten were sunk. The most numerous, and also the most typical, were the 38 ships of the *Cleveland* class. They were good all-round fighting ships, seeing much action from the Mediterranean and across the Pacific fighting to the final surrender of Japan, without the loss of a single ship of the class.

Of the 441 destroyers of the US Navy's fleet, 59 were lost. The most famous were the *Fletcher* class which made up 176 of the total number of destroyers built; 19 were lost, predominantly to Kamikaze attack. Good all-round combat ships, they bore the brunt of much of the sea fighting against the Japanese, accounting directly for the sinking of ten

Japanese destroyers and 21 submarines and assisting in the destruction of numerous other ships.

Fletcher Class Destroyers	
Displacement	2,900 tons
Crew	273
Armament	5 x 5in guns & 10 x 21in torpedo tubes
Engine/motor	Two turbines, 60,000hp, max. speed 38 knots
Dimensions	Length: 376ft 5in Beam 39ft 7in

Fletcher *class destroyer*

Right: *The* Fletcher *class destroyer USS Cassin Young (DD 793) moored at the Charlestown Memorial Naval Shipyard. She honors Captain Cassin Young, who earned the Medal of Honor during the attack on Pearl Harbor on December 7, 1941. He was later killed during a surface action with Japanese forces at the Battle of Guadalcanal.*

Iowa Class Battleships	
Displacement	58,000 tons
Crew	1,921
Armament	9 x 16in, 20 x 5in guns
Armor	Max: 440mm. Min: 152mm
Engine	Four turbines, 212,000hp, max. speed 32 knots
Dimensions	Length: 887ft 3in Beam 108ft 2in

Right: A Cleveland *class cruiser.*

Below: *A battleship of the* Iowa *class.*

Above: The battleship USS Pennsylvania *with other battleships in line ahead.*

Cleveland Class Cruisers	
Displacement	14,000 tons
Crew	1,285
Armament	12 x 6in & 12 x 5in guns
Armor	Max: 165mm
Engine	Four turbines, 100,000hp, max. speed 32 knots
Dimensions	Length: 610ft 1in Beam 66ft 4in

Chindwin River back to India. Of 3,000 Chindits, nearly a third do not get back to India

Far Eastern Theater General Events
December, 1942 Stilwell begins building the Ledo Road, Assam to China via north Burma
Jan 12, 1943 US land on Amchitka and build an airfield to attack Kiska
Feb 18, 1943 US bombard Attu
Feb 21, 1943 US occupy Banika and Pavuvu, north-west of Guadalcanal
March, 1943 Japanese reorganize in Burma: General Kawabe commands Burma Area Army
March 3–5, 1943 Battle of the Bismarck Sea. US intercept Japanese convoy bound for Lae and Salamaua, sinking all 8 transports
March 6, 1943 US bombard Munda on New Georgia
March 8, 1943 Japanese offensive up Yangtse River, essentially a large-scale raid
March 11, 1943 US Fourteenth Air Force established in China under Chennault
March 12–15, 1943 Pacific Military Conference, Washington plans to clear Solomons and New Britain
March 26, 1943 Battle of the Komandorski Islands (Bering Sea). US squadron turns back Japanese supply convoy for Attu and Kiska. Uniquely in the Pacific, this is a daytime fleet action in which carriers play no part
March 28, 1943 US plans capture of Rabaul
March 31, 1943 Nimitz plans reconquest of Attu
April 18, 1943 Japanese CinC Combined Fleet Admiral Yamamoto killed over Bougainville, after 'Magic' intelligence forewarns US of his itinerary

Warsaw Ghetto Uprising
April, 19 to May 8, 1943 Warsaw Ghetto uprising by Jews. Uprising is brutally suppressed by the Germans. Over 50,000

STALIN	
Dates	1879–1953
Background	Bolshevik Revolutionary
Offices	Dictator of the USSR and Commander of the USSR's Armed Forces

In 1937 seven of the top Red Army commanders were charged with conspiracy against Stalin and were convicted and executed. Another 30,000 members of the armed forces were also executed, including half of all the army officers. This was all instigated by Stalin's paranoia. He secretly agreed to partition Poland in September 1939 and then conquered Lithuania, Latvia and Estonia and incorporated them into the Soviet Union. Resistance was short-lived and brutally repressed. People from the military, commercial, professional or cultured classes were generally imprisoned or executed. Stalin then suffered a disastrous setback when the Soviets invaded Finland and

Left: *A Soviet idealized portrait of Stalin.*

Below: *He arrives for the Yalta Conference in 1945.*

came up against the dogged resistance of the Finns. Stalin was reluctant to believe the rumors of Germany's impending invasion of the Soviet Union in 1941, calculating that it would not happen until 1942. His military experience was limited, and showed itself, so he turned to the generals he could trust. Stalin's forte was political negotiation. He showed great cunning in his dealings with Roosevelt and Churchill. His constant urging for a second front created some friction within the Allies. By means of commisars Stalin made it very clear to Soviet soldiers who might be thought to have let down the Soviet Union that they would be severely punished. He extended this rule after the war to Soviet soldiers who had been captured: they were to be considered traitors. The Soviet people lived in fear of both Stalin and Hitler and thus had no option but to stand and fight. As the war progressed and the Soviet armies advanced west, the countries that came under Stalin's control would continue to remain so. They were not liberated, they were conquered. Political opposition to Stalin was not tolerated, and this was to lead to the forty years of the 'Cold War'.

Above: *Stalin with his Foreign Minister, Molotov.*

Jews die
RUSSIA: Soviet Kharkov Offensive
Jan 3, 1943 Germans begin evacuation of the Caucasus area south of the Manych River
Jan 13–18, 1943 Soviet offensives across the Don River by the Bryansk and Voronezh Fronts encircle Hungarian Second Army and Italian Eighth Army
Jan 27, 1943 80,00 men of the encircled Hungarian and Italian armies surrender creating a 200-mile gap in the Army Group B front
Jan 27, 1943 Hitler sanctions withdrawal of Army Group Don behind the Donets
Jan 30, 1943 Soviet Bryansk and Voronezh Front offensive encircles two-thirds of German Second Army
Feb 4, 1943 Soviet amphibious landing near Novorossisk
Feb 8, 1943 Soviets take Kursk
Feb 14, 1943 Soviets take Rostov and Voroshilovgrad
Feb 15–17, 1943 Soviets eliminate Demyansk salient
Feb 16, 1943 Germans evacuate Kharkov
Feb 17, 1943 Hitler visits Army Group South HQ at Zaporozhe and agrees to von Manstein's plans for counterattack
Feb 20, 1943 Von Manstein's offensive surprises the Soviet Voronezh and South-West Fronts
Feb 20, 1943 Soviets take Pavlograd and Krasnograd, closing on the Dnieper River
Feb 28, 1943 Germans reach the Donetz near Izyum
March 4–15, 1943 The second phase of Manstein's offensive retakes Kharkov
March 18, 1943 Germans take Belgorod. Von Manstein has now eliminated the Soviet salient south of Kursk; the spring thaw and resulting mud postpones further operations against the Kursk salient

ALEUTIANS
May 11, 1943 US land on Attu, supported for the first time in the Pacific by aircraft

ATROCITIES

The list of atrocities committed during the war is large and, sadly, many of the perpetrators were never punished. Typical was the massacre in the French village of Oradour-sur-Glane in June 1944 by the German 2nd Waffen SS Panzer Division. It was carried out in revenge for local resistance activity. The Germans herded all the villagers, men, women and children, into some barns and the village church and then set the buildings alight. As people tried to flee they were shot down. A few did manage to escape. The Germans then looted and burned the village. Oradour-sur-Glane now stands, unoccupied, as a memorial.

In 1942 the Czech village of Lidice was razed to the ground, the 198 men of the village were shot and the 293 women and children were abducted or imprisoned in reprisal for the assassination of the top-ranking SS man Reinhard Heydrich. In the Soviet Union and Greece the burning of villages was a routine reprisal after any sabotage incident. In late March and early April 1945, 250 Dutchmen were killed in retaliation for the death of another senior SS officer who was accidentally shot. In October 1941, 3,000 innocent Yugoslavs were killed over a two-day period, in retaliation for attacks made on the occupying forces.

Below: *Victims of mass panic – dead civilians in Chungking, June 5, 1941, after 4,000 died stampeding to reach shelter during a Japanese air raid.*

As a matter of course, German Waffen SS units did not take military prisoners. In France in May 1940, soldiers of the British Royal Norfolk Regiment were captured by the Germans. They were then lined up against a farmhouse wall and shot. The 97 soldiers were murdered by troops of the 2nd SS Totenkopf (Death's Head) Regiment. In 1944, at Malmédy in Belgium, SS troops shot 129 US prisoners, 86 of whom died.

Atrocities occurred on both sides. In Sicily, at Biscari, in the summer of 1943, 74 Italian and two German prisoners were shot by US troops. There is a documented account of Japanese prisoners being marched into the jungle and massacred by vengeful Borneo tribesmen as their Australian captors looked on.

The Japanese believed surrender was shameful and often shot their prisoners. When Japanese troops captured the Chinese city of Nanking, and during what is referred to as the 'Rape of Nanking', between 200,000 and 300,000 people were slaughtered.

Below: Jewish civilians being led away to their fate by German troops during the destruction of the Warsaw Ghetto, Poland, 1943.

A US Liberator heavy bomber.

The USAAF remained convinced that daylight bombing would achieve the best results by using aircraft with a very heavy defensive armament that could fight their way through to the target. Even so, they would suffer heavy casualties. Early in the war the RAF had suffered high casualties in daylight raids, and they switched to night bombing in an attempt to reduce them.

Level bombing during the first years of the war was a very imprecise art, especially at night. Collateral damage was always high. Aircraft would rain down hundreds of bombs in order to get a few hits on a target such as a factory, and often they would completely miss it. Navigation at night was almost impossible. The Luftwaffe were the first to use radio beams to aid their aircraft during their nocturnal Blitz on Great Britain during 1940–41. The RAF at the time were lucky even to find the target at night, and daylight raids had proved to be far too costly in terms of casualties. Things improved for the British in 1942 with the Gee navigational aid, providing navigators with a fix from radio pulses transmitted by three ground stations, the pulses intersecting at the target.

Area-bombing of urban centers was adopted when precision bombing could not be achieved, the target being an entire city with its factories and people. It was hoped that this would undermine the morale of the civilian population. It worked in a few places. The Netherlands surrendered after Rotterdam's town centre had been flattened by German bombers, but area-bombing did not undermine the will of Britons, Germans or Japanese to continue to fight the war.

The firestorm was achieved by using a combination of high explosive and incendiaries. The high-explosive bombs would be dropped to break up buildings, making them more susceptible to the incendiaries. Huge numbers of small incendiary bombs would be dropped over a whole city. When areas caught fire, the air above would become hot and rise rapidly. At ground level cold air would then rush in, feeding the fire with oxygen and making it burn ever more vigorously. As the fires joined up, wind speeds in excess of 150mph could be generated, which would in turn continue to fuel the fires. The most notable examples of this tactic occurred in Hamburg in 1943, Dresden

Right: German Dornier Do17 bomber.

Left: British Blenheim light bomber.

in 1945 and Tokyo in 1945: 40,000 people were killed in Hamburg, as many as 150,000 in Dresden and 100,000 in Tokyo.

Dive-bombing made it possible for pin-point accuracy to be achieved. Targets such as bridges and ships could be taken out with amazing accuracy. A typical Stuka attack would commence from about 10,000 feet in an 80-degree dive, the drag of the aircraft's fixed undercarriage and the dive brakes preventing the speed from increasing too rapidly. This made for a stable aircraft during the 15-second dive. The pilot centred the bombsight on the target, released his bomb-load at 2,200 feet, then automatically pulled out of the dive. Another successful dive-bomber was the US Navy's Douglas Dauntless. This aircraft sank four Japanese aircraft carriers at the decisive Battle of Midway. As the war progressed, the slow dive-bomber was always vulnerable to fighters and it was eventually supplanted by the fighter-bomber.

Torpedo-bombers brought many mighty warships to bay, for instance the battleships at Taranto and Pearl Harbor, and also crippled the *Bismarck* before her destruction by British battleships. Torpedo-bombers would attack from an altitude of 100 feet or less and might split up, approaching from different directions. At 1,000 yards from the target the torpedo would be released. A 45-knot torpedo launched at 1,000 yards takes 40 seconds to reach a ship. In that time the ship would travel 2,000 feet if moving at 30 knots. Aim was important: the torpedo had to hit the water flat to run true to the target or else it might dive straight down or porpoise. The torpedo was designed to run at a pre-set depth just below the surface.

British Swordfish torpedo-bomber

from an escort carrier

May 29–30, 1943 Japanese carry out big banzai-style charges, but are beaten off

May 30, 1943 US secure Attu after a hard fight in foul weather. Most surviving Japanese commit suicide

June, 1943 Japanese begin evacuating Kiska by submarine

July 28/9, 1943 Under cover of fog, Japanese complete evacuation of Kiska unknown to the Americans

Aug 15, 1943 Kiska landings by 34,000 US and Canadians; but the Japanese are long gone

Western Theater General Events

May 8, 1943 Island of Pantelleria bombardment by air begins

May 9, 1943 Allies deceive Hitler into thinking their next target will be Greece. The body of a British officer washed ashore in Spain carries bogus plans

May 12–15, 1943 Allied 'Trident' conference, Washington

May 16/17, 1943 'Dambuster' raid on Mohne, Sorpe and Eder dams in the Ruhr

May 23/4, 1943 Düsseldorf bombed

May 24, 1943 Disastrous U-boat losses in May – 41 boats – cause Dönitz temporarily to withdraw from the North Atlantic

May 29 to June 3, 1943 Allied Algiers Conference

May–June, 1943 Tito's partisans are trapped by the Germans in Montenegrin mountains, but escape with heavy loss

June 11, 1943 British secure Pantelleria: the Italian garrison does not resist

June 13, 1943 Kiel daylight raid: USAAF suffer heavy losses

June 14/15, 1943 Oberhausen bombed, first use of Serrate night-fighter detector

June 20/1, 1943 Friedrichshafen, first 'shuttle' raid, Lancasters from Britain landing in N. Africa

NEW GEORGIA

June 21, 1943 US land on New Georgia at

① The Kharkov Offensive, January–March 1943

② The Battle of Kursk, July 1943

③ The Russian Autumn Offensive, July–November 1943

④ The Soviet Winter Offensive, December 1943 to May 1944

⑤ Operation 'Bagration', June–December 1944

⑥ Germany and Berlin, January–May 1945

1943–1945

The Battle of Kursk, July 1943

The Russian salient north of Belgorod, centering on Kursk, became the focus of attention on both sides. On July 5, the Germans attacked it from north and south in an attempt at envelopment. The Battle of Kursk was decisive and the greatest tank battle ever fought. The Soviets, forewarned by intelligence decrypts, were well prepared and counterattacked, halting the German advance by 13th. It was the last major German offensive on the Eastern Front.

The Russian Autumn Offensive, July–November 1943

There now began a series of rolling offensives by the Russians, based on the principle of shifting attacks, from Smolensk to the Black Sea. Hitler's stubborn refusal to give ground made it difficult for Manstein and the other Army Group commanders to use more mobile

defensive tactics effectively. On August 23 the Russians took Kharkov once again; by September 22 they were beginning to cross the Dnieper, and on November 6 they retook Kiev.

Right: 'Liberation', Soviet style. Jubilant civilians wave as a column of Su-76 self-propelled guns speed through the streets.

KONEV

Rank attained	Marshal
Dates	1897–1973
Background	Career soldier; military commissar during Russian Civil War; Funz Military Academy
Commands	Kalinin Front, 1941; West Front, 1942; Steppe Front, 1943; Second Ukrainian Front, 1943; First Ukrainian Front, 1944
Campaigns/ Battles	Moscow, 1941; Kursk, 1943; Berlin, 1945

Second only to Marshal Zhukov, Ivan Konev displayed great capability in handling armies. During the Battle of Moscow he commanded the Kalinin Front in the supporting, but decisive, struggle on the northern flank at the time of the battle. He became prominent at the Battle of Kursk, and during the 1943–44 offensives he played a prominent part in the Soviets' advance west. He led the one million men of the First Ukrainian Front that fought the Battle of Berlin. His forces played a prominent part in the envelopment of the city and then the final victory. Three days after this his forces then advanced south and entered Prague.

Segi Point

July 3–4, 1943 US make new landings on New Georgia

July 17/18, 1943 Japanese counterattack on New Georgia. Allied morale deteriorates seriously

July 25, 1943 Reinforced and with fresh units, US forces begin major attack

Aug 1, 1943 Japanese withdraw inland

Aug 5, 1943 US take Munda

Aug 13, 1943 US activate Munda airfield

Aug 25, 1943 US secure New Georgia

RUSSIA: Battle of Kursk

The Kursk salient is seen by both sides as of significance. The Germans plan a major encirclement operation; the Soviets construct three lines of defense and deploy a force ready to counter-strike once the Germans have been repulsed

July 5, 1943 After a night bombardment, German Ninth Army attacks from the north while Fourth Panzer Army and Group Kempff attack from the south. These two pincers are aimed at Kursk

July 5–13, 1943 Battle of Kursk, Operation 'Citadel'

July 12, 1943 Soviets counterattack the southern pincer at Prokhorovka in the largest tank battle of World War II and halt the German advance

July 15, 1943 Soviets counterattack the northern pincer

July 16, 1943 The Germans begin to fall back

July 17, 1943 South of the Kursk salient, Soviet South-West Front thrusts toward Kharkov

Kursk is the last major German offensive on the Russian front. For the Soviets it marks the beginning of a series of massive offensives that will take them to Berlin and Vienna

Far Eastern Theater General Events

June 14, 1943 Chinese complete the expulsion of Japanese from western Hupeh following the Japanese offensive toward

BRITISH EMPIRE AND DOMINION FORCES

The countries of the British Empire covered one quarter of the world's land surface. From the Caribbean, African, Indian, and all the other colonies, troops and personnel played a crucial role in supporting the Allied cause in World War II.

Over one million Canadians enlisted in the armed forces. Of these, 42,000 were killed and over 54,000 were wounded. As well as sending troops to the UK, the Canadians sent them to assist in the defence of Hong Kong. In August of 1942, at the tragic débâcle at Dieppe, over half of the 5,000 Canadians involved were lost. Large numbers were present in Sicily, Italy and the invasion of Europe, where the Canadian 1st Army fought through to the enemy's surrender in Germany. Many Canadian airmen served with the RAF making their greatest contribution in Bomber Command. The Royal Canadian Navy made a huge contribution to winning the Battle of the Atlantic, as well as serving on many of the other naval fronts.

During the war nearly one million Australians enlisted in the armed forces. Nearly 27,000 died and 24,000 were wounded. The Army fought particularly well in the North African, Balkan and Syrian campaigns and against the Japanese in Malaya, New Guinea and Borneo. The Royal Australian Navy made a considerable contribution to the sea battles in the

Mediterranean and in the South Pacific campaigns. Australian airmen served in the RAF as well as the RAAF, seeing action in Europe, the Middle East, Malaya and the South Pacific.

As a ratio of her population, New Zealand suffered the greatest numbers killed of all the member countries of the Empire – over 11,500 out of a population of less than 1¾ million, with nearly 16,000 wounded. The New Zealanders fought in much the same campaigns as their fellow ANZACs, the Australians.

At the start of the war the Indian Army comprised 350,000 professional volunteers but by the end of the conflict this had risen to 2½ million – the largest volunteer army in history.

Below: *Australian troops about to embark for Egypt, where they made a vital contribution to the campaign in the Western Desert.*

It suffered 24,000 killed and 64,000 wounded. Indian troops fought in North Africa, East Africa, Italy, Syria, Iraq, Malaya and Hong Kong, and of particular note was their victory in Burma against the Japanese.

South Africa raised nearly 335,000 volunteers, losing nearly 9,000 dead and over 8,000 wounded. The South Africans fought against the Axis in the North and East African campaigns, as well as in Italy. Many South African airmen fought with the RAF and SAAF squadrons, fighting in Madagascar and the Central Mediterranean, and for a while they made up almost one third of the strike power of the Western Desert Air Force.

Above: Indian troops in training.

Above: *The New Zealand cruiser* Achilles, *which fought at the Battle of the River Plate.*

Changsha

June 29, 1943 MacArthur launches the 'Cartwheel' offensive against Rabaul, the main Japanese base in the area. This involves the clearance of the Solomons including Bougainville, and New Georgia

July 6, 1943 US bomb Bougainville

July 20, 1943 US Joint Chiefs of Staff direct Admiral Nimitz to capture the Gilbert Islands

July 5/6, 1943 Naval clash in the Gulf of Kula off New Georgia

July 12/13, 1943 Battle of Kolombangara. Naval night battles north-west of New Georgia as US squadrons attempt to intercept Japanese 'Tokyo Express' supply convoys to the island

Aug, 1943 The Allies deem Rabaul effectively neutralized, isolated by advances on New Guinea and neighboring islands

Aug, 1943 Japanese award 'independence' to Burma in the form of a one-party state run by Ba Maw

Aug 6/7, 1943 Battle of the Gulf of Vella. US prevents Japanese reinforcements to New Georgia

Aug 17–18, 1943 Over 200 US aircraft from an airfield built secretly 60 miles west of Lae strike Japanese airstrips in the Salamaua–Lae area on New Guinea, leaving only 38 Japanese aircraft serviceable

Aug 15, 1943 US landings on Vella Lavella

Sept, 1943 Japanese decide upon a 'Minimum Defensive Area' – in the east, the Kurile Islands, the Marianas and Carolines in the Central pacific; in the south the west of New Guinea; in the west, Burma and Malaya

Sept, 1943 Reconstruction of the Burma Road begins, some 25 miles of it having been destroyed in 1942 to halt the Japanese

Sept 27, 1943 Chiang Kai-shek executes Mao Zedong's brother, Mao Zemin

Sept 28 to Oct 2, 1943 Japanese evacuate Kolombangara, sandwiched between US forces on Vella Lavella and New Georgia

October, 1943 P-51 Mustangs of US Tenth

JUNGLE WARFARE

The jungle is an extremely challenging environment in which to survive, let alone fight. To soldiers from Europe and America it was a strange, fearsome place, and moving and fighting in it was a nightmare. Many were ready to classify the jungle as impenetrable, since it appeared only as an obstacle to movement, rather than as an asset. Because of this attitude, the British paid a penalty during the campaign for Malaya in 1941: the Japanese were also unused to jungle – many of their soldiers were from temperate environments – but they realized that it created a good environment, making for concealment and for outflanking maneuvers.

Careful training in survival skills was essential, and these had to be learnt by Western soldiers. Maintaining good health and hygiene to avoid sickness and learning the skills of navigating the jungle where it was impossible to see much farther than ten yards ahead enabled the troops to survive as well as fight. Essential skills such as tracking, jungle patrolling, clearing villages, watching for booby- traps and ambush had to be learnt. Learning how to get within ten yards of the enemy without being seen was also vital. Troops had to acclimatize to cope with the heat and humidity, and also torrential rain, mud, insects, wild animals and the potential for sickness, especially malaria and dysentery in the hot and sticky conditions – sickness often caused more casualties than the enemy.

The close-quarters fighting often encountered in the jungle demanded special equipment such as carbines, automatic weapons and machetes. The proper use of camouflage helped to make up for an enemy with superior numbers.

Units such as the Chindits, who operated deep behind enemy lines in northern and central Burma, became experts in jungle combat. For many months they lived in, and fought the enemy in, the jungles of Japanese-held territory, totally reliant on air-drops for their supplies. The environment led to the loss of many men, both in combat and to sickness.

The US Marines and soldiers operating in the tropics of the Pacific Ocean also became masters of the art of jungle combat as they pushed the Japanese back.

Below: GIs in a typical jungle environment in New Guinea.

Above: Filipino volunteers carry supplies into the jungle and mountains to reach US 1st Cavalry Division troops during fighting on Leyte, 1944.

Below: British troops advancing into the Burmese jungle following the path of an M3 Lee tank. Tanks occasionally proved useful in a jungle environment.

RESISTANCE MOVEMENTS

Every country occupied by the Axis formed resistance movements against their occupation. There were two forms of resistance, passive and active.

Passive, non-violent acts, on their own could not dislodge a determined occupying power but they sometimes did save lives, modify the occupying forces' policies and assist Allied military operations.

The Netherlands offered mostly passive resistance and because it did have an effect the Germans took very harsh reprisals against the people.

In October 1943, after a tip-off from a German attaché, the Danish resistance organised the escape to neutral Sweden of most of their Jewish population, who otherwise were to be arrested. In Berlin, attempts to deport Jews who were married to non-Jews met with spontaneous opposition and the deportations were stopped. In Bulgaria, mass opposition forced the Jewish deportations to be halted.

Railway workers across Europe organised go-slows at critical times during the war. For example, during the summer of 1944 the general attitude of non-cooperation seriously limited the availability of the railway system of France to the German Army at the time of the Normandy landings.

Active resistance included such policies as killing and sabotage. Several Allied secret services, for example the British SOE and the American OSS, often assisted in providing arms, explosives or specialist equipment.

The French resistance, the Maquis (literally, 'scrub') centred on the River Rhône, did not really become active until 1942. It was politically divided between the Communists and the Gaullists. When the Allies landed in France in 1944 it assisted the Allied troops. On August 19, 1944 the Maquis rose against the German occupation forces in Paris. Six days later the city fell to the troops of the Free French Army.

The Polish resistance warned the British of the development of the V-2 rocket and even managed to smuggle a sample engine to England. There were two Warsaw uprisings. The first was in April–May 1943 by the Jews in the Ghetto established there by the Germans. Even though inspired, it was crushed. The second uprising began on August 1, 1944, the resistance movement hoping that the Russians would come to its aid. It lasted for two months and the Russians, who were on the outskirts of the city, did not attempt to help. The Germans crushed the rising and 250,000 Poles died.

Below: *Jewish resistance fighters during the uprising of the Warsaw Ghetto, Poland, 1943.*

Above: Parisians resist the Germans and help to retake Paris, August 1944.

German forces occupied parts of Italy when the country signed an armistice with the Allies. Many Italian soldiers in the occupied areas resisted, most groups being organised by the Communists. By the spring of 1944 their numbers in the mountains were in the region of 100,000. During the summer of that year the Nazis unleashed a terrible offensive upon them and the resistance forces were devastated. Their final act was the capture and execution of Mussolini.

The mountains of Yugoslavia were perfect for guerrilla operations. There were two groups, the Çetniks and the Communists under Tito but these did not operate in unison and eventually ended up fighting each other. The Communists won and Tito became the leader of that country.

In Czechoslovakia, the resistance was made up of many groups. One group of exiles, flown in from London, assassinated Reinhard Heydrich, the Reichsprotektor and second most powerful man in the SS.

Norwegian resistance was mostly passive, but in November 1942 they helped to destroy the Germans' heavy water plant vital to the production of an atomic weapon. This set the German atomic program back by two years.

In the USSR, the partisans operated behind enemy lines, gathering intelligence and disrupting the German lines of communication. This type of warfare became very brutal, neither side paying any attention to suffering caused to the local people, and no quarter was given by either side.

Air Force begin operating in the China-Burma-India theater. They are soon followed by Air Commando units
Oct 6, 1943 Battle of Vella Lavella: US seek to intercept Japanese evacuation of the island

Western Theater General Events
July 4, 1943 Death of Sikorski, leader of the Free Poles, in an air crash
July 9/10, 1943 Gelsenkirchen, last raid in Battle of the Ruhr
July, 19, 1943 Allies bomb Rome
July 24 to Aug 3 Hamburg raids cause firestorm killing some 50,000. First use of 'Window' anti-radar decoy by RAF
July 25, 1943 Mussolini arrested. Marshal Badoglio forms a new government in Italy
July 25, 1943 Hitler sends Rommel with German troops into northern Italy following the fall of Mussolini
Aug 1, 1943 Ploesti oilfields: US bombers take severe losses
Aug, 1943 Italians open negotiations with the Allies, who demand unconditional surrender
Aug 8, 1943 Mussolini sent to Maddalena Island off Sardinia
Aug 13–23, 1943 Allied 'Quadrant' conference, Quebec
Aug 13, 1943 Allies bomb Rome
Aug 14, 1943 Italians declare Rome an open city
Aug 17, 1943 Schweinfurt: US bombers again take severe losses. USAAF bombing is halted until Sept 6
Aug 17/18, 1943 Peenemünde V-weapon research site raided
Aug 23/4, 1943 Berlin raided: but RAF suffer heavy losses
Sept, 1943 ELAS, Greek Communist resistance army, seizes weapons of surrendered Italians in Greece. Tito's men do the same in Yugoslavia
Sept, 1943 U-boats renew attack on Allied convoys in N Atlantic
Sept 3, 1943 Italy signs armistice with the

At the Casablanca Conference in January 1943, the Allies faced up to the fact that the long-planned invasion of north-western Europe could not be attempted until 1944. In the meanwhile, the clearance of Tunisia would lead to the invasion of Sicily, thereby making safe the central Mediterranean for Allied shipping and providing a possible stepping stone to Italy.

The Allies launched what would be the second largest amphibious operation in the European Theater of Operations, eight divisions landing on a 100-mile front.

A deception plan ('Mincemeat') involving the planting of false documents, suggesting an Allied invasion of Greece, on a corpse dumped in the sea off Spain appeared to work, but there were still some 230,000 Axis troops in Sicily to be dealt with, including two good German armored divisions.

Montgomery's British Eighth Army landed on the south-east coast, aiming to drive directly north on Messina. Patton's US Seventh Army landed on the south coast, but, while Montgomery's troops fought their way through mountainous terrain including the volcano, Mount Etna, Patton seized the opportunity of more open terrain for a spectacular, fast drive on Palermo, which he entered on July 23. His troops then turned east, the advance along the north coast aided by several amphibious 'hops'. Both armies entered Messina on August 17, but some 70,000 Germans and 60–70,000 Italians escaped to the Italian mainland.

On July 25, 1943, Mussolini's government fell and the new Italian prime minister, Marshal Badoglio, began secret negotiations with the

Allies, which led to an armistice on September 3. The following day, XIII Corps of British Eighth Army crossed the Strait of Messina and advanced into Calabria, slowed by German demolitions and rearguard actions.

On the 8th the Italian armistice was announced, and the following day Clark's US Fifth Army landed at Salerno, south of Naples, while Montgomery made a secondary landing at Taranto. Since the fall of Sicily, the Germans had moved 16 divisions into Italy, which now became an occupied country. Allied hopes of a quick campaign were soon dashed. On 12–13th, German counterattacks almost drove the Americans back into the sea. Three days later, elements of Eighth Army linked up with Fifth Army, while the Germans fell back slowly to a prepared position south of Rome. This was the Gustav (Winter) Line, which took advantage of the mountainous terrain of central Italy interspersed with fast-flowing rivers (the Garigliano, Sangro, Rapido, and Liri).

On the eastern side of the mountains, Eighth Army landed 78th Division at Bari on September 22/3, and on November 20 the Sangro River was crossed, just south of the Gustav Line.

In the west, the advance from the Salerno beachhead was checked by the swollen waters of the Volturno, bridges destroyed. In the east, Eighth Army advanced to Ortona by December 27 before running out of steam. Then, in the west, the dominant position of Monte Cassino, overlooking the coastal plain, became the focus of a succession of costly attacks. The Allies were destined to struggle against the Gustav Line for more than seven months.

The Allies' attempt to break this deadlock was an amphibious landing at Anzio, between the Gustav Line and Rome. But the commander, Lucas, took too long to consolidate the beachhead before attempting to break out. By the 30th, Kesselring had organized a series of counterattacks that almost succeeded in eliminating the beachhead. Lucas was replaced by Truscott, but the Alles were in no shape to break out. Neither had simultaneous attacks on the Gustav Line, including two Battles of Monte Cassino, made significant progress.

Left: American troops firing a 155mm gun ('Long Tom') artillery piece, Italy, winter 1943/44.

Allies, effective 8th

Sept 9, 1943 Germans use radio-controlled bomb to sink Italian battleship *Roma* en route to surrender
Sept 10, 1943 British forces invade the Dodecanese but fail to seize Rhodes
Sept 11, 1943 Germans evacuate Sardinia
Sept 12, 1943 Daring German rescue of Mussolini from Gran Sasso in the mountains north-east of Rome by Skorzeny's special forces. Mussolini becomes head of a puppet Italian government in northern Italy
Sept 15/16, 1943 Dortmund–Ems Canal, first use of 12,000lb 'Tallboy' bomb
Sept 16, 1943 Soviets take Novorossisk
Sept 22, 1943 British X-craft midget submarines damage *Tirpitz* in Altenfjord

SALAMAUA/LAE
Sept 4, 1943 Australian 9th Division lands near Lae in New Guinea
Sept 5, 1943 US paratroops take the airstrip there
Sept 11, 1943 Japanese evacuate from Salamaua to Lae
Sept 12, 1943 Australians take Lae and its airfield
Sept 16, 1943 Australians take Salamaua
Sept 22, 1943 Australians land east of Lae near Finschhafen on Huon Peninsula

ALLIED LIBERATION OF SICILY
July 10, 1943 Allies invade Sicily. Patton's Seventh Army lands on the south coast; Montgomery's Eighth Army to the south-east
July 10, 1943 Syracuse taken
July 12, 1943 The beachheads secure, Allies advance inland
July 13/14–16, 1943 Battle for the strategically important Primasole Bridge after British air/sea landings on the east coast
July 16, 1943 Patton begins rapid advance towards Palermo while German defense is stubborn around Catania on the east coast
July 23, 1943 Patton's forces take Palermo

THE SOVIET ARMY

When the Germans invaded the USSR (Operation 'Barbarossa') in June 1941, the Red Army on paper seemed impressive with nearly 5½ million troops plus another 5 million reservists. They possessed 20,000 tanks, of which 1,800 were the latest KV or T-34 types and superior to the best the German Army had. The invading army had just over 3½ million men and 3,600 tanks. The Red Army forces should have been sufficiently capable of repelling any aggressor.

The largest Soviet army formation was the front: this controlled between five to seven armies, which were each made up of several corps of between three to nine divisions. A division, depending on type, consisted of a brigade of four regiments each of three battalions, plus an anti-aircraft battalion.

The 61 Red Army tank divisions (10,500 troops) would each have 375 tanks, twice as many as the equivalent Panzer formation. A rifle (infantry) division had nearly three times as many machine-guns as a German infantry division. The Red Army raised 400 divisions during the war.

Serious shortcomings within the Soviet Army first became apparent during its invasion of Finland in November 1939. The purges and executions of the officer class by the paranoid Stalin during 1937–8 had left the Army poorly trained and inefficient with regard to leadership.

There seemed to be nothing the Soviet Army could do to halt the German Blitzkrieg. In the great encirclement battles of 1941, 26 Soviet armies were destroyed, the Germans taking over 2 million Soviet troops as prisoners of war and also capturing 7,500 tanks and 13,000 artillery pieces. The trend continued into 1942 with another 11 armies eliminated and 600,000 prisoners, 2,500 tanks and 4,500 guns taken. The number of Soviets killed and wounded was appaling as each Soviet counter-offensive achieved nothing and the German advance continued.

In the summer of 1942 the Soviets began to form complete Tank Armies, each comprising two tank corps plus all the ancillary units, aimed purely at massive offensive operations. These Soviet 'steamroller' tactics were not the most subtle, as they had to be able to absorb huge numbers of casualties. This is what Stalin exploited. The Soviets had an abundance of men and factories, which were now turning out ever more tanks and guns with which to arm them.

The Red Army soldier's equipment was simple, cheap and usually reliable but crudely manufactured. If it was damaged or broke down one simply replaced it – one of the benefits of mass production on a huge scale.

Despite the setbacks, the Soviet soldier continued to defend stubbornly and with

Below: A propaganda photograph showing snow-camouflaged Soviet troops advancing on exercise.

growing skill and improved leadership during the winter of 1942/43 the tide was turned at Stalingrad. The Soviets succeeded in surrounding and eliminating the 20 divisions of the German Sixth Army, consisting of nearly 250,000 men. They then defeated the big German summer offensive of 1943 at the great tank battle of Kursk.

The Soviet Army would not taste retreat again as the 'steamroller' began to push the enemy steadily back – all the way to the gates of Berlin by April 1945.

Throughout the war the Soviet Army's losses were extremely high: in the region of ten million servicemen were killed and 18 million wounded, and over five million were taken prisoner. Tank losses were enormous, with nearly 100,000 destroyed or captured.

Above: KV-1 tanks, paid for by donations from collective farmers, being presented to Soviet troops.

The crudely produced but very effective PPSh 41 submachine-gun. It could be fitted either with a 35-round box-magazine or a 71-round drum magazine.

then swing east for Messina

July 28, 1943 1st Canadian Div takes Agira in central Sicily

July 31, 1943 Patton's troops take San Stefano, halfway along the north coast en route to Messina

Aug 3, 1943 Axis forces begin evacuation across the Strait of Messina

Aug 5, 1943 Montgomery takes Catania after a long battle

Aug 7, 10, 1943 US amphibious landings on the north coast

Aug 17, 1943 Patton's troops enter Messina. But the Axis have evacuated successfully

RUSSIA: Soviet Autumn Offensive

Aug 5, 1943 Soviets take Orel and Belgorod while the Germans fall back to the Hagen Line before Bryansk

Aug 11–17, 1943 German counterattack east of Kharkov halts the Soviet advance

Aug 12, 1943 Hitler orders construction of the East Wall defense line

Aug 23, 1943 Soviets retake Kharkov

Aug 26, 1943 Soviet Central Front strikes Army Group Center in the south

Aug 30, 1943 Soviet Central Front takes Taganrog, threatening German forces in the Taman Peninsula

Sept 6, 1943 Soviets take Konotop

Sept 8, 1943 Hitler confers with von Manstein and sanctions evacuation of the Taman Peninsula

Sept 10, 1943 Soviets take Mariupol by amphibious attack

Sept 14, 1943 Soviet Central and Voronezh Fronts attack toward Kiev

Sept 16, 1943 Germans evacuate Bryansk

Sept 21, 1943 Soviets take Chernigov

Sept 25, 1943 Soviets take Roslavl and Smolensk

Sept 26, 1943 Voronezh Front creates bridgeheads across the Dnieper River

End Sept, 1943 Von Manstein has withdrawn behind the East Wall

Oct 6, 1943 Soviets attack between

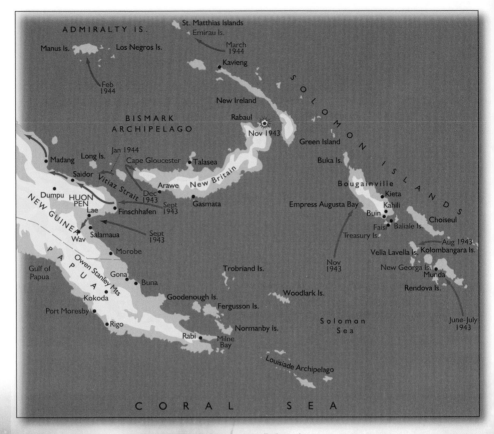

ADMIRALTY IS.

St. Matthias Islands
Emirau Is.

Manus Is.   Los Negros Is.   March
1944
Kavieng

Feb
1944

New Ireland

S
O
L
O
M
O
N

BISMARK
ARCHIPELAGO

Rabaul

Nov 1943

Green Island

Jan 1944

Madang   Long Is.   Cape Gloucester   Talasea

Buka Is.

Saidor   Vitiaz Strait

Arawe   New Britain

Bougainville

Kieta

Dumpu   HUON
PEN

Dec
1943   Sept
1943   Gasmata

Empress Augusta Bay   Kahili

I
S
L
A
N
D
S

Lae
NEW GUINEA   Finschhafen

Buin
Fais   Baliale Is.   Choiseul

Wau   Sept
1943   Salamaua

Treasury Is.

Aug 1943

Morobe

Vella Lavella Is.   Kolombangara Is.

Gulf of
Papua   Owen Stanley Mts   Gona
PAPUA   Buna

Trobriand Is.   Nov
1943   New Georgia Is.
Munda

Kokoda

Woodlark Is.   Rendova Is.

Port Moresby   Goodenough Is.

Fergusson Is.

June-July
1943

Rigo

Solomon
Sea

Rabi   Normanby Is.

Milne
Bay

Louisiade Archipelago

C O R A L   S E A

Below: *American troops mopping up on Bougainville. As with the other island campaigns, there was much hand-to-hand fighting, the Japanese attempting to infiltrate American lines by night.*

LUCKY
LEGS II

North of Buna and Gona, the Japanese established bases at Lae and Salamaua on March 8 1942, but these were only reinforced in January–February 1943, with a build-up of aircraft based on a number of airstrips including Wau, inland from Salamaua. In accordance with the strategic decision to clear the Solomons and New Britain and capture the main Japanese base at Rabaul, General MacArthur planned Operation 'Cartwheel', which he launched in June. This included the need to secure the east coast of New Guinea.

On 17–18 August, from an airfield built secretly 60 miles west of Lae, some 200 US aircraft struck the Japanese airfields in the area, leaving just 38 Japanese aircraft serviceable. With air supremacy, the Allies could now attack, and on September 4–5 forces landed, taking Lae and Salamaua by 16th. Six days later Australian troops landed at the tip of the Huon Peninsula, and took Finschhafen on October 2. Japanese resistance centered on the Sattelberg height, which was taken on December 8. After mopping-up operations, the Allies now attacked north, the Japanese withdrawing before them.

On January 2 1944 landings at Saidor almost cut off the retreating Japanese, whose main base was now Wewak. Landings at Hollandia and Aitape further along the coast now isolated the Japanese at Wewak, who held out until May 10 1945.

German Army Groups North and Center toward Vitebsk
Oct 16, 1943 Soviet Steppe and South-West Fronts attack toward the Dnieper
Oct 23, 1943 Soviets take Melitopol
Nov 3, 1943 Soviets attack from the Dnieper bridgehead at Lyutezh
Nov 6, 1943 Soviets take Kiev
Autumn, 1943 German Army Group North constructs the Panther defense line as a fallback
Nov 12, 1943 Soviets take Zhitomir, effectively breaching the German East Wall
Nov 18, 1943 Germans retake Zhitomir
Nov 26, 1943 Soviets take Gomel

NEW GUINEA
Oct 2, 1943 Australians take Finschhafen, but stiff reisistance persists inland
Dec 8, 1943 Sattelberg Mountain, Japanese focus of resistance west of Finschhafen, is taken. After mopping up, the Australians pursue the Japanese north
Jan 2, 1944 US landing at Saidor on New Guinea just fails to cut off the Japanese retreat north from the Huon Peninsula

BOUGAINVILLE
Oct 27–8, 1943 New Zealand and US troops land on islands near Bougainville as feints
Nov 1, 1943 Large-scale US invasion of Bougainville, which is heavily garrisoned by the Japanese
Nov 5, 1943 Admiral Halsey's carrier air attack on Admiral Kurita's powerful naval force at Rabaul averts their intervention in Bougainville operations
Nov 7–8, 1943 Japanese counterattack US Marines on Bougainville
Jan 16, 1944 US Marines replaced by Americal Army Division. The beachhead is enlarged
March 8/9, 1944 Japanese make major attack on US Bougainville beachhead
March 24, 1944 Final Japanese attack on the US Bougainville beachhead fails; they

The Nazis established some 15,000 camps within Germany and the occupied countries. Some were small, temporary camps; others were so large they had sub-camps and their own railway lines. At the end of the war, facing defeat, the Nazis destroyed many of the camps as they retreated.

Dachau, the first concentration camp, opened on March 22, 1933. Its first inmates included political prisoners such as Communists, Social Democrats and people the Nazis considered 'undesirable' such as Jewish intellectuals, Jehovah's Witnesses, homosexuals and criminals. Above the main gates was the slogan 'Tolerance is a sign of weakness'. The sign above Auschwitz's gates was 'Arbeit macht frei' – 'Work makes you free'.

The Danish people pulled off a unique operation in a country-wide effort to rescue Danish Jews from the Nazis. Secretly alerted on September 28, 1943 by a German diplomat that the Nazis were getting ready to deport

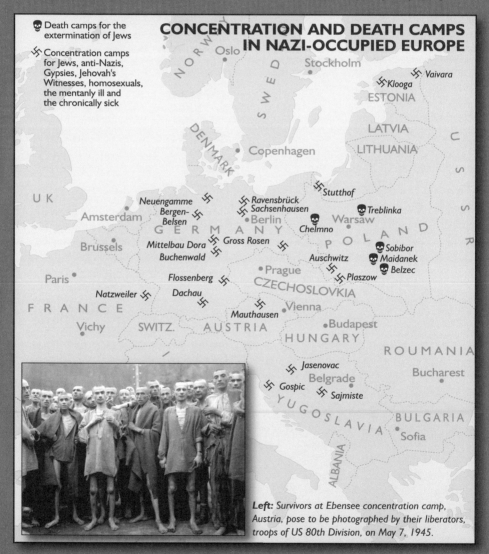

CONCENTRATION AND DEATH CAMPS IN NAZI-OCCUPIED EUROPE

☠ Death camps for the extermination of Jews

卐 Concentration camps for Jews, anti-Nazis, Gypsies, Jehovah's Witnesses, homosexuals, the mentally ill and the chronically sick

Left: Survivors at Ebensee concentration camp, Austria, pose to be photographed by their liberators, troops of US 80th Division, on May 7, 1945.

Jews from Denmark, Danish politicians passed the word to the resistance movement. This warned every Jewish household to flee and arranged for fishermen on the east coast to ferry people across the sea to neutral Sweden.

Most of the 8,000 Jews in Denmark lived in Copenhagen. They made their way across the country, helped and hidden by fellow Danes, to the coast, where in small groups on little boats, they were taken to safety. 7,220 Jews and 680 non-Jews were taken to Sweden in a fortnight.

The national effort rescued all but 475 Danish Jews, most of whom were too ill or frail to make the trek to the coast. Even then, Danish officials hassled Germany with concerns over their people, ensuring that nearly all the concentration-camp prisoners survived the war.

As a national effort involving royal family, politicians, resistance and ordinary people, the Danish effort was unique. In Norway, the church and ordinary people succeeded in smuggling about 1,000 Jews – roughly half the country's Jewish population – to neutral Sweden. Bulgaria refused to hand over any of its Jews to the Nazis, but it did not protect Jews in territories it had recently annexed. And it was Germany's original Axis ally, Italy, which, to start with, also provided official protection for Jews in its territories.

Above: Of the extermination of the Jews, Reichsführer Heinrich Himmler said, 'This is a glorious page in our history ...' His ideal camp commandants were passionless, fundamentally disinterested individuals whose adherence to orders was never in doubt and to whom murder meant nothing.

On June 10, 1940, the fascist **Benito Mussolini** of Italy declared war on Britain and France in alliance with Germany. In North Africa Italy was getting the worst of the combat until the Germans intervened, and the same was true in Greece. In June 1941 he declared war on the Soviet Union and the United States. He was deposed in June 1943 and arrested. He was rescued by the Germans several months later. Little more than a puppet of Germany, he then set up fascist state in northern Italy. On April 27, 1945, he was arrested by Italian partisans, along with his mistress, and on the next day they were both executed. Their bodies were hung, upside down, in a Milan square beside those of other fascists.

Count Ugo Cavallero served successfully during World War I and became the Supreme Commander of the Italian Armed Forces in East Africa in 1938. He took over as Chief of Comando Supremo on December 6, 1940. He also became Commander of Italian forces fighting against Greece on December 30, 1940. After the Italian occupation of Greece, he returned to Italy. He then became Chief of General Staff of the three armed forces. He was a friend of General Kesselring. He was promoted to Field Marshal in 1942. After the defeats in Russia and the loss of Libya, Cavallero was removed from the Comando Supremo in 1943, and following Mussolini's fall in the same year he was arrested. The Italian King set him free, but he was re-arrested along with many fascist leaders. He wrote a memorandum claiming he was an anti-fascist and that he had plotted against Mussolini. With the Italian surrender in 1943, the Germans took him as they wanted to give him command of the remaining Italian forces loyal to the Germans but the SS obtained the memorandum

that he had written earlier and they surmised that he was an anti-fascist. Cavallero committed suicide on September 14, 1943, probably at the Germans' instigation.

The highly regarded **Admiral Angelo Iachino** became C-in-C of the Italian Fleet in December 1940, replacing Admiral Campioni a month after the disaster at Taranto. Prior to this promotion he had commanded the Italian cruiser force, which had acquitted itself well in action against the Royal Navy. His ships were always plagued by lack of fuel oil and their lack of sonar and radar. He also had the problem of too much control from the high command in Rome, complaining that they interfered with orders, even down to the minor naval units. He was in his flagship *Vittorio Veneto* commanding the Italian ships at the Battle of Matapan, where they suffered a major defeat. There is no doubt that Iachino was also badly served by his

MUSSOLINI	
Dates	1883–1945
Background	Journalist; World War I soldier
Offices	The leader of the Fascist Party; Italian dictator, *Il Duce*

CAVALLERO	
Rank attained	Marshal
Dates	1880–1943
Background	Career soldier, Modena Military School
Commands	C-in-C East Africa, 1938; Comando Supremo, 1940; C-in-C Greece, 1940; C-in-C General Staff, 1941

Above: Mussolini at the Munich Conference in 1938, with Göring to his right and Hitler to his left.

Cavallero   Iachino

air reconnaissance, and his fleet was hampered by the fact that it did not possess an aircraft carrier to provide constant air cover. As the war progressed, the lack of fuel for his ships increasingly handicapped the ability of his men to train at sea and of his ships to carry out major sorties.

IACHINO

Rank attained	Admiral
Dates	1889–1976
Background	Career sailor
Commands	Cruiser Force, 1940; C-in-C Italian Fleet, 1940–43

pull back on 27th and fighting subsides

ITALY: Allied Landings

Sept 3, 1943 British XIII Corps crosses from Messina to the toe of Italy

Sept 9, 1943 Allied landings at Salerno by Clark's US Fifth Army and at Taranto by Montgomery's Eighth Army

Sept 9–17, 1943 Battle of Salerno

Sept 10, 1943 Germans occupy Rome and von Vietinghoff's Tenth Army deploys before the Salerno beachhead

Sept 16, 1943 The three Allied forces in southern Italy link up

Sept 23, 1943 Allies advance from Salerno

Western Theater General Events

Oct 3, 1943 Germans take Cos in the Dodecanese

October, 1943 Portugal permits Britain use of the Azores as air base against the U-boats

Oct 9, 1943 Anklam/Marienburg aircraft factories (USAAF)

Oct 14, 1943 Schweinfurt hit by USAAF again; but again the bombers suffer heavy losses

Oct 31, 1943 Moscow conference of Allied foreign ministers

Oct, 1943 to Jan, 1944 Further German offensives against Tito's Yugoslavs

Nov 12, 1943 Germans attack Leros, held by British and Italians. They take the island by 16th. The Allies evacuate all other garrisons in the Dodecanese

Nov 18/19, 1943 Aerial Battle of Berlin begins. Four attacks this month cause extensive damage and kill c.4,500

Nov 23–6, 1943 Allied 'Sextant' Conference, Cairo

Nov 28 to Dec 6, 1943 Allied 'Eureka' Conference, Tehran

To Dec, 1943 Generally from north of Vitebsk to the Baltic, the frontlines are relatively stable

Dec, 1943 Battle of Berlin: four more raids this month

Dec 13, 1943 Long-range Packard-Merlin-engined P-51B Mustang fighters fly first

BRITISH AND DOMINION GENERALS

In 1914 at the beginning of World War I, **Bill Slim** enlisted as a private soldier; he eventually became a Field Marshal. He transferred to the Indian Army in 1919. He commanded two Indian Divisions, seeing active service in Sudan, Syria, Iraq and Iran before going to Burma in 1942 and taking command of the 1st Burma Corps. As he arrived, British forces were retreating the 900 miles from Rangoon into India. He built up the morale of XVIII Corps and then took command of the 14th Army and launched an offensive into Burma in December 1943. In 1944 he defeated an impressive Japanese counterattack at the Battle of Imphal/Kohima in India, inflicting 50,000 casualties on them. By 1945 his troops had fought all the way back to Rangoon, defeating the Japanese Army in Burma. He had achieved one of the greatest land victories over the Japanese, inflicting nearly 350,000 casualties on them. An experienced soldier, Slim was greatly liked and admired as a military commander. He inspired confidence and was held in great affection by his men.

Above, top row: Slim and Wavell. **Second row:** *Cerar and General Orde Wingate. The latter came to prominence in the Burma campaign as leader of the Chindits, a special force that carried out a number of successful behind-the-lines operations, supplied by air. He died in an air crash during one of these forays in 1944.*

SLIM

Rank attained	Field Marshal
Dates	1891–1970
Background	Career soldier, enlisted as a private
Commands	5th Indian Division, 1940; 10th Indian Division, 1941; I Burma Corps, 1942; XVIII Corps, 1943; 14th Army, 1943
Campaigns	Sudan, 1940; Syria/ Iraq/Iran, 1941; Burma/India, 1942–45

WAVELL

Rank attained	Field Marshal
Dates	1883–1950
Background	Career soldier; Sandhurst Military Academy, wounded in WWI
Commands	C-in-C Middle East Command, 1939–41; C-in-C India, 1941–43
Campaigns	North Africa, 1939–41; East Africa, 1940; Greece, 1941; Syria/ Iraq/Iran,1941; Burma, 1943

Sir Archibald Wavell was a well-respected soldier whose military career began during the Boer War. He lost an eye fighting in World War I. During 1940–41 he defeated the Italians in North and East Africa, capturing 110,000 troops. In March 1941, after these successes, the best of his military units were sent to the Balkans during the ill-fated attempt to help the Greeks, at the same time as Rommel was striking into Libya. Wavell was forced into retreat as trouble also flared in Iraq and Syria. His offensives against Rommel in May and June 1941 came to naught. He was then transferred to India as C-in-C. His defeat in Burma by the Japanese was followed by his failed counter-offensives in 1942. He was promoted to Field Marshal and given the political post of Viceroy of India. Always under-resourced and pressured by London, this talented general was poorly used.

Top: General Sir Alan Brooke, Chief of the Imperial General Staff, and General Sir Harold Alexander, Allied Supreme Commander in the Mediterranean. Second row: General Sir Claude Auchinleck, C-in-C Middle East after Wavell; and Lieutenant-General Arthur Percival, who surrendered Singapore to the Japanese, the greatest British defeat ever.

Having served with distinction during World War I, **General Henry Crerar** was appointed Chief of the Canadian Staff in 1941. He commanded the 1 Canadian Corps during the Italian Campaign and then was appointed to command the 1st Canadian Army for the invasion of Normandy. In late 1944 he took command of the largest military force ever led by a Canadian – some 500,000 men, consisting of 13 divisions made up of Canadians, Britons, Americans, Belgians, Dutchmen and Poles. There were tensions between him and General Montgomery, his commanding officer. Not a charismatic man, he was not well known for inspiring his men, but he was a very proficient planner and administrator. He had the good fortune of having as his second-in-command the inspirational and inventive Lieutenant General Simonds. Crerar was the 'executive' commander of the 1st Canadian Army and Simonds the battlefield commander.

escort mission to Kiel.

Dec 16/17, 1943 First 'Crossbow' raid against some 100 German V-1 launch sites begun by RAF No. 617 Sqn ('Dambusters')

Dec 26, 1943 Battle of the North Cape: British battleship *Duke of York* sinks German battlecruiser *Scharnhorst* which is attempting to intercept Arctic convoy JW55B

By the end of 1943 Germany has effectively lost the Battle of the Atlantic

Far Eastern Theater General Events

Oct 5–6, 1943 US bombards Wake Island

October: Burma, 1943 Stilwell's Chinese continue advance in northern Burma, building the Ledo Road en route to China Completion of the Japanese Burma–Thailand railway. 61,000 Allied prisoners plus 270,000 natives have been forced to build 260 miles of railway through one of the most unhealthy places on earth. Conservative estimates are that 12,000 Allied prisoners died together with 90,000 natives

October: Borneo, 1943 Chinese population of British Borneo stage an uprising against the Japanese, seizing Jesselton, but are subsequently defeated. Many are executed

Oct 6, 1943 Admiral Mountbatten becomes Supreme Allied Commander South East Asia Command with Stilwell as his deputy. Mountbatten visits Chiang Kai-shek. General Slim takes command of new Fourteenth Army

Nov 1, 1943 British advance in the Arakan

Nov 1/2, 1943 Battle of Empress Augusta Bay. US naval forces beat off an attack by the Japanese intending to disrupt the US landings on Bougainville

Nov 5 and 11, 1943 Admiral Halsey launches major air stikes on Rabaul from carriers *Saratoga* and *Princeton*, inflicting heavy damage on the Japanese squadron there and forcing its evacuation to Truk

Nov 24/5, 1943 Battle of Cape St. George. US intercept reiforcements for Buka Island,

The US Army in September 1939 had a strength of 190,000. By the end of the war it had a strength in excess of 6,000,000 – a relatively small army when compared with size of the population and with that of other nations.

The United States deployed nine field armies during the course of the war – First, Third, Seventh, Ninth and Fifteenth Armies fought in North-West Europe, Fifth in Italy and Sixth, Eighth and Tenth Armies in the Pacific. Two armies, Second and Fourth, were stationed in mainland Amrica and were concerned with training and administrative duties. Each Army consisted of two or more corps, of which 26 were formed in total. They

each usually consisted of three divisions together with ancillary and support units.

The division was the basic fighting formation, and during the course of the war 90 divisions were deployed, 68 in Europe and 22 in the Pacific. The majority were infantry divisions. Each division had approximately 14,500 men of three regiments of three battalions, plus supporting arms. Sixteen of these were armored divisions and these had an established strength of 263 tanks, but three – the 1st, 2nd and 3rd Armored Divisions – had 390 tanks. The armored divisions were all deployed to Europe. There they suffered badly due to the superiority of German tanks and anti-tank weaponry they were fighting against, but eventually they won

Above: Emplaning a four-wheel-drive Willys Jeep, of which over 650,000 were built.

Below: An M3 halftrack and M4 Sherman tank.

Above: A 'Deuce and a Half' 2½ ton truck, of which over 750,000 were built.

through. The main US tank, the Sherman, was reliable, but it was too lightly armed and armored.

Tanks were important during mobile offensive warfare but, as General Patton said, it was the US artillery that gave the infantry and tanks the necessary edge over their enemy.

Five airborne divisions were raised, the 13th, 11th, 17th, 82nd and 101st. These élite units had fewer troops – less than 13,000 or, in the case of the 11th, only 8,500.

Generally the GI was the best-equipped soldier of the war. American technological innovation and manufacturing techniques not only supplied him with good equipment, but also a vast range and large quantities of it.

Such items as the M1 Garand semi-automatic rifle, the GMC 2½-ton truck and the ubiquitous Willys Jeep were war winners.

During the early part of the fighting the inexperienced US Army had some hard lessons to learn, being opposed by the battle-hardened Japanese and Germans. The early loss of the Philippines and the mauling the GIs received at the battle for the Kasserine Pass in Tunisia in 1942 not only caused the loss of men and matériel but generated a loss of confidence. But the lessons were gradually learnt and the war was won.

The US Army fought in 34 specific campaigns, suffering over 820,000 casualties, including nearly 183,000 killed.

north of Bougainville
Dec 15, 1943 US make decoy landing on south coast of New Britain
Dec 4, 1943 Kwajalein and Wotje in the Marshall Islands bombed by US carrier aircraft
Dec 26, 1943 US main landings on New Britain at Cape Gloucester

GILBERT ISLANDS
Nov 10–13, 1943 Invasion fleet for the Gilbert Islands sails from Pearl Harbor and from the New Hebrides
Nov 20, 1943 Tarawa and Makin landings by Marines and Army troops respectively. Amtrac LVTs first used. During the first critical day, the US troops are pinned down on the beaches
Nov 21, 1943 Second wave landings on Tarawa. Fanatical Japanese counterattacks result in some of the heaviest combat of the Pacific war
Nov 21, 1943 US land on Apamama and secure it the same day
Nov 23, 1943 Tarawa and Makin secured by the US after Japanese fight to the death

ITALY
Oct 1, 1943 Foggia captured by Eighth Army; Naples by Fifth Army
Oct 3–6, 1943 Battle of Termoli
Oct 9, 1943 Fifth Army reaches the Volturno River but bad weather aids the German defenders
Oct 12–15, 1943 Crossing of the Volturno Line
Nov 5–15, 1943 First Battle for Camino
Nov 8, 1943 Eighth Army reaches the Sangro River
Nov 20, 1943 Eighth Army crosses the Sangro
Nov 20–8, 1943 Heavy rain halts operations
Nov 28, 1943 Eighth Army attacks Gustav Line
Nov 29 to Dec 1, 1943 Battle of the Sangro River
Dec 2–10, 1943 Second Battle for Monte

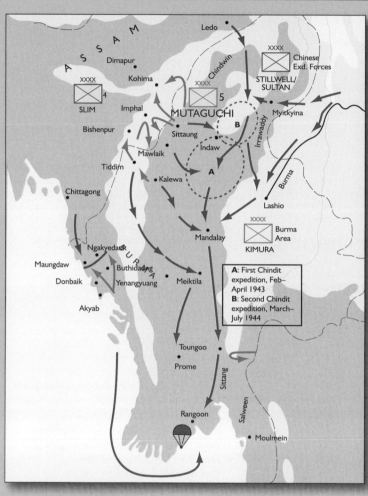

A: First Chindit
expedition, Feb–
April 1943
B: Second Chindit
expedition, March–
July 1944

Left: Burma, showing the principal Chindit expeditions, the Japanese attempted invasion of India, repulsed at the Battle of Imphal-Kohima, and the final advance of Fourteenth Army and the Chinese to liberate the country.

Below: During the Burma campaign the use of mules proved vital for carrying heavy equipment through the jungle, even dismantled artillery pieces, which were then reassembled for use against the Japanese.

The first tentative steps back into Burma by the Allies were not a success. In December 1942 an advance down the coast was intended to prepare the way for the ambitious 'Anakim' Plan, an amphibious assault on Rangoon combined with offensives in northern Burma. (In the event, that plan was abandoned, not least because landing craft were never in sufficient supply for such a major operation; the capture of Rangoon was eventually carried out from the sea, but the conditions for it had been created by decisive victories inland.)

The 14th Indian Division advanced to Maungdaw, the Japanese falling back to prepared defenses at Donbaik, with tunnels and bunkers. These repulsed successive attacks, and the campaign subsided into a sort of stalemate. In March, the Japanese reinforced the area and counterattacked, each side attempting to encircle the other. On May 14 the Japanese recaptured Maungdaw just before the monsoon broke. The campaign did little to bolster Allied morale, the Japanese being seen as superior jungle troops.

A better indication of Allied potential in these tropical conditions came with the first Chindit expedition, during February to April 1943. This was a deep penetration raid by special forces raised by Orde Wingate, their purpose being to sabotage Japanese communications and hit the enemy where he least expected it. They would travel light and be supplied entirely by air. The first incursion took them some 200 miles into Japanese-held Burma, and they succeeded in demolishing railway bridges and cutting the Mandalay–Myitkyina track. As the enemy reacted and began to close in on them, Wingate split his force into small groups who exfiltrated back across the Irrawaddy and Chindwin Rivers. Losses were high, sickness and exhaustion taking a heavy toll, but morale in the Allied lines was boosted by this evidence that the Japanese could be beaten in the jungle.

Camino: Fifth Army resumes attacks toward the Gustav Line
Dec 4–7, 1943 First Battle of Orsonga; subsequent battles 18th and 23rd
Dec 20–8, 1943 1st Canadian Div takes Ortona
January, 1944 Eisenhower and Montgomery depart the Italian theater to prepare for the invasion of North-West Europe

BURMA
Jan 7, 1944 Japanese high command decides upon the invasion of India in March by General Mutaguchi's Fifteenth Army from Burma
January, 1944 Allied plan is for Stilwell to continue building the Ledo Road to establish firm communications between India and China; for the Chinese to enter northern Burma from Yunnan province; and for Wingate's Chindits to interdict Japanese communications farther south
February, 1944 Merrill's Marauders, based on the Chindits, join Stilwell's Chinese forces. Their role will be to infiltrate and outflank the Japanese
Feb 3, 1944 Japanese offensive in the Arakan area, outflanking the Allied line inland to Taung Bazaar, intending to encircle the defenders
Feb 6–24, 1944 Japanese attack Allied 'Admin Box' defensive position at Ngakyedauk, which is supplied by air
Feb 26, 1944 Japanese attacks on the 'Admin Box' repulsed, they fall back
March 11, 1944 British retake Buthidaung, east of Maungdaw, then redeploy two divisions north to the Imphal-Kohima area
Feb 5, 1944 Chindits enter Burma from Ledo

MARSHALL ISLANDS
Jan 30/1, 1944 US landing on unoccupied Majuro
Feb 1, 1944 US landing on other islands in the group including Roi and Namur. These

Chester Nimitz joined the United States Navy in 1905. During World War I he was chief of staff of the US Atlantic Submarine Force. Promoted to Rear-Admiral in 1938, Nimitz was placed in charge of the Pacific Fleet after the attack on Pearl Harbor. He was a firm believer in an offensive rather than a defensive war and in gaining the initiative over the enemy. He met regularly with Admiral King and General MacArthur, their first objective being to establish a line of communication across the South Pacific to Australia, resulting in the Battle of the Coral Sea. With the aid of excellent intelligence he then planned and executed the decisive US naval victory at the Battle of Midway. He

NIMITZ	
Rank attained	Fleet Admiral
Dates	1885–1966
Background	United States Naval Academy, Annapolis
Commands	Pacific Fleet, 1941; C-in-C Naval Operations, 1945

landed forces on the island of Guadalcanal: thus leading to another decisive US victory. Nimitz employed the effective strategy of making a series of amphibious landings on islands across the Central Pacific as a means of approach to the Japanese home islands. He also fought a number of major naval battles that led to the virtual destruction of the Imperial Japanese Navy, and his submarines gradually eliminated the Japanese merchant marine. An affable but determined man, he was one of the ablest stategists the US Navy has ever produced. The Pacific war was won by his strategy.

Frank Fletcher saw service as a destroyer captain during World War I. In January 1942, as Rear-Admiral Fletcher, he was given command of a carrier task force. He delayed his task force's arrival at Wake Island because of a controversial decision to refuel, resulting in the loss

of the island to the Japanese before US naval forces could arrive. He supported the reinforcing of other vital strategic islands in the South Pacific. He then raided Japanese positions in the Central Pacific, New Guinea and the Solomon Islands and turned back the Japanese at the Battle of the Coral Sea. He saw his flagship, the USS *Yorktown*, sink under him at the Battle of Midway. He has been criticised for withdrawing his naval forces too precipitately at the Battle of Guadalcanal leaving the US Marines who were defending the island isolated. At the Battle of the Eastern Solomons he was again criticised for being overcautious. He then became C-in-C Northern Pacific, transporting aid to Russia via the western route. He remained at this post until the war's end.

FLETCHER	
Rank attained	Vice-Admiral
Dates	1885–1973
Background	United States Naval Academy, Annapolis
Commands	Task Force 17, 1942; C-in-C Northern Pacific, 1942

During World War I William 'Bull' Halsey served in the US Destroyer Force. In 1940 he was the most senior carrier admiral, with the rank of Vice-Admiral. His carriers were, fortunately, not at Pearl Harbor during the Japanese attack. He was the Commander of Task Force 16 in April 1942 during the 'Doolittle Raid',

Far left: King.
Second left: Fletcher.
Left: Halsey.

Below: The US battleship Missouri with other ships of the US fleet anchored in Tokyo Bay at the end of the war.

the first bombing attack on Japanese soil. By November 1942 he was C-in-C South Pacific Forces and Area, remaining in command of US Forces in that area for the next 18 months. In June 1944 he took command of the Third Fleet and was designated Commander Western Pacific Task Forces. During the Battle of Leyte Gulf his carriers were lured away from the focal point of the battle by the Japanese decoy carrier force and the US forces narrowly avoided disaster. Again his judgement was

HALSEY

Rank attained	Admiral
Dates	1882–1959
Background	United States Naval Academy, Annapolis
Commands	Task Force 16, 1942; C-in-C Southern Pacific, 1942; Third Fleet, 1944

called into question when he took his ships into the teeth of two typhoons, as a result of which three destroyers were lost. Subsequent to the Okinawa campaign in 1945, his forces struck at Tokyo and the Japanese home islands. His flag was flying on USS *Missouri* in Tokyo Bay when the formal Japanese surrender was signed on board. A pugnacious man, with an impulsive nature, he was nicknamed 'Bull' Halsey, but he earned the loyalty of his commanding officer, Nimitz, when he advocated taking to the offensive as soon as possible at the beginning of the war.

are secured next day

Feb 1–4, 1944 US landing and capture of Kwajalein in the Marshalls after one of the most intensive naval artillery bombardments of the Pacific war

Feb 18–23, 1944 Eniwetok invaded and captured. Other islands in the Marshalls are bypassed and do not surrender until the end of the war

Far Eastern Theater General Events

Feb 17–18, 1944 Operation 'Hailstone': massive air raids on Truk from 9 US carriers destroy 265 aircraft and 140,000 tons of shipping, effectively neutralizing the Japanese base

Feb 29, 1944 US land in the Admiralty Islands north-west of Rabaul and establish airfield by March 7

March, 1944 General MacArthur is directed by the US Joint Chiefs of Staff to prepare the Allied invasion of the Philippines. He will deploy the largest forces yet assembled in the Pacific

March 12, 1944 US Chiefs of Staff designate the Philippines and Formosa as next targets

March 20, 1944 US land on Emirau Island, north of Rabaul, which is now encircled

BURMA: Second Chindit Expedition

March 5–12, 1944 Chindits are flown to sites just north of the Irrawaddy near Indaw and establish fortified zones. They cut the Mandalay–Myitkyina railway and repel Japanese attacks

March 24, 1944 General Wingate killed in an air crash

March 24, 1944 Chindits fail in attempt to take Indaw but repulse more Japanese attacks on their fortified areas

May 17, 1944 Chindits handed to Stilwell's command

June 6–27, 1944 Chindits capture Mogaung. Most Chindits, in searing temperatures, are now sick and exhausted

August, 1944 Last Chindit elements flown

Victory was made possible by the Allies' industrial superiority, particularly that of the United States, which possessed the necessary raw materials, skilled manpower and industries. In the USA there was a massive increase in food production, of which 10% was exported to allies through Lend-Lease. There was rationing, but the US civilians ate more, and better, than they did before the war. In the factories there was a huge increase in employment and production, which caused many families to move from small towns and rural areas to the big industrial cities. The average working week rose from 38 hours to 47. Productivity increases were dramatic: for example, it took only a third as many work hours to build a ship in 1945 as it did in 1943. There was a huge increase in the number of women working in heavy industry, replacing the men in the workforce.

British women played a very important part in the war effort, replacing many of the men who normally worked in the factories and heavy industry. In Britain, blackouts were enforced immediately and children evacuated. During the Blitz many British cities were bombed, starting with London in early September 1940. During one period London was bombed for two and a half months continuously, night after night. The people had to contend with austerity, strict rationing and

bombing, but in general the British stoicism shone through and civilian morale remained high. British democracy carried on, and by-elections continued to be held. British men and women were directed to work in any industry that was thought necessary by the government. Young men often were conscripted to work in the coal mines as opposed to military service.

In Germany, in the early years of the war, domestic rationing was not at first introduced, but as the war progressed it became necessary, although civilian morale remained high. In the German-occupied countries, food was seized and shipped back to the German people. The Nazis resisted the need for women to undertake compulsory work service for ideological reasons. Instead, women were paid a generous allowance by the state to stay at home and have babies. The Nazi state outlawed listening to any foreign radio stations. Any criticism of the state was an offense, and many offenses were punishable by death. At first the bombing of German population centres was light, but it became increasingly intense and by the time the Americans entered the war, alongside RAF Bomber Command, city after city was devastated, culminating in the horrific raid on Dresden at the end of the war.

When the Germans invaded the USSR the Council for Evacuation proved essential for

Below: American shipyard welders – women taking on jobs formerly the preserve of men.

Right: Londoners sheltering at Aldwych station in the London Underground during the Blitz.

Soviet survival, in particular for the women and children. Over 16 million people were evacuated by the Council plus 10 million refugees. Many people went east to the factories and steelworks constructed in the Urals and beyond, to build the weapons to win the war. Some areas of the Soviet Union did welcome the Germans, initially as liberators from the sufferings under Stalin, but this was unfounded optimism. Life for the Soviet citizen was very hard, and the people suffered from every form of privation.

The Japanese people found that gradual changes in normal civilian life were being made. From 1939 controls were placed on daily necessities which became more and more severe as the conflict progressed. Military priorities started to dominate life. All group travel began to be forbidden. Education was reduced, and limits on working hours of women and children were waived. Then American bombers started to attack Japan's towns and cities in earnest and hundreds of thousands of people were killed in the bombing and incendiary raids. By 1945 Japan's economy and society were starting to come apart. The US naval blockade caused severe raw material and food shortages. After the two atomic bomb raids and the surrender, on September 2, 1945, Japanese society was physically and mentally disarmed.

out from Burma to India

ITALY: Anzio and Monte Cassino

Jan 17, 1944 Fifth Army attacks across the Garigliano River but is halted before Monte Cassino

Jan 22, 1944 Anzio landings by Allied VI Corps establishes beachhead which fails to be exploited

Jan 24 to Feb 11, 1944 First Battle of Monte Cassino

Jan 25 and 30, 1944 Allied VI Corps attempts to break out of the Anzio beach-head

Feb 3, 1944 German counterattack almost destroys the Anzio beachhead

Feb 15, 1944 The Allies destroy the monastery of Monte Cassino from the air

Feb 16–18, 1944 Second Battle of Monte Cassino

Feb 16–19, 1944 Another German coun-terattack at Anzio almost succeeds

Feb 28 to March 3, 1944 Continued German attacks on the Anzio beachhead

March 15–25, 1944 Third Battle of Monte Cassino

The Germans have failed to dislodge the Allies at Anzio, while the Allies have failed to break out of the beachhead or to take the strategic position of Monte Cassino – stale-mate. Both sides prepare to renew opera-tions in the spring

BURMA: Imphal/Kohima

March 5–6, 1944 Stilwell's Chinese defeat Japanese at Maingkwan and Walawbaum

March 7/8, 1944 Japanese begin their planned invasion of India by advancing from Fort White toward Tiddim, taking the Allies by surprise. 17th Indian Division there begins withdrawing north

March 14, 1944 Japanese advance toward Tamu but are held by 20th Indian Division. Repeated attacks fail to break through over the next three months

March, 19, 1944 Japanese attack Shangshak, north-east of Imphal, toward Kohima but are held there for a week.

In October 1943 the Japanese completed construction of their Thailand–Burma railway, illegally using slave labor and prisoners of war, thousands of whom were literally worked to death in appalling conditions. Meanwhile from Ledo in Assam, Stilwell's Chinese pushed forward, building a road to link with the Burma Road, which Chinese from Yunnan were repairing. That same month, Admiral Mountbatten arrived as Supreme Allied Commander South East Asia Command, and plans began to be formulated for a combined offensive from India and China. Before this could be put into effect, however, the Japanese struck.

While a division advanced up the Arakan coast, three divisions of General Mutaguchi's Fifteenth Army advanced toward the communications center of Dimapur in Assam, from where they planned to thrust into India – one element of their planning being that the Indian people would rise up aganst the British. The decisive battle came at Imphal–Kohima, the latter enduring a siege of two weeks and having

to be supplied by air. By the end of April the Japanese offensive had ground to a halt, but it took another two months to push them back from the Assam frontier. Their coastal advance had also been repulsed in February at Ngakyedauk, where another air-supplied defensive position, the 'Admin Box', had defied all Japanese assaults.

As these decisive events were taking place, a second Chindit expedition had been flown into Burma north of Indaw, establishing air-supplied defensive positions codenamed 'Broadway', 'Aberdeen' and 'White City', which the Japanese attacked unsuccessfully. The Chindits spent some five months within Japanese-controlled territory before being evacuated, longer than planned. Again losses were heavy, malaria and general exhaustion gradually reducing their combat effectiveness. By the time they were evacuated in August 1944, the 9,000 men had lost over 3,600 killed, wounded or missing.

In May, the Chinese advanced from Yunnan, while Stilwell's forces were progress-

ing from the north-west toward Myitkyina and Mogaung. In August they succeeded in linking the two roads, re-establishing land communications with China.

In November the Allied offensive that would eject the Japanese from Burma began. Crossing the Chindwin at Sittaung and Kalewa, Slim pushed his forces in two directions – a move on Mandalay and a wider outflanking thrust to Meiktila, aiming to cut off the two Japanese armies to the north and then move against Rangoon. On March 3, 1945 the Allies took Meiktila, and Mandalay fell seventeen days later. A desperate counterattack at Meiktila had to be fought off before, at the end of March, Slim was able to propel his forces speedily south along the Irrawaddy, to take Rangoon before the monsoon set in. On 1–2 May there were air and sea landings south of Rangoon, and the Burmese capital, evacuated by the Japanese, was liberated on the 3rd.

Final operations in Burma were to prevent the breakout of Japanese troops trapped to the west by the Allied thrust down the Irrawaddy. This Japanese offensive failed by the beginning of August, leaving the Allies with mopping-up operations in the lead-up to surrender on the 28th.

Above: Gurkhas advancing with Lee tanks to clear the Japanese from the Imphal–Kohima road.

Left: Troops and supplies crossing the Irrawaddy River near Tigyiang, Burma, December 30, 1944.

Meanwhile the Japanese cut the Imphal–Kohima road, and Kohima is reinforced

April 5–18, 1944 Japanese besiege Kohima, which is resupplied by air

April 18, 1944 Japanese attack Imphal from the north-east but are halted at Sengmai

Imphal-Kohima is the turning-point in Burma

April, 1944 Stilwell's Chinese continue their advance toward Myitkyina and Mogaung

April 18, 1944 British relieve Kohima

April 21, 1944 The Japanese offensive has been fought to a standstill

April 22, 1944 British begin pushing the Japanese back from Kohima

April 26, 1944 A series of Japanese attacks toward Imphal from Tiddim in the south is stopped near Bishenpur, though fighting continues. The Japanese are now short of supplies

May 11, 1944 Chinese offensive begins from Yunnan across the Salween River

May 13, 1944 Increased fighting between Tiddim and Bishenpur

May 17, 1944 Merrill's Marauders take Myitkyina airfield but cannot take the town

June 22, 1944 Imphal-Kohima area cleared of Japanese

July 11, 1944 Japanese terminate their operation to invade India and withdraw across the Chindwin River, sickness, hunger and casualties – together with inadequate preparation – having sapped their strength

RUSSIA: Soviet Winter Offensive

Dec 24, 1943 Soviet First Ukrainian Front attacks from the Kursk salient

Jan 8, 1944 Soviets take Kirovograd

Jan 14–15, 1944 Soviets launch major offensive to clear the Leningrad area

Jan 25–8, 1944 Soviets encircle two German corps west of Cherkassy

Jan 26, 1944 Soviets end Leningrad blockade

Jan 27, 1944 Soviets attack west from Korosten

SOVIET TANKS

T-26 Tank

Weight	10.1 tons
Crew	Three
Armament	45mm gun and two 7.62mm MG
Armor	Max: 25mm. Min: 10mm
Engine	GAZ T-26, 88hp, speed 17mph
Dimensions	Length: 15ft 3in. Width: 8ft 0in. Height: 7ft 8in
Production	11,000+

T-26 tank.

T-34/85 tank.

T-34 Tank

Weight	28 tons (T-34/85 32 tons)
Crew	Four
Armament	76.2mm gun (later 85mm) and two 7.62mm MG
Armor	Max: 47mm. Min: 16mm
Engine	V-2 V-12, 500hp, speed 32mph
Dimensions	Length: 21ft 7in. Width: 9ft 10in. Height: 8ft 0in
Production	40,000+

KV-1 Tank

Weight	43 tons
Crew	Five
Armament	76.2mm gun and three 7.62mm DT machine-guns
Armor	Max: 75mm. Min: 35mm
Engine	V-2K V-12, 550hp, speed 22mph
Dimensions	Length: 22ft 3in. Width: 10ft 11in. Height: 10ft 8in
Production	10,000+

KV-1 tank.

Below: *Soviet infantry advance with a T-34/76 tank.*

When they entered the war the Russians had the largest tank force in the world but, owing to military incompetence, they lost some 17,500 to the 2,500 Panzers of the German Army during the first months of the fighting.

The early T-26 and BT-7 series of tanks were of good design, as were most other Soviet tanks apart from the large multi-turreted T-35 and the giant KV-2.

Soviet tanks were crudely built compared with their German counterparts. Even so, the T-34 series of tanks can be considered as possibly the best all-round tanks of the war, possessing good speed, reliability, protection and fire-power and being simple to maintain.

The KV-1 took the Germans by surprise at the start of Operation 'Barbarossa'. It was virtually invulnerable to German anti-tank gun fire other than from the 88. Its successor, the IS-2 'Stalin', could even challenge the mighty Tiger tank on even terms.

IS-2 'Stalin' tank.

IS-2 'Stalin' Tank	
Weight	45.5 tons
Crew	Four
Armament	122mm gun and three 7.62mm DT machine-guns
Armor	Max: 120mm. Min: 14mm
Engine	V-2 V-12, 513hp, speed 23mph
Dimensions	Length: 32ft 2in. Width: 10ft Height: 8ft 11in
Production	2,350

Jan 30, 1944 Soviets attack into the Dnieper bend

Feb 12, 1944 Soviets take Luga between Lakes Peipus and Ilmen

The Soviet Leningrad offensive isolates Finland, which tries to begin negotiations with the USSR

Feb 15–17, 1944 German troops encircled west of Cherkassy finally get permission from Hitler to break out

Feb 22, 1944 Soviets take Krivoy Rog

March 1, 1944 Soviets reach the Panther Line on the Estonian border to which Eighteenth Army has withdrawn

March 4–6, 1944 Soviet offensive south of the Pripet River and across the Bug River

March 10, 1944 Soviets take Uman

March 13, 1944 Soviets take Kherson

March 17, 1944 Soviet Second Ukrainian Front reaches the Dniester River

March 25, 1944 Soviets reach the border of Roumania at the Prut River

March 28, 1944 German First Panzer Army encircled east of Podgaitsy

March 30, 1944 Hitler sacks Manstein and von Kleist

March 30 to April 7, 1944 German First Panzer Army breaks out

April 2, 1944 Soviets enter Roumania

April 8, 1944 Soviets attack in the Crimea

April 10, 1944 Soviets take Odessa

May 5–12, 1944 Soviets assault Sevastopol and secure the Crimea

Far Eastern Theater General Events

April 17, 1944 Japanese Ichi-Go offensive in southern China. The Japanese overrun Fourteenth Air Force airfields

April 29–30, 1944 Final air strike by US carrier aircraft on Truk wrecks what ships and installations remain. The Japanese base is destroyed

April/May, 1944 Chennault and his Fourteenth AF fly missions against the Japanese in China, provoking an offensive to capture the US bases. An argument between Chennault and Stilwell erupts over

THE PACIFIC: 'ISLAND HOPPING'

The Gilberts

Admiral Nimitz at Pearl Harbor received the directive to take the Gilbert Islands on July 20 1943. Occupied by the Japanese since December 1941, this group of sixteen atolls was perceived as posing an air threat to US-Australia sea communications; it would also lead directly to the Marshalls and Marianas.

The US operation, 'Galvanic', was launched on November 20, Marines going ashore at two islands, Tarawa and Makin. The latter was not heavily defended and the island was secured by 23rd.

Tarawa, although taken in the same length of time, was an altogether different proposition – and became one of the epic battles of the war. Here the Japanese had built pillboxes, bunkers and fortifications all over the island, and the garrison was some 5,000 men. Because of the coral reefs, landing craft were largely replaced by Amtrac amphibious tractors for the first time. The first wave, on 20th, met withering fire and was at first pinned down on the beach. After the first, critical day, a second wave of

Marines landed next day. A succession of attacks and counterattacks took place, the Japanese surging forward in *banzai* all-out attacks. On 23rd, the Marines finally had control of the entire island after 76 hours of the hardest fighting in the Pacific to date. Of the Japanese troops garrisoning the island, only 176, wounded and taken prisoner, remained alive.

The Marshalls

Next on Nimitz's central Pacific thrust were the Marshall Islands, a group of 36 atolls including Kwajalein, largest atoll in the world. The capture of these islands and their airfields would put pressure on the Japanese main base at Truk, just under 1,000 miles to the west.

The lessons of Tarawa were incorporated in a brilliantly conducted landing operation (Operation 'Flintlock'). Intelligence intercepts revealed that the Japanese had transferred their main garrisons to the outlying islands; consequently these were subjected to heavy air attack and bypassed. Some 300 warships provided the most intensive artillery

Below: US troops of the 7th Division using flamethrowers to force Japanese soldiers from a blockhouse on Kwajalein Island in the Marshall Islands, February 4, 1944.

bombardment of the war, as the main landing on Kwajalein went in on February 1, 1944. The island was secured within three days, while other islands, including Roi and Namur were taken by the 2nd. The capture of the Gilberts together with massive air attacks forced the Japanese Combined Fleet to evacuate Truk (to Singapore). On February 17–18 in Operation 'Hailstone', aircraft from 9 US carriers destroyed 265 aircraft and 140,000 tons of shipping here; a final attack on April 29/30 destroyed what remained.

The Marianas

The Marianas group, midway between New Guinea and Japan, consists of 15 islands, principal of which are Saipan and Guam. From the former to Toyko is 1,200 miles, so that its capture would put Japan itself within range of America's new B-29 heavy bombers.

On July 15 the first wave of US troops landed on Saipan, taking heavy casualties across the coral reefs through which frogmen had blown gaps. Resistance was even heavier than expected, and it took much longer to secure the island than planned, against fanatical opposition. On July 6/7 the last great *banzai* charges (the war's largest) were beaten back and the island was secured on the 9th, that day witnessing the tragic suicides of many civilians who leapt over the 220-foot cliffs at Marpi Point.

The landings on Guam were delayed by the length of time it had taken to capture Saipan, and by the threat of Japanese naval intervention, which was averted at the Battle of the Philippine Sea. On July 21, after 13 days of bombardment from the air and naval artillery, the US troops landed, ways through the formidable beach defenses having been cleared by frogmen. From cliffs overlooking the beaches, the Japanese pioured fire on the attackers, but by nightfall two beachheads had been established. It took until 31st for these to link up, and after repelling heavy counterattacks, the island, together with Tinian, invaded on July 24, was declared secure on August 10,

Mopping up in the Marianas lasted well into 1945, and the last Japanese soldier did not surrender until 1972. On October 12 1944 the first B-29 touched down on Saipan.

allocation of resources

May, 1944 Japanese Prime Minister Tojo is under increasing pressure as the war turns in favor of the Allies. He will be forced to resign on July 18 after the loss of Saipan and the defeat at the Battle of the Philippine Sea; his replacement is General Koiso

June 5, 1944 Bangkok bombed by US B-29s from Chengtu in China, first combat mission for the new bomber

June 11, 1944 US carrier aircraft begin strikes on the Marianas to 'blanket' Japanese air bases there and take complete control of the skies

June 15, 1944 First B-29 bombing mission from mainland Asia to Japan. 50 B-29s strike steelmills on Kyushu

June 15–16, 1944 US carrier aircraft bomb the Bomin Islands including Iwo Jima

July 16, 1944 Australian warships of Allied Task Force 74 bombard Japanese pocket of resistance near Aitape on New Guinea

June 18, 1944 Japanese take Changsha

PAPUA-NEW GUINEA: Hollandia

April 22, 1944 US landings at Hollandia and Aitape

April 24, 1944 Australians take Madang and then press on north up the coast after the retreating Japanese

May 27, 1944 US land on Biak Island near Wadke, but resistance here is strong

June 30, 1944 US secure Biak Island

July, 1944 Allies land on Numfoor Island

July 30 US land at the NW tip of New Guinea

MARIANAS

June 13, 1944 Admiral Toyoda, CinC Japanese Fleet, orders Admiral Ozawa to stop the invasion of Saipan and to destroy the US carriers. He has 9 carriers of various sizes against the 15 of US Admiral Spruance's Fifth Fleet, which are organized as Task Force 58 under Admiral Mitscher

June 15–17, 1944 US landings on Saipan,

LEMAY

Rank attained	General
Dates	1906–1990
Background	Career airman
Commands	C-in-C of 305th Bombardment Group, 1942; 20th Bomber Command, 1943; 21st Bomber Command, 1945

LeMay   Spaatz

Curtis E. LeMay was one of the architects of the US bomber offensives against Germany and then Japan. A strict disciplinarian and a great tactician, he became the youngest two-star general in the US Army, commanding a bomber group. By leading raids personally, he gained the action experience to develop better defensive formations. In July 1944 he transferred to the China/Burma/India theatre to command the 20th Bomber Group. He then commanded 21st Bomber Command, greatly improving the bomber offensive against Japan. He switched to night-time, low-level, area incendiary bombing. The devastation caused to Japan's cities was on a spectacular scale.

Carl Spaatz saw action in 1916 on the Mexican border and then during World War I. He was one of the earliest of US aviators. He favored daylight precision bombing. Firstly he commanded the US Eighth Air Force then the North African theater, including the Twelfth Air Force, fighting in Tunisia and Sicily. When he returned to the UK he became Commanding General of the Strategic Air

EAKER

Rank attained	Lieutenant-General
Dates	1896–1987
Background	Career airman
Commands	C-in-C Eighth USAAF, 1943; C-in-C Allied Air Forces Mediterranean, 1943.

infantry officer before learning to fly and joining the United States Air Service. Promoted to Brigadier-General in 1942, Eaker was appointed C-in-C of Eighth Bomber Command under Carl Spaatz. Arriving in England in February 1942, he set up US Army Bomber Command at High Wycombe. In February 1943 he headed the US Air Force in Algiers. Eaker was a strong advocate of daylight bombing raids: the USAAF would concentrate on daylight bombing whereas the RAF would bomb at night. He was promoted to Lieutenant-General in June 1943, commanding Mediterranean Allied Air Forces.

SPAATZ

Rank attained	General
Dates	1891–1974
Background	Career airman
Commands	Eighth USAAF, 1942; C-in-C Allied Air Forces North Africa, 1943; US Stategic Air Force, Europe, 1943; US Stategic Air Force, Pacific, 1945

Force. In 1945 he transfered to the Pacific, directing the bombing of Japan.

Ira Eaker led the first US bombing raid on Germany in 1942. Texas-born he was an

HARRIS

Rank attained	Air Chief Marshal
Dates	1892–1984
Background	Royal Flying Corps
Commands	No 5 Bomber Group, 1939; C-in-C Bomber Command, 1942

Arthur Harris joined the Royal Flying Corps in 1915. At the outbreak of World War II he spent the early months in the USA purchasing aircraft for Britain. He then served under Charles Portal, C-in-C of RAF Bomber Command, and became C-in-C himself in

1942. At the time, the Allied bombing campaign was ineffective and Harris set out to implement a new and more efficient strategy. Under his leadership the Command developed the technique of saturation, or area, bombing. He argued that night-time 'blanket' bombing of urban areas was the only way to defeat Germany, undermining civilian morale and destroying any factories within the cities. Attacks were launched on Germany's major population centers, sometimes involving as many as a thousand bombers. The campaign killed an estimated 600,000 civilians and destroyed or seriously damaged some 6,000,000 homes. During the war Bomber Command lost over 57,000 men killed. 'Bomber' Harris commanded great respect and loyalty from his subordinates and his bomber crews, but his request for a campaign medal for Bomber Command was refused. The morality of the bombing campaign will always be debatable.

Eaker   *Harris*

Harris (left) and Eaker (right)

with heavy casualties across the reefs
June 25, 1944 US take Mount Tapotchau on Saipan
July 6/7, 1944 Japanese final suicide counterattack on Saipan
July 8, 1944 Start of 13-day bombardment of Guam
July 9, 1944 Saipan secured. Surviving Japanese troops, women and children throw themselves off Marpi Point cliffs
July 21, 1944 US land on Guam
July 24, 1944 US land on Tinian
July 25/6, 1944 US repulse Japanese counterattacks on Guam
July 31, 1944 US Guam beachheads link up
Aug 10, 1944 US secure Guam

Western Theater General Events
Aug, 1943 to June, 1944 'Crossbow' raids: RAF/USAAF bomb some 100 suspected V-weapon launch sites in France and Belgium
Jan 3, 1944 First 'Overlord' conference, London, for Normandy invasion
By the end of February over a million US troops have been transported across the Atlantic
Jan, 1944 Berlin raided 5 times
Feb 20/1, 1944 'Big Week' begins: 6-day offensive on German fighter and ball-bearing factories from British and Italian bases. But German aircraft industry rapidly recovers
Feb 15/16, 1944 RAF bomb Berlin; but defences there are strong
March 4, 1944 Berlin daylight raid by USAAF
March 6/7, 1944 Trappes, first pre-invasion raid
March 30/1, 1944 Nuremberg: 'Pointblank' bombing campaign ends. Raid marks highest RAF loss rate of the war
March, 19, 1944 Germans occupy Hungary
March 22, 1944 Roumanian dictator Antonescu meets Hitler in Berlin to discuss defense of Roumania
March 24/5, 1944 Last major RAF raid of the aerial Battle of Berlin: distance, weather and German defenses have made it too

Affectionally known as the 'Wooden Wonder', the all-wood constructed de Havilland Mosquito was the fastest RAF bomber of World War II, entering sevice in May 1942. Used for pinpoint raids and Pathfinder operations it spearheaded the bombing campaign against Germany. There were also very successful night-fighter variants operating in home defense, shooting down over 600 German raiders as well as 600 V-1 flying bombs. They also flew intruder missions in support of RAF bomber night raids on Germany, shooting down German night-fighters.

Arguably the most important Luftwaffe bomber of WWII, the Ju 88A remained in front line service from first weeks of war until the last. Its operational debut was on 26 Sept 1939, attacking British warships in the Firth of Forth. It participated in the Norwegian and French campaigns and played a major role during the Battle of Britain. Subsequently it saw action on all fronts from the Arctic to North Africa and Russia. It scored notable successes against Allied shipping, both merchantmen and warships. The Ju 88 bomber was adapted for various fighter roles, particularly the successful night-fighter versions.

The Northrop P-61 Black Widow was the first USAAF night-fighter designed as such

from the outset. They first entered service in the Pacific theatre in mid 1944. Their first recorded victories were on the night of 6–7 July 1944. It became the standard USAAF night fighter during the final year of the war equipping all such squadrons both in the Pacific and European theaters. Two squadrons were employed at night against incoming V-1s from July 1944. First Luftwaffe aircraft a Black Widow destroyed was over France in August 1944. They also operated on deep intruder operations attacking ground targets such as locomotives, supply convoys and bridges as well as enemy aircraft.

De Havilland Mosquito	
Weight	21,600lb max.
Crew	Two
Armament	Maximum bombload 4,000lb. Fighter – 20mm cannon and four 0.303in machine-guns in nose, eight 3in rocket projectiles under wings.
Range	3,500 miles
Engines	2 Rolls-Royce Merlin 1,3480hp, max. speed 425mph
Dimensions	Length: 40ft 6in. Wing span: 54ft 2in. Height: 15ft 3in
Production	7,781 all marks

Above and below: *The British Mosquito, which also saw service with the USAAF.* **Right**: *The P-61 Black Widow.*

Junkers Ju 88A-4

Junkers Ju 88A-4

Weight	30,865lb max.
Crew	Four
Armament	One forward-firing 7.92mm MG in cock-pit, one 13mm machine-gun in fuselage nose, two rearward-firing 7.92mm machine-guns in cock-pit and one 13mm machine-gun in ventral nose gondola. Maximum bombload 7,935lb.
Range	1,696 miles
Engines	2 Junkers Jumo 211J-1 1,340hp, max. speed 280mph
Dimensions	Length: 47ft 2⅔in. Wing span: 65ft 7½in. Height: 15ft 11in
Production	15,000 all marks

Northrop P-61B Black Widow

Weight	38,000lb max.
Crew	Three
Armament	Four 0.5in machine-guns in remote-controlled rotating turret and four forward firing 20mm cannon in the lower fusolage, plus four bombs of up to 1,600lbs each carried underwing
Range	3,000 miles max.
Engines	2 Pratt & Whitney 2,000hp R-2800-65, max. speed 366mph
Dimensions	Length: 49ft 7in. Wing span: 66ft 0in. Height: 14ft 8in
Production	742

The US used a total of 105 carriers, of which 72 were the small and slow escort carriers. Ten carriers of all types were lost. It was the fleet-type carriers that formed the striking force of the Navy and 17 of these were the excellent *Essex* class. There were also nine light fleet carriers of the *Independence* class. No *Essex* class carriers were lost but several were badly damaged, typically by Kamikazes.

The Carrier Task Forces of the US Navy's Pacific Fleet were crucial to winning the war against Japan. Early examples were Task Forces 16 and 17, operating with just three fleet aircraft carriers during the Battle of Midway in June 1942.

Admiral Halsey's Third Fleet and Admiral Spruance's Fifth Fleet were merged in 1944, Spruance and Halsey taking it in turns to command. When Spruance was in command it was called the Fifth Fleet, with Halsey the Third Fleet. This was at the time the most powerful fleet in the world, the backbone being the fast carrier groups.

The doctrine of mass air strikes had evolved, employing hundreds of aircraft at the same time rather than dozens. At the US victory at the Battle of the Philippine Sea, in June 1944, Task Force 58 (the Fast Carrier Task Force) swept all before it. It consisted of five Task Groups. At the front was the Battle Line, Task Group 58.7, consisting of a large circle of seven battleships with asso-

ciated cruisers and destroyers on picket duty. Slightly north of them was Task Group 58.4, with three carriers plus cruisers and destroyers. To the east were the three major carrier groups Task Groups 58.1, 58.2, 58.3, all with two fleet carriers and two light fleet carriers, plus attendant cruisers and destroyers. The carriers in each Task Group cruised in a diamond formation, surrounded by five cruisers and then by 12–15 destroyers in a four-mile circle around them, providing anti-submarine and anti-aircraft defense.

Independence Class Carrier	
Displacement	14,500 tons
Crew	1,569
Armament	30 aircraft
Engine/motor	Four turbines, 100,000hp, max. speed 31 knots
Dimensions	Length: 600ft 0in Beam 73ft 0in

Essex Class Carrier	
Displacement	30,000 tons
Crew	2,682
Armament	90 aircraft
Engine/motor	Four turbines, 150,000hp, max. speed 32 knots
Dimensions	Length: 872ft 0in Beam 96ft 0in

Above: An Independence class light fleet carrier.

Below: Essex class fleet carriers, December 1944.

Above: The escort carrier USS Altamaha with her flight deck crammed with P-51 fighters.

Below: USS Enterprise at Pearl Harbor in May 1942; one month later she would distinguish herself at the Battle of Midway.

expensive

April to June, 1944 Further German offensives against Tito's Yugoslavs

April 3, 1944 British make first of a series of six unsuccessful air attacks on *Tirpitz* in Altenfjord

Late May Schnorkel breathing device on U-boats begins widespread deployment

May 14–17, 1944 Lebanon conference on Greek affairs

May 25, 1944 German special forces fail in attempt to seize Tito at Drvar

June 12, 1944 Germany commissions first high-speed *Elektroboot* U-boat

June 13, 1944 German V-1 flying-bombs launched against London. Soon 100 a day are being launched

June 14, 1944 RAF resumes daylight bombing

July 7, 1944 Caen tactical area-bombing

July 20, 1944 Attempt on Hitler's life at Rastenburg fails

July 27, 1944 Homberg, first major RAF daylight raid

BATTLE OF THE PHILIPPINE SEA

June 18, 1944 Japanese scout aircraft locates TF58 200 miles west of Saipan. Admiral Ozawa plans to hit the Americans with his aircraft, which have a longer range than the Americans' before TF58 comes within their offensive range

June, 19, 1944 Japanese 373-plane attack on the US carriers is detected by radar 150 miles away, giving time for the US to launch its interceptors. Only minor damage is suffered by the US carriers, but 243 Japanese aircraft are downed for the loss of just 29 Americans. The Japanese survivors fly on to Guam to refuel and rearm, but 50 more are lost there. Meanwhile US submarines sink 2 Japanese carriers including flagship *Taiho*

June 20, 1944 Ozawa pulls back to keep out of range, abandoning plans to renew his attacks, but the US fleet is chasing and launches a dusk attack at extreme range. One carrier is sunk, 2 others badly

AMPHIBIOUS WARFARE

Between 1939 and 1942 amphibious techniques were poor. The Japanese Army was probably the best during this period, developing the necessary expertise as well as specialised landing craft. The Germans carried out a well-organised amphibious invasion of Norway in 1940, but they were not fully geared for an assault on Great Britain and the German Army balked at the idea.

The most vulnerable and important moment of an amphibious landing is when the first wave of troops hits the beach and the complex timing of the sea bombardment and air support comes fully into play.

After the disastrous raid on the French port of Dieppe by the British and Canadians in August 1942, some very serious lessons had to be learnt – a very thorough surveying of the beach beforehand, a heavy naval and air bombardment prior to disembarkation, support vessels covering the beach as the troops land, the need to develop specialised equipment, landing ships and landing craft, and the efficient co-ordination of landing supplies on the beach. Many of these lessons had not been fully absorbed in time for the Allied landings in North Africa three months later. Needless numbers of troops were drowned, each man

Above: *US Marines hit the beach.*

Below: *The LST (tank landing ship or 'Landing Ship, Tank') was built during World War II to support amphibious operations by carrying vehicles, cargo and troops directly on to the beach.*

being overburdened with gear and there being nothing adequately to bridge the gap between the shore and the landing vessels. Thankfully the landings were largely unopposed. These lessons were learnt for the subsequent landings on Sicily and Italy and also for the D-Day landings, the largest and most complex amphibious operation the world has ever seen.

The US Marines were the masters of amphibious operational techniques. As in most things, experience counts, and the US Marines certainly got plenty of that as they made their spectacular island-hopping offensive across the Pacific Ocean.

Above: *Australian troops storm ashore in the first assault wave to hit Balikpapan on the southeast coast of oil-rich Borneo, July 1945.*

damaged, 2 oilers are sunk and damage inflicted on other ships. 20 US aircraft are lost, 65 Japanese
This is a mortal blow to the Japanese carrier fleet. Ozawa has but 35 aircraft left. US dub the battle 'The Great Marianas Turkey-Shoot'. It is the largest carrier battle of the war. 80 US aircraft are lost during the night-time return, running out of fuel or crash-landing. But almost all the aircrew are saved

Far Eastern Theater General Events
Summer, 1944 to early, 1945 Nearly 50 B-29 raids from China strike Japan 9 times and also hit targets in Manchukuo, Korea, Formosa, China and south-east Asia
Second half of, 1944 B-29 bombing missions from India to Japan sustain heavy losses
Sept 4, 1944 Japanese take Lingling airfield in China
Sept 15, 1944 US forces land on Morotai and on Peleliu in the Palaus
Oct 3, 1944 MacArthur and Nimitz are directed to invade Luzon, northern main island of the Philippines, while Nimitz is to attack Iwo Jima then Okinawa

NORTH-WEST EUROPE:
Allied Invasion of Normandy
Many small-scale Allied intelligence-gathering operations are undertaken on the French coast prior to the Normandy invasion, including sand-sampling by frogmen from midget submarines
Massive Allied naval forces including battleships support the Normandy landings and beachhead operations with the ability to lob shells some 15 miles inland
June 4, 1944 D-Day postponed from 5th to 6th because of bad weather
June 5/6, 1944 Allied deception operations 'Glimmer' and 'Tractable' indicating landings in the Straits of Dover and near le Havre
June 5/6, 1944 BBC transmits coded signal to the French Resistance announcing D-Day
June 6, 1944 D-Day: Allies land 155,000

From 1942, the demand for an Allied 'second front' against the Germans mounted – voiced by Stalin, to take pressure off the Eastern Front, and increasingly by elements of the British public, who had no idea of the size of such an undertaking. When it came, the invasion of France was the result of a massive build-up of troops, weapons and *matériel* in Britain, much of it transported across the Atlantic, and much meticulous planning.

The Germans expected such an attack, and built an impressive system of fortifications along the coast of France, equipped with artillery emplacements, and constructed massively of reinforced concrete. Coastal waters were mined and beaches strewn with obstacles against landing craft and tanks. Allied air superiority had now made mobility a problem for the Germans, especially as a result of a pre-invasion bombing campaign against centres of communication, railways and roads. Rommel, in command of the defenses from January 1944, clearly saw that the Allies must be defeated on the beaches and not allowed to penetrate inland.

Most probable, the Germans believed, was a landing in the Pas de Calais, the closest point between England and Europe. Allied deception schemes, including the creation of a phantom army with authentic-sounding radio traffic, persuaded the Germans to station their Fifteenth

Army in this area. The actual landing site, however, was the 50-odd-mile stretch of beaches between the Seine estuary and the Cotentin Peninsula. Here, in contrast to the Pas de Calais, were long beaches and fewer cliffs. Allied special forces spent months covertly examining the beaches and reconnoitering, while the troops destined for the invasion trained hard.

The five target beaches were designated Utah, Omaha, Gold, Juno and Sword, the first two, at the Cotentin end, destinations for US First Army; the other three for British Second Army (with a major Canadian component).

D-Day, June 6, 1944

Unseasonably bad weather forced the postponement of D-Day from June 5 to the 6th, when a mighty armada of ships put more than 150,000 men ashore. They were preceded by airborne landings on the flanks of the intended beachheads by the US 101st and 82nd Airborne Divisions in the west and the British 6th Airborne Division in the east, the latter to secure the flank against 21st Panzer Division, known to be in the area.

Specialised armoured vehicles – including floating tanks and mine-clearing vehicles – plus bombing and naval bombardment enabled the Allies to establish themselves ashore, but not all objectives were attained. On Omaha beach the

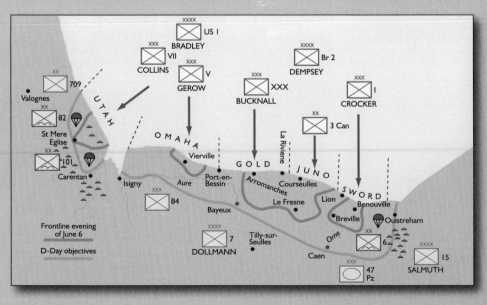

Above: GIs approaching the D-Day beaches in their landing craft, June 6, 1944.

cliffs posed difficulties that led to heavy casualties, and in the east the British failed to take Caen, where the 21st Panzer Division actually were. Meanwhile, Hitler, convinced that this was but a feint, refused to deploy two more panzer divisions until too late.

For the next seven weeks the battle for the beachheads raged, as Allied troops and equipment poured in, protected from the weather by artificial 'Mulberry' harbors. (At Dieppe, in August 1942, the attempt by Canadian and British troops to capture a port failed disastrously, and the Allies realized that effectively they must build their own.) The Germans meanwhile fed in reinforcements.

The beachhead, united on the second day, gradually expanded, and a series of British attempts to take Caen failed – Operation 'Goodwood' most disastrously on July 18, when 400 tanks were lost. That day St-Lô fell to the Americans, the Cotentin Peninsula including Cherbourg, having been secured by June 27.

Above: US infantrymen with a wrecked German tank.

troops in Normandy and secure beachheads

June 7–8, 11–14, 1944 Canadian and British forces attack Caen but fail to take it

June 11–14, 1944 British 7th Amd Division thrust halted at Villers-Bocage

June 12, 1944 All beachheads are now linked up

June 12, 1944 Carentan Peninsula, less Cherbourg, secured by US forces

June 17, 1944 Hitler confers with Rommel and von Rundstedt at Soissons

June, 19–22, 1944 Storms in the Channel damage Mulberry harbors and slow the Allied build-up of supplies

June 22–7, 1944 Allies assault and take Cherbourg

June 26–30, 1944 British Operation 'Epsom' fails to break out west of Caen

June 29, 1944 Hitler confers with Rommel and von Rundstedt at Berchtesgaden and refuses evacuation of Normandy

July 3, 1944 US First Army attacks toward St-Lô

July 4, 1944 Canadians fail in attempt to take Carpiquet airfield

July 8–11, 1944 British Operation 'Charnwood' takes part of Caen

July 18, 1944 British and Canadian Operation 'Goodwood' secures Caen but is halted at Bourgebus Ridge

July 18, 1944 US take St-Lô

July 17, 1944 Rommel wounded by RAF air attack

July 25–7, 1944 Operation 'Cobra': US forces launch attack in the east which finally breaks out of the beachhead

July 31, 1944 US take Avranches

FINLAND:
June 10, 1944 Soviets attack on the Finnish front

June 20, 1944 Soviets take Viipuri

RUSSIA: Operation 'Bagration'
June 9, 1944 Soviet summer offensive Operation 'Bagration' begins in the north

June 22, 1944 Operation 'Bagration' begins

Nicknamed 'Old Blood and Guts', George S. Patton came from a Californian family with a strong military background and he always wanted to be a soldier. He fought in the Mexican Campaign of 1916 and in World War I, when he was assigned to tanks. Between the

wars he reverted to the old horsed cavalry. In 1940 he commanded a brigade of the newly-formed 2nd Armored Division and later that year, after promotion to Major General, the command of the whole division and then the 1st Armored Corps. In November 1942 he commanded the Western Task Force that successfully landed in French Morocco. In the Sicilian Campaign he commanded the US Seventh Army. Unfortunately two incidents occurred in which he accused soldiers of cowardice because they were suffering from combat fatigue. This was reported in the press and he was relieved of command for eleven months as a consequence. In January 1944 he was given command of the US Third Army. He launched a series of armored thrusts from Normandy across France to the German border. He then relieved the besieged town of Bastogne during the Battle of the Bulge. In March 1945 his forces drove deep into Germany, Austria and Czechoslovakia at the war's end. He was promoted to four-star general in April 1945. He was hailed as the outstanding American general of the war, a flamboyant, aggressive and meticulous commander, deeply religious and widely read. He died in a car accident in December 1945.

Below: Infantrymen of Patton's 10th Infantry Battalion, Third Army, in action.

PATTON

Rank attained	Lieutenant General
Dates	1885–1945
Background	Career soldier; Virginia Military Institute; West Point Military Academy
Commands	2nd Armored Division, 1940; 1st Armored Corps 1942; Western Task Force, Operation 'Torch', 1942; II Corps, 1942–43; Seventh Army, 1943; Third Army, 1944; Military Governor of Bavaria, 1945
Campaigns	North-West Africa, 1942–43; Sicily 1943; North West Europe, 1943–45

BRADLEY

Rank attained	General
Dates	1893–1981
Background	Career soldier; West Point Military Academy
Commands	82nd and 28th Divisions, 1942; II Corps, 1943; First Army, 1943; Twelfth Army Group, 1944
Campaigns	North Africa, 1943; Sicily, 1943; North-West Europe, 1943–45

Bradley.

Omar Bradley taught at West Point before the war and later served on the General Staff. Early in 1942 he commanded and trained the 82nd and 28th Divisions in the United States Army. He was then transferred to North Africa as deputy to General Patton in II Corps. Bradley took over command when Patton left, leading the corps through the remainder of the North African Campaign, capturing Bizerta and taking 40,000 prisoners. He then led his corps in Sicily. He left II Corps and took command of the First Army in Great Britain prior to the invasion of France. He commanded the US forces at D-Day and led the First Army in France until taking command of the 12th Army Group which consisted of four armies, a post that he held until the end of the war.

During the Battle of the Bulge he behaved with great coolness, stemming a German breakthrough. His men then sealed the Ruhr Pocket, capturing 335,000 enemy soldiers. He was promoted to a full general in March 1945. At the end of the war he commanded more men than any other US general in history – 1,300,000. A man of common sense, he was highly regarded by those who served under him, nicknaming him the 'GI's General'. Eisenhower thought that he was the best of the battlefield commanders.

General 'Vinegar Joe' Stilwell was a cantankerous and difficult man to work with – hence his nickname. An anglophobe, he had an implacable dislike of the British. He served in World War I, had two tours of duty in China before the war and was the US military attaché in Peking from 1935 to 1939. He was sent to China in 1942 as Chiang Kai-shek's chief of staff and the commander of the Chinese Fifth and Sixth Armies. He was driven from Burma by the Japanese but returned in 1943. Friction with Chiang over troop deployments resulted in his withdrawal from the theater of operations in 1944. He went on to command US Tenth Army in the battle for Okinawa.

Stilwell.

STILWELL

Rank attained	General
Dates	1883–1946
Background	Career soldier; West Point Military Academy
Commands	Commander US Forces China, 1942; Chinese Fifth and Sixth Armies, 1942; Deputy South-East Asia Command, 1943; Tenth Army, 1945
Campaigns	Burma/China, 1942–44; Okinawa, 1945

The Normandy Breakout, July 25

The 'Cobra' offensive, launched on July 25 by US First Army, was a 'right hook' while on the Allied left the battle for Caen tied down the bulk of the German defending armor. On July 31 the Americans took Avranches, and the following day the exploitation of the breakout was taken over by the newly deployed US Third Army, under Patton. As his spearheads thrust toward Brest, Lorient and the Loire, a German counterattack at Mortain, just 20 miles from Avranches, attempted to sever the communications of the advancing Americans on August 7. After a week the attack had been repulsed, and Patton's tanks were nearing Chartres and Orléans. On August 21, Patton's troops approaching from the south linked up with the Canadians and Poles from south of Caen. To their west, in the 'Falaise pocket', some 50,000 men of German Seventh Army had been encircled and captured. German resistance in Normandy was broken, and the Allies advanced rapidly north-east toward Belgium and the Rhine.

South of France

Initially codenamed 'Anvil', subsequently 'Dragoon', this was a secondary landing by American and French forces, using ships and troops diverted from Italy. Landings were in the Fréjus–Cannes area on August 15, and German resistance was weak. Toulon and Marseilles were rapidly taken and US Seventh Army (Patch) and French First Army (de Lattre de Tassigny) drove up the Rhône, taking Lyons on September 3.

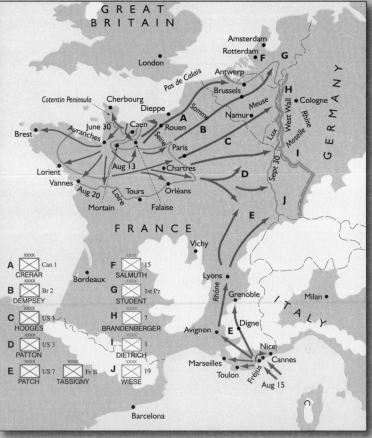

Right: US troops advance in the densely-hedged bocage country immediately inland from the beachheads.

Right: Allied tanks advance. In the foreground is an M10 Achilles tank destroyer; behind it a Churchill Crocodile flame-thrower.

Paris, Brussels, Antwerp

The Allied armies now sped north on a wide front, entering Paris on August 25 and Brussels on September 3, while the Germans fell back towards their West Wall ('Siegfried') defense line, built before the war. As Allied lines of supply lengthened, operations were inhibited by shortages of fuel, which had to be brought via the Mulberry harbors in Normandy and, from the beginning of September, Cherbourg. A strategic debate – broad versus narrow front – ensued, since the port of Antwerp, taken on September 4, could not become operational until the north side of the Scheldt River had been cleared.

in the center

June 27, 1944 Soviets take Vitebsk

July 4, 1944 Soviets take Minsk

July 13–22, 1944 Soviets attack north of Ternopol and trap German forces at Brody

July 10, 1944 Hitler moves HQ to Rastenburg, East Prussia

July 13, 1944 Soviets take Vilna

July 20, 1944 Soviets reach the Polish border at the Bug River

July 22, 1944 'Lublin Committee' set up for Communist administration of Poland, independent of the existing government in exile in London

July 23, 1944 Soviets take Lublin

July 26, 1944 Soviets take Narva

July 26, 1944 Soviets reach the Vistula River

NORTH-WEST EUROPE:
Allied Breakout from Normandy

July 30, 1944 British 'Bluecoat' offensive toward Vire

Aug 6–7, 1944 US reach Lorient and Brest, which they besiege

Aug 6/7–15, 1944 German counterattack 'Luttich' repulsed

Aug 7/8, 1944 Canadian 'Totalize' offensive toward Falaise

Aug 8, 1944 US take Alençon and thrust north toward Argentan and Falaise to trap the German Fifth Panzer and Seventh Armies

Aug 16, 1944 Canadians take Falaise. Germans continue eastward evacuation through the narrowing neck of the pocket

Aug, 19, 1944 Paris uprising

Aug 21, 1944 Falaise pocket closed. 50,000 Germans surrender

Aug 25, 1944 French and US troops enter Paris

Aug 26, 1944 De Gaulle enters, and takes control of, Paris

Aug 31, 1944 British take Amiens

Sept 3, 1944 British take Brussels

Sept 4, 1944 British take Antwerp

Sept 11, 1944 US patrols cross German

OPERATION 'MARKET GARDEN': THE ARNHEM BATTLE

While the advance continued toward the Rhine, Montgomery was given an opportunity to strike across the mouths of the Rhine River, outflank the West Wall and enter Germany via the Netherlands. Operation 'Market Garden' was an ambitious use of airborne troops on a scale not seen since Crete. Three airborne divisions would seize bridges across the canals at Eindhoven, the Maas, Waal and Rhine Rivers, while the tanks of British XXX Corps would advance and link up with each in turn. The operation was launched on September 17, British 1st Airborne taking the Arnhem bridge across the Rhine while the US 101st Airborne Division took the canal bridges and 82nd Airborne took the Maas crossing.

The advancing armor linked up successfully as far as the Waal at Nijmegen, but the unexpected presence of two SS Panzer divisions near Arnhem prevented the British and Polish paratroops holding the bridge there long enough for support to arrive. On 26th some 7,000 were captured, and the attempt to end the war before the end of 1944 had failed.

Left: Lines of C-47 transport planes are loaded with men and equipment at an airfield from which they took off for Holland September 17, 1944.

Below: British airborne troops moving into Arnhem shortly after landing. Heavy equipment, such as the jeep and 6pdr anti-tank gun shown here, were landed by gliders.

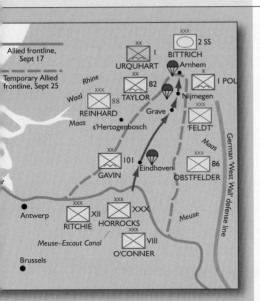

border
Sept 12–15, 1944 US First Army attacks German West Wall defense line

SOUTHERN FRANCE
Aug 15, 1944 Allied 'Dragoon' ('Anvil') landings in Provence
Aug 28, 1944 Allies take Marseilles and Toulon
Sept 3, 1944 French take Lyons

NORTH-WEST EUROPE: Arnhem
Sept 17–26, 1944 Battle of Arnhem ('Market Garden')
Sept 20, 1944 Allies take Nijmegen bridge
Sept 21, 1944 Germans retake Rhine bridge at Arnhem. Polish paras drop south of the river
Sept 26, 1944 British armor reaches the Poles south of the Rhine, but British 1st Airborne Div remains cut off in Arnhem and is forced to surrender

Western Theater General Events
Sept–Dec, 1944 US operations in the Roer River and Hüertgen Forest areas
Oct 1 to Nov 8, 1944 Canadians clear the Scheldt estuary
Oct 2, 1944 US attack West Wall north of Aachen
Oct 12–17, 1944 British attack west of Venlo
Oct 21, 1944 US take Aachen
Nov 1–8, 1944 British and Canadian amphibious attack secures Walcheren
Nov 9, 1944 Patton attacks in the Saar valley
Nov 14, 1944 French offensive into the Belfort Gap
Nov 16, 1944 US launch thrust for Cologne
Nov 22, 1944 French secure Mulhouse
Nov 23, 1944 US enter Strasbourg
Nov 26, 1944 Scheldt estuary open. This becomes the Allies' main port of supply
Dec 7, 1944 Allied commanders meet at Maastricht. Eisenhower confirms broad

Above: The town of Nijmegen, Holland, and the Nijmegen Bridge over the Waal (Rhine) River in the background. The town was heavily damaged during the fighting.

AIRBORNE FORCES

Airborne troops can be landed by parachute, by large troop-carrying gliders or by conventional transport aircraft.

The Soviets were the first to form airborne units in the 1930s, but they made little use of them during the war.

The German Luftwaffe formed their first airborne troops in 1938 and they were the first to use them operationally during the invasion of the West in 1940, most notably in the taking of the powerful fort of Eben Emael in Belgium.

The largest German air landing was against Crete in 1941. Even though successful, 4,000 men were lost out of 15,000 involved.

British and US airborne units made airborne assaults during the invasion of Sicily in 1943. During the successful D-Day invasion three airborne divisions were landed by parachute and glider, the US 82nd and 101st divisions, and the British 6th Division. Three months later, during operation 'Market Garden', Allied airborne troops were to take important bridges

Above: *A British Horsa glider, capable of transporting 25 troops, a light artillery piece or a Jeep.*

in Holland. The courageous attempts to capture the bridge at Arnhem ended in a failure for the British and Polish troops involved.

The Allied crossing of the Rhine in March 1945 was the largest air landing carried out on a single day – 22,000 troops.

Airborne forces were employed during the Pacific and Far Eastern campaigns but never to the extent that they were in Europe.

Airborne troops were always highly motivated and particularly well trained, but airborne operations always generated high casualty rates. This is due to the nature of airborne operations, the troops being relatively lightly equipped and generally employed upon highly risky undertakings. When fighting enemy units with tanks and heavy artillery, as at Arnhem, they find themselves at a huge disadvantage. After the battle for Crete, Hitler decided that large-scale airborne operations were too costly, and from then on German airborne troops were used as conventional infantry, albeit with considerable success.

Above: A German paratrooper, distinguishable by his special helmet and special parachute smock.

front strategy

BURMA: Fourteenth Army's offensive

Aug 3, 1944 Stilwell's Chinese take Myitkyina town, which causes the Japanese in north Burma to pull back, their lines of communication threatened. Then comes the monsoon, forcing operations to halt

Mid–August, 1944 Burma Road reconstruction completed

Late Aug, 1944 Japanese push Chinese back to the Salween River

Sept 16, 1944 Allied Combined Chiefs of Staff direct Mountbatten to clear Burma of the Japanese

Merrill's Marauders are subsequently disbanded and replaced by Mars Force

Sept 26, 1944 Japanese armies in Burma move to an essentially defensive posture. General Kimura intends to hold a line from Akyab via Mandalay to Lashio

Nov 1, 1944 General Sultan's forces advancing north from Myitkyina take Lungling

Nov, 19, 1944 Slim begins the Fourteenth Army general offensive on a 140-mile front, initially, crossing the Chindwin at Sittaung

Dec 3, 1944 Fourteenth Army crosses the Chindwin at Kalewa and Mawlaik, linking up with Sultan's right flank. Japanese resistance (Fifteenth Army) is initially slight

Dec 15, 1944 Chinese occupy Bhamo

Dec 18, 1944 Slim plans to feint toward Mandalay with XXXIII Corps while thrusting farther south to Meiktila with IV Corps to cut Kimura's lines of communication

ITALY: Diadem and Rome

May 11/12 to June 4, 1944 Operation 'Diadem', Allied offensive to breach Gustav Line and take Rome

May 15, 1944 Germans begin withdrawal to Dora (ex-Adolf Hitler) Line

May 18, 1944 Monte Cassino finally falls to the Poles

May, 19, 1944 Fifth Army takes Gaeta

May 22–3, 1944 Eighth Army penetrates

General Alexander, now in command of 15th Army group, redeployed his forces, moving the bulk of Eighth Army (now commanded by Leese) to the west of the Apennines. On May 11 he launched Operation 'Diadem', a coordinated series of assaults on the Gustav Line, on Monte Cassino, a breakout from Anzio and a thrust to Rome.

Polish II Corps took Monte Cassino on the 18th; the French Expeditionary Force made excellent progress; and XIII punctured the Gustav Line, while Fifth Army broke through on the coast. On the 23rd a reinforced VI Corps broke out of the Anzio perimeter, linking up with the advance from the south two days later. The Allies now confronted a further German defense line, the Caesar Line. A possible envelopment of German Tenth Army was controversially wrecked by Clark's decision to swing the axis of his attack west toward Rome instead of to Valmontone in the mountains. On 1–2 June, Clark attacked the west end of the Caesar Line with 11 divisions. The tired defenders were finally forced to retire, and Kesselring declared Rome an open city, which Clark's US forces entered on June 4.

The Italian theater now became secondary to events farther north, the Allies losing six divisions (including the invaluable French mountain troops) to the 'Anvil' landing in the south of France. Kesselring meanwhile retired to lines of defense based on the Arno River via intermediate positions including the Albert Line (Grosseto to south of Ancona).

In July and August the Allies advanced to the Arno, beyond which lay a new German prepared position, the Gothic Line. The eastern side came under attack on August 30, forcing a succession of seven river crossing battles that brought the Allies to Rimini on September 21 and to Ravenna on December 4. Winter weather then forced a pause in operations. The Allied attack was resumed in April 1945, the Germans being forced back into the open countryside of the Po valley – Hitler had forbidden retreat into the Alps. On April 21, Bologna fell to the Allies as their advance became a rapid series of drives spreading out north of the Appenines.

Historians still debate the rights and wrongs, priorities and decisions of the Italian campaign, which can be seen as a diversion of German forces from the Eastern Front, but also as an Allied diversion from the overriding priority of the Normandy invasion. Kesselring, Hitler's commander in Italy, fought a tenacious defensive campaign that, combined with spells of bad weather and mud, frustrated the Allies, used up resources that had not initially been intended for this theater, and dragged out the conflict in the peninsula to the very end of the war.

Left: American M4 Sherman tanks come ashore from a landing ship at Anzio. These vessels were specially designed with flat bottoms to allow them to come as close to shore as possible enabling men and vehicles to disembark directly on to a beach.

Right: Moving up through Prato, Italy, men of the 370th Infantry Regiment have yet to climb the mountain which lies ahead. April 9, 1945.

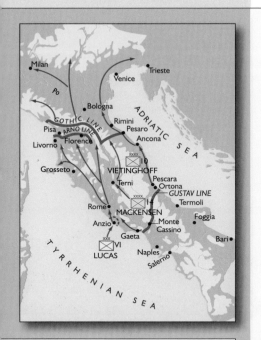

Dora Line
May 23, 1944 Allies finally break out of the Anzio beachhead
May 24, 1944 Germans begin withdrawal to Caesar Line, just south of Rome
June 3–4, 1944 Germans evacuate Rome and withdraw to Albert Line then Arno Line. Meanwhile major (and final) defenses are prepared farther north at the Gothic Line
June 4, 1944 Clark's Fifth Army enters Rome
July 5–15, 1944 Battles for the Arezzo Line
July 18, 1944 Allies take Ancona
July, 19, 1944 Allies take Livorno
July 20–30, 1944 Battles for the Trasimene Line
Aug 4, 1944 Allies reach Arno Line
Aug 4, 1944 Allies take Florence
Aug 30 to Sept 2, 1944 Battle for the Gothic Line
Aug 25 to Sept 21, 1944 Operation 'Olive': Allied Eighth Army pushes forward to the eastern Gothic Line on the Foglia River
Sept 2, 1944 Allies take Pisa
Sept 6, 1944 Allies take Lucca
Sept 4–9 and 12–21, 1944 Battles of Coriano
Sept 12 to Oct 27, 1944 Fifth Army attacks the Gothic Line in the west and penetrates toward Bologna suffering heavy losses
Sept 21, 1944 Fifth Army takes Fiorenzuola
Sept 21, 1944 Greek Bde of Eighth Army takes Rimini
Sept 22 to Dec 29, 1944 Battles of the Rivers: Uso, Fiumicino, Savio, Ronco and Lamonte
Oct 11, 1944 Eighth Army reaches the Rubicon
Dec 4, 1944 I Canadian Corps enters Ravenna
Dec 26–8, 1944 German counterattack in Serchio valley
Dec 29, 1944 Onset of winter leads to

The US seriously neglected tank development between the two world wars, but with the outbreak of conflict in Europe in 1939 there was an expansion of tank production which eventually became phenomenal: between July 1940 and the war's end production totalled over 88,000.

The bulk of the USA's production was taken up by the M4 Sherman, which served with all the main Allied forces, including the Soviets.

US tanks proved to be not only very reliable but (especially in the case of the Sherman) also adaptable, and could be upgraded in a desperate attempt to match the ever more powerful tanks of the German Army. However, the sheer quantity of US tanks proved to be the war winner.

Left: M4 Sherman.

Below: M3 Lee/Grant.

M3 'Lee/Grant' Medium Tank	
Weight	27 tons
Crew	Six
Armament	75mm gun, one 37mm gun and 3 or 4 .30in Browning machine-guns
Armor	Max: 50mm. Min: 13mm
Engine	Wright Continental, 340hp, speed 32mph
Dimensions	Length: 18ft 6in. Width: 8ft 11in. Height: 10ft 4in
Production	4,924

M4 Sherman Medium Tank	
Weight	30 tons
Crew	Five
Armament	75mm gun, one .50in and three .30in Browning machine-guns
Armor	Max: 51mm. Min: 19mm
Engine	Wright Continental, 400hp, speed 25mph
Dimensions	Length: 19ft 2in. Width: 8ft 9in. Height: 9ft 0in
Production	50,000

Below: M5 Stuart light tanks on reconnaisance.

M24 Chaffee

M24 Chaffee Light Tank

Weight	19 tonnes
Crew	Five
Armament	One 75mm gun, one .50in and two .30in Browning machine-guns
Armor	Max: 38mm. Min: 9.5mm
Engine	Cadillac Twin 44T24 110hp each, max. speed 35mph
Dimensions	Length: 18ft 0in. Width: 9ft 8in. Height: 8ft 1½in
Production	4,415

M26 Pershing Heavy Tank

Weight	41 tons
Crew	Five
Armament	One 90mm gun, one .50in and two .30in Browning machine-guns
Armor	Max: 102mm. Min: 7mm
Engine	Ford V-8, 500hp, max. speed 20mph
Dimensions	Length: 28ft 10in. Width: 11ft 6in. Height: 9ft 1in
Production	2,428

M26 Pershing

cessation of operations

FINLAND
Aug 25, 1944 The Finns ask Soviets for peace terms and an armistice is signed on Sept 19
Oct 7–15, 1944 Soviets take Petsamo, northern Finland
Nov 29, 1944 Soviets secure northern Finland

RUSSIAN FRONT
Aug 1, 1944 Polish uprising in Warsaw fails to get Soviet support. Despite aid parachuted from the West, the Germans suppress the rising by Oct 2
Aug 23, 1944 Antonescu deposed in Roumania by King Carol. German troops there lose heavily as they withdraw
Aug 20, 1944 Soviets invade Roumania, trapping 20 German divisions between the Dniester and Prut Rivers
Aug 30, 1944 Soviets secure Ploesti oilfields in Roumania
Aug 31, 1944 Soviets enter Bucharest
Sept 1, 1944 'Rat Week' air offensive by Allied Balkan Air Force to block German evacuation of Greece and southern Yugoslavia
Sept 8, 1944 Bulgaria changes sides and declares war on Germany
Sept 11, 1944 Soviets repulse German/ Hungarian counterattack in Roumania and take Targu Mures
Sept 14, 1944 Soviet offensive in Estonia and Latvia
Sept 22, 1944 Soviets take Tallinn
Sept 24, 1944 Soviets cross Transylvanian Alps to the Hungarian border
Sept 28, 1944 Soviets attack toward Belgrade in conjunction with Tito's partisans from the south-west
Oct 5–10, 1944 Soviets advance in Lithuania to the Baltic coast, trapping German forces in the Courland Peninsula
Oct 11, 1944 Soviet-Hungarian armistice
Oct 13, 1944 Soviets take Riga
Oct 15, 1944 Germans kidnap Hungarian

The origins of the SS (Schutzstaffeln, or Protection Squad), or 'Black Shirts', date back to 1923 when Hitler formed the Stabswache (Head-quarters Guard), his personal bodyguard. From small beginnings it expanded rapidly when Himmler was appointed as its head in 1929.

Himmler wanted to create a state security force that was made up of a racial élite, to be in the vanguard of National Socialism. Until 1934 it was in the shadow of the much larger, and rival, SA (Sturmabtielungen–Storm Troopers) under the leadership of Ernst Röhm. During the 'Night of the Long Knives', in June 1934, the SS assassinated all the members of the SA leadership, thus supplanting it as the dominant organisation within the Nazi party.

Himmler then incorporated the German police forces into the SS, thus assuming total control of the German domestic security force which in 1939 was nearly 250,000 strong.

The SS was a complex political, commercial and military organisation made up of three

Left: Heavily armed Waffen SS soldiers during the German counter-offensive in the Ardennes (Battle of the Bulge), December 1944.

Right: A German propaganda poster promoting the Waffen SS.

separate and distinct branches. The Allgemeine-SS (General SS) was the main branch, serving in a political and administrative role. The SS-Totenkopfverband (SS Death's Head Organisation) and, later, the Waffen-SS (Armed SS), were the other two branches that made up the structure of the SS.

The Gestapo (Geheime Staats-Polizei – Secret State Police) was formed by Hermann Göring in 1933. In 1939 it came under the control of Reinhard Heydrich, Himmler's subordinate in the SS. Even though it retained its individual identity, the Gestapo was, in effect, merged with the SS. The confinement of suspects without trial was normal, and the use of torture during interrogation was commonplace.

The Waffen-SS were independent combat units of the SS, not being part of the Army or the police. By 1939 their strength was 18,000. By June 1941 this had grown to 150,000 and by the end of 1944 it had reached 600,000. The Waffen-SS operated under the tactical control of the German Army but enjoyed preferential treatment with regard to military equipment. Well known for its toughness in battle, the SS had a tendency not to take prisoners. Their members were looked upon as an élite force.

dictator Horthy

Oct 20, 1944 Soviets take Debrecen, Hungary

Oct 29 to Dec 5, 1944 Soviets attack and encircle Budapest

Nov 6, 1944 Tito's Yugoslavs enter Monastir

Nov 13, 1944 Germans evacuate Skopje

Nov 21, 1944 Albanian partisans take Tirana and Durazzo

Nov 23, 1944 Soviets take Cop, strategic rail junction in Hungary

Nov 24, 1944 Soviets clear Saaremo Island in the Gulf of Riga

Nov 28, 1944 Soviets near confluence of the Danube and Drava

Nov 29, 1944 Germans evacuate Scutari

Dec 4, 1944 Soviets advance on a wide front in Hungary to Lake Balaton

Dec 7, 1944 Badescu forms new government in Roumania

Dec 9, 1944 Soviets reach Danube north of Vac

Dec 9, 1944 Serbia and Macedonia cleared of German troops

Dec 15, 1944 Soviets enter Czechoslovakia at Sahy

Dec 29, 1944 Hungarian provisional government declares war on Germany
The battle for Budapest continues

Far Eastern Theater General Events
Oct, 1944 Stilwell replaced by Wedemeyer. His field command is taken by General Sultan

Oct 12, 1944 First of many B-29 heavy bombers lands on Saipan preparatory to the strategic bombing of Japan. B-29s are all redeployed from China to the Marianas. Those in India follow

Oct 12–16, 1944 US Third Fleet carriers strike Formosa and Luzon. Some 500 Japanese defending aircraft are lost against 89 US machines

Oct, 19, 1944 Japanese Admiral suggests the establishment of a suicide force of fliers to attack US carriers. These are the

KAMIKAZE

In 1281 Japan was threatened with a Mongol invasion. When it seemed that the invading Mongol fleet was about to overwhelm the Japanese, a huge typhoon arose, destroying the Mongols. This typhoon that saved Japan became known as the Kamikaze or 'Divine Wind'. Late in World War II it was apparent that Japan was losing the war. With a last-ditch effort to turn the tide on their flagging fortunes, the Japanese resorted to suicide tactics and titled these Kamikaze.

Organised into 'Special Attack' groups, Kamikaze pilots used their aircraft, mostly fighters loaded with bombs, to crash into enemy ships, killing themselves and hopefully sinking the ship. *Bushido* enabled these pilots

Right: Kamikaze pilots.

Below: The carrier USS Bunker Hill *after being hit by a Kamikaze.*

to come to terms with this form of attack and embrace their death.

Japan also developed a number of specialised suicide weapons such as the Baka. This rocket-powered, piloted missile was carried to within 50 miles of the target by a medium bomber. After being dropped it would glide towards the target, then, activating its rockets' engines, increase its speed and dive into the target, exploding its one-ton warhead. The Baka, once in flight, was difficult to stop, but its mother

plane was extremely vulnerable to marauding US fighters and many were caught before they reached their targets.

There were also explosive motor torpedo boats, human torpedoes and midget submarines but these never proved as successful as aircraft in attacking ships. Kamikaze tactics were also employed against US B-29 bombers.

The first Kamikaze attacks occurred in June 1944, and they reached their zenith in April 1945 during the Allies' invasion of Okinawa, sinking 36 ships and landing vessels and damaging 368.

These tactics would have been very much part of the Japanese defence of their home islands in the event of an invasion.

Above: USS Bunker Hill *was hit on May 11, 1945. Out of a crew of 2,600, 372 personnel were killed.*

Below: Yokosuka D4Y3 Suisei *diving at the carrier* USS Essex, *November 25, 1944.*

Kamikaze

Oct 21, 1944 First official Kamikaze attack hits HMAS *Australia*

Oct 25, 1944 First large scale deployment of Kamikaze aganst the US escort carriers at Leyte Gulf

Nov 7, 1944 US forces secure Peleliu

Nov 24, 1944 US bombers make first raid on Japan from Saipan. 80 unescorted B-29s hit the Nakajima factory in Tokyo

Dec 8, 1944 US aircraft from the Marianas bomb Iwo Jima

Dec, 1944 and Jan, 1945 US high-level precision bombing causes damage to Japanese industry but is hampered by bad weather and wind, and the new B-29s experience mechanical teething troubles

Dec, 1944 US renew offensive on Bougainville but seriously underestimate Japanese numbers and make slow progress. Fighting on the island continues until the end of the war

PHILIPPINES

The Philippines are defended by General Yamashita's Fourteenth Area Army

Oct 14, 1944 US Philippine invasion force sails from Hollandia on New Guinea and Manus in the Admiralty Islands to land in Leyte Gulf

Oct 17, 1944 US Rangers take Suluan Island at the mouth of Leyte Gulf. This alerts Japanese defenses

Oct 20, 1944 US main landings in Leyte Gulf by General Kreuger's Sixth Army after 4hr barrage. A fleet of more than 700 ships lands 160,000 men. This day MacArthur also makes his personal return to the Philippines

Oct 23 to early Dec, 1944 Japanese convoy 45,000 men plus supplies to Ormoc on Leyte, suffering heavy casualties en route

BATTLE OF LEYTE GULF – the largest naval engagement of all time

Oct 23, 1944 US submarines spot Kurita's fleet off Palawan and sink 2 cruisers,

On the day the Americans landed in Leyte Gulf, the Japanese fleet began what would be it's last big offensive operation. From Japan's Inland Sea the fleet's last four operational carriers, with escorts, sailed south. From the fleet anchorage in Brunei Bay, a far more powerful force of surface ships – including *Yamato* and *Musashi*, the largest battleships in the world – sailed north-east. The plan was for the carrier force (Ozawa) to lure the carriers of Halsey's Third Fleet north, away from the American invasion fleet, which would then be destroyed by the heavily-gunned ships of the southern force (Kurita). Carrier and land-based aircraft would strike Halsey as he moved north, and the new Kamikaze suicide aircraft would take out the escort carriers of Kinkaid's Seventh Fleet at Leyte.

On October 23, US submarines spotted Kurita's fleet off Palawan and sank 2 cruisers, crippling a third. The Americans had been in the dark about this operation because of a Japanese code-change, and Kurita had kept strict radio silence – but not so Ozawa, whose aim was to attract Halsey's attention.

On the 24th, Japanese aircraft sank the carrier *Princeton* off Luzon while, before going north to hit Ozawa's carriers, Halsey launched four strikes on Kurita in the Sibuyan Sea, damaging a cruiser and sinking *Musashi*. Kurita turned back; Halsey took this to be a retreat; and late in the day he turned north against Ozawa – without telling Kinkaid. The Japanese decoy operation was working.

During the night, Kurita reversed course and took his battleships and cruisers through San Bernardino Strait, to the north of Samar and Leyte. Kinkaid's Seventh Fleet was now being threatened by a pincer attack, for Kurita had earlier detached a force under Shima and Nashimura to transit Surigao Strait to the south of Leyte.

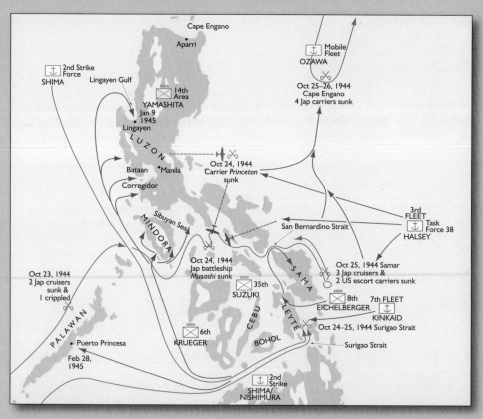

Here, on the 25th, took place the last great surface action of the war. Admiral Oldendorf deployed 6 battleships, with cruisers, destroyers and torpedo-firing PT boats across Surigao Strait, and practically annihilated Nashimura's force, both battleships *Fuso* and *Yamashiro* going down. *Shima*, following, turned about.

To the north, however, Kurita's heavy ships – including 4 battleships and 5 heavy cruisers – emerged to surprise Sprague's 6 escort carriers and 7 destroyers and destroyer-escorts. Three of the latter were sunk together with a carrier; damage was inflicted on almost all the other ships. As the seriousness of the situation became clear, Spruance called Halsey to return. But then, seemingly inexplicably, Kurita turned away, possibly suspecting a trap, possibly through lack of fuel. Kamikaze suicide aircraft now struck at Sprague's ships, sinking another escort carrier. Many US aircraft, unable to return to their ships because of damage caused by Kurita and the kamikazes, were saved by landing on the partially complete airfield ashore on Leyte.

North of Luzon, Halsey was meanwhile destroying Ozawa's carriers off Cape Engaño. He then returned south, reaching Leyte 23 hours later – far too late to trap the retreating Kurita. Nevertheless, the final great intervention by the Japanese fleet had been repulsed and the last of its carriers sunk.

Above: MacArthur returning to the Philippines.

crippling another

Oct 24/5, 1944 Nishimura and Shima's squadrons pass through the Sulu Sea toward Surigao Strait to strike the US invasion fleet from the south

Oct 24, 1944 *Battle of the Sibuyan Sea* – Admiral Halsey's Third Fleet strikes Kurita, sinking giant battleship *Musashi* and crippling a heavy cruiser.

Japanese bombers cripple US light carrier *Princeton*. She sinks after her magazines explode, also causing over 400 casualties aboard cruiser *Birmingham* alongside

Oct 24/5, 1944 Late in the day, Halsey turns north to find Ozawa's carrier force, and during the night Kurita reverses course to pass through San Bernardino Strait and hit the US Leyte invasion fleet from the north

Oct 25, 1944 *Battle of Surigao Strait:* Admiral Kinkaid (US Seventh Fleet) deploys Oldendorf's battleships, cruisers, destroyers and PT boats across the strait. As the Japanese approach they open fire, sinking 5 of the 7 ships including battleships *Fuso* and *Yamashiro*

Oct 25, 1944 *Battle off Samar:* Kurita's force surprises the escort carriers of Admiral Sprague, who flees, calling back Halsey. One carrier is sunk, others are badly damaged, but Kurita does not press his advantage and turns back. Kamikaze attacks further damage Sprague's carriers

Oct 25, 1944 *Battle of Cape Engaño:* Halsey locates Ozawa's fleet and sinks the carriers before turning south too late to trap Kurita

Oct 26, 1944 US carrier aircraft and B-24s pound the retiring Japanese squadrons

PHILIPPINES

By Nov 2, 1944 US forces have taken most of Leyte Island

Dec 7, 1944 US forces land at Ormoc, on the western coast of Leyte Island

Dec 10, 1944 Ormoc taken by US forces, but destroyed in the process

DWIGHT D. EISENHOWER

At the age of 28 this popular, outgoing Texan was given the task of forming the US Army's first tank corps during World War I. From the Operations Branch in Washington he was sent to Great Britain in 1942 to lead the American staff there. He was a good choice in achieving the harmony needed within the Allied Forces' HQ. He commanded the invasion of French North Africa in November 1942. He was promoted to four-star general in February 1943. In December 1943 he was appointed as Supreme Commander in the Mediterranean theatre of operations. Then, in January 1944, he was appointed as the Supreme Commander of the Allied Expeditionary Forces for the invasion of Europe. He was not a fighting general in the mould of Patton or Bradley but, as President Roosevelt believed, the best politician among any of the military commanders – which was exactly what the job called for. He did, however, insist on the 'broad front' strategy instead of the 'narrow front' as urged by Montgomery and Patton. The narrow front strategy might have ended

EISENHOWER	
Rank attained	General of the Army
Dates	1890–1969
Background	Career soldier; West Point Military Academy
Commands	Operations Division, 1942; US Commanding General, European Theater of Operations, 1942; Supreme Allied Command, Europe. 1943–45
Campaigns	North Africa, 1942–43; Sicily 1943; Italy 1943; North-West Europe, 1943–45

the war earlier with powerful, deep thrusts into German territory, making for Berlin, while the broader front was the slower but less risky option. He ended the war being looked upon as a hero, as much by the British as by the Americans. After the war he went on to be twice elected US President.

Below: Eisenhower (second from right), brought considerable charm and diplomacy to his role in coordinating the efforts of the disparate forces from Allied nations under his command.

Above: General Eisenhower gives a pep-talk to US paratroopers in England prior to making one of the first assaults during the invasion of Europe, June 6, 1944.

Above: General Dwight D. Eisenhower, Supreme Allied Commander, at his headquarters in the European theater of operations, February 1, 1945. He wears the five-star cluster of the newly-created rank of General of the Army.

Dec 15, 1944 US forces land unopposed on the south coast of Mindoro
Dec 25, 1944 US forces secure Leyte Island

Western Theater General Events
Aug 12, 1944 Churchill and Tito confer in Naples
Aug 21, 1944 Churchill and Papandreu, leader of the Greek Social Democratic party confer in Rome
Sept 8, 1944 German V-2 rocket offensive against London begins
Sept 8, 1944 Germans begin evacuating Aegean and then Greece
Sept 12–14, 1944 Allied 'Octagon' Conference, Quebec
Sept 15, 1944 British severely damage *Tirpitz*
Sept 17 to Oct 3, 1944 Lull in German V-2 attacks on London as Allies capture forward launch sites
Sept 21, 1944 Tito visits Stalin
Sept–Oct, 1944 Allied operations to clear Aegean of German forces
Sept 23/4, 1944 Dortmund-Ems canal breached
Oct, 1944 Belgian cities attacked by V-1s
Oct 9–19, 1944 Churchill and Stalin confer in Moscow ('Tolstoy' conference)
Nov 7, 1944 Roosevelt re-elected President of the USA for unique 4th term
Nov 8, 1944 Germans begin moving nearly 40,000 Jews from Budapest to concentration camps in Germany
Nov 12, 1944 Third British air attack on *Tirpitz* succeeds, eliminating the German threat to Arctic convoys
Dec 25, 1944 Churchill visits Greece

GREECE: Liberation and Civil War
Oct 4, 1944 British force (Scobie) lands at Patra in Greece
Oct 8, 1944 Germans evacuate Corinth
Oct 12, 1944 Germans evacuate Athens
Oct 18, 1944 British liberate Athens
Oct 31, 1944 Germans evacuate Salonika

Closing on the Rhine

The next two and a half months were spent in forcing forward to the Rhine and in clearing the Scheldt waterway to open the port of Antwerp for Allied resupply. This task was entrusted to the Canadian First Army, aided by commandos. On November 8 the island of Walcheren was secured, and by the end of the month ships were entering Antwerp. On November 16 US First and Ninth Armies thrust east of Aachen (Operation 'Queen') towards the Roer River, but progress was slow. Farther south, US and French armies advanced in a broad line from the Swiss border to Luxembourg, taking Strasbourg on November 23.

Battle of the Bulge: the Ardennes

On December 16 Hitler launched the last major German offensive in the west. Concentrating some 30 divisions in the Ardennes area, the Germans took the Allies completely by surprise, hitting a weak sector of the line and thrusting rapidly across the Our River toward the Meuse. The plan was then to sweep north-east, take Antwerp and trap the British, Canadians and two US Armies. But the German forces were insufficient for the task, while narrow roads and snow slowed the progress of their armored columns. A celebrated siege at Bastogne, reinforced by the US 101st Airborne on 19th, was raised on

Right: GIs examine a giant King Tiger tank, heaviest of the war, knocked out during the Ardennes campaign.

Below: The Ardennes area abounded in tree-lined roads that were easy to defend.

Boxing Day. By now, the offensive had ground to a halt just short of Dinant. Patton, Simpson and Hodges wheeled their armies to hit the sides of the 'bulge' in the front, and by the end of January the lines were restored to their early December positions.

Nov 5, 1944 British land at Salonika
Dec 3, 1944 Civil War breaks out in Athens: vicious street fighting ensues
Jan 11, 1945 Ceasefire in Greece as British secure Athens
Feb 12, 1945 Peace of Varkiza proves temporary, civil war returning in 1946–9

NORTH-WEST EUROPE: German Ardennes Offensive (Battle of the Bulge)
Dec 16 to Jan 28, 1944 German Ardennes offensive (Battle of the Bulge)
Dec 16, 1944 German forces launch surprise attack aiming at Antwerp
Dec 18, 1944 Germans cross Amblève River
Dec 18/19, 1944 Germans reach Bastogne and US 101st Airborne reinforces the defense
Dec 22, 1944 Germans encircle Bastogne
Dec 26, 1944 Bastogne relieved
Dec 31, 1944/Jan 1, 1945 Germans launch 'Nordwind' offensive into Alsace
Jan 1, 1945 Germans launch 'Bodenplatte' air offensive on Western Allied airfields, destroying 300 aircraft on the ground
Jan 16–26, 1945 Allies take Roermond triangle
Jan 16, 1945 Allies 'pinch out' the 'Bulge'
Jan 23, 1945 Allies take St-Vith

Far Eastern Theater General Events
By the beginning of 1945 US forces have built up so that MacArthur has almost a million and a half men; Nimitz has 6,000 ships; and there are 37,000 aircraft
Jan 20 Curtis LeMay takes command of the US strategic bomber force and agrees with Arnold that incendiary bombing is the way forward
March 9/10, 1945 First big US incendiary raid on Tokyo. 300 B-29s deliver 2,000 tons of incendiaries creating a firestorm that destroys a quarter of the city and kills 85,000
March 11/12, 1945 Nagoya air raid
March 13/14, 1945 Osaka air raid

CHINESE ARMED FORCES

The Nationalist and Communist Chinese forces, sworn enemies, nevertheless agreed a rapprochement in order to face the common foe, the Japanese.

The Nationalist Chinese forces, led by Chiang Kai-shek, had about 1,500,000 men in 1937 when the Japanese invaded China. During the first year they lost nearly 1 million men to the Japanese. The remainder of them traded space for time as the Japanese advanced into central and southern China. These advances slowed and came to a stop as a war of attrition developed. As the Japanese slowly began to cut off access to the rest of the world, Nationalists eventually became reliant on only one supply route, the Burma Road, to bring in military aid. Their army was short of such items as tanks and medium and heavy artillery and their air force had been all but destroyed by mid-1938. By 1940 the American General Chennault established his 'Flying Tigers' to aid the Nationalists. These US

Right: *Chinese Communist troops with captured Japanese tanks.*

Below: *A P-40 Hawk of the 'Flying Tigers'.*

volunteer pilots and P-40 aircraft never numbered more than 200. By the war's end the Nationalists had some 300 divisions each with a strength of some 10,000.

The Communists of Mao Zedong were the Japanese forces' main opponents in the north of China. Within a few months of the start of hostilities the Communists had three divisions established behind enemy lines. Initial losses were heavy. especially during the 'Hundred Regiments' Campaign' of 1940. In 1937 they had 90,000 troops but by 1945 they had some 900,000, with local militia units as well as regular units.

Altogether Chinese military casualties numbered over 1,300,000 killed and 1,750,000 wounded during the eight years of combat.

Above: Chinese Communist leader Mao Zedong.

Above: Chinese nationalist leader Chiang Kai-shek with his wife.

March 18, 1945 US Fifth Fleet (Spruance) attacks Kyushu. Carriers *Franklin* and *Wasp* are hit by Kamikaze

March 18/19, 1945 Nagoya and Kobe bombed

April 7, 1945 P-51 Mustang fighters begin escorting B-29 bombers on missions to Japan

May 14 for a month, 1945 US bombers strike Japan's six most imortant cities – Tokyo, Nagoya, Kobe, Osaka, Yokohama, Kawasaki. 500-bomber raids devastate the cities and kill over 100,000 civilians

April 3, 1945 The invasion of Japan: US Joint Chiefs of Staff direct Nimitz and MacArthur to begin planning

April 5, 1945 Russia tells Japan that it will no longer adhere to their 1941 non-aggression pact

April 5, 1945 Admiral Suzuki becomes prime minister of Japan

April 6, 1945 Battleship *Yamato* sails from Japan's Inland Sea on a suicide mission to intervene in the Okinawa landing

April 6–7, 1945 Kamikaze attacks on US Okinawa invasion fleet hit 28 ships and sink 3. In the period to June 22, some 1,900 Kamikaze sorties are flown

April 7, 1945 *Yamato* sunk off Kyushu, together with its escorts

May 1, 1945 Australian and Dutch forces land at Tarakan in Borneo

May 10, 1945 Allies take Wewak on New Guinea

May 25, 1945 Directive for the invasion of Japan: 'Olympic', invasion of Kyushu on Nov 1; 'Coronet', invasion of Honshu on March 1 1946

BURMA

Jan 14–16, 1945 British XXXIII Corps crosses the Irrawaddy north of Mandalay, then repulse Japanese counterattacks on the bridgeheads

Jan 21, 1945 British Commandos land on Ramree Island, south of Akyab, having taken Myebon. They then secure Cheduba

US NAVY SUBMARINES

US Navy submarines played a decisive role in driving Japanese warships and merchant vessels from the Pacific Ocean. The US Navy conducted the most successful campaign of unrestricted submarine warfare against Japan, much superior to that which the Germans fought in the Atlantic against the Allies. During the fighting the Japanese merchant marine lost over 2,300 vessels, eight and a half million tons of shipping, US submarines accounting for five million tons of this – 1,300 ships. US submarines also sank over 600,000 tons of warships, nearly 30% of the total, including eight aircraft carriers, one battleship and eleven cruisers.

Of the total of 288 US submarines deployed throughout the war, 52 were lost, 48 of them in the Pacific. American submariners comprised some 1.6% of Navy personnel but suffered the highest loss rate in all the US Armed Forces, with 22% killed.

There were several early submarine classes, of mixed quality, serving with the US Navy during the war. The oldest was the S class, a World War I design. There were also large fleet types, culminating in the 228 boats of the *Gato*, *Balao* and *Tench* Classes, which were the classic boats of the US Navy's wartime mass-production programs. These three classes were virtually identical, and were, arguably, the finest submarines of the war.

Right: *At the periscope.*

Below: *USS* Hackleback, *a* Balao *class submarine. On her first patrol, in March 1945, she sighted the Japanese giant battleship* Yamato *but was unable to attack because of the strength of the escorting force.* Yamato *was sunk the following day, from the air.*

Gato/Balao/Tench Classes	
Displacement	2,400 tons
Crew	80/81
Armament	6 x 21in torpedo tubes forward, 4 aft. 1–2 x 4in/5in guns and various AA guns
Engine/motor	5,400hp surfaced, 2,740hp submerged, max. speed surfaced 20 knots, submerged 8.75 knots
Dimensions	Length: 311ft 9in Beam 27ft 3in

Above: A dramatic photograph of a torpedoed Japanese destroyer sinking, photographed through the periscope of a US submarine.

Above: Looking forward along the deck from the stern of a US submarine.

Jan 22, 1945 British take Monywa, on the Chindwin River west of Mandalay

Jan 27, 1945 Sultan and the Chinese from Yunnan meet at Mongyu, linking the Ledo to the Burma Road and reopening India-China communications

Jan 28, 1945 British reach Yeu, north of Schwebo

Feb 12, 1945 Indian troops cross the Irrawaddy at Myinmu

Feb 14, 1945 Indian troops cross the Irrawaddy south-west of Mandalay at Nyaungu, some 60 miles from Meiktila

Feb 22, 1945 Indians advance from Nyaungu toward Meiktila

Feb 27, 1945 Indians reach outskirts of Meiktila

March 3, 1945 Indians take Meiktila, but the Japanese counterattack

March 4, 1945 Japanese take Taungtha, cutting the lines of communication to Meiktila, which has to be supplied by air for three weeks and is under heavy attack by the Japanese

March 7, 1945 Chinese take Lashio

March 20, 1945 Mandalay secured by British XXXIII Corps

March 28, 1945 Japanese abandon attempts to retake Meiktila

March 30, 1945 Allies advance directly south from Meiktila, racing to reach Rangoon before the monsoon rains set in. The advance gains momentum

April 6, 1945 General Honda's 33rd Army almost encircled south of Pyawbwe and practically destroyed

April 21–5, 1945 British take the Yenangyaung oilfields

April 23, 1945 Japanese evacuate Rangoon

May 1, 1945 Gurkha parachute troops land at Elephant Point, just south of Rangoon

May 2, 1945 'Dracula' landings on the coast south of Rangoon by British XV Corps from Akyab and Ramree

May 2, 1945 British take Prome, isolating Japanese defenders in the Arakan area

V-1 Flying Bomb	
Guidance	Preset compass and auto pilot
Weight	4,800lb
Warhead	1,875lb
Range	125–250 miles
Engine	Argus pulse-jet engine, max speed 350mph
Dimensions	Length: 27ft 3in Wing Span: 17ft 4in
Production	Over 30,000

V-2 Rocket	
Guidance	Preset, gyroscopic
Weight	28,650lb
Warhead	2,150lb
Range	200 miles
Engine	Liquid-fuelled rocket motor, max speed 3,500mph
Dimensions	Length: 46ft 1in Fin span: 11ft 8in
Production	10,000

The V-1 and V-2 were Hitler's so called 'vengeance' weapons, which were supposed to turn the tide of war in Germany's favor during the last year of the fighting. Although inaccurate, they did cause a great many civilian casualties and a lot of damage, but they failed in their purpose.

The V-1 was nicknamed the 'Doodlebug' by the British and the 'Buzz Bomb' by the US. The first fell on London on June 13, 1944, and by the end of the war they had caused over 6,000 British deaths and nearly 18,000 injured. Of the 10,000 or more launched against London, however, only 3,500 got through, the

Above: A German V-1 flying bomb. These, effectively unguided, pilotless aircraft containing high-explosive, can be seen as forerunners of modern cruise missiles, which are directed to their targets by sophisticated global-positioning systems. By contrast, the V-2 rockets were ballistic missiles; their technology, transmitted by German scientists after the war, led, when armed with nuclear warheads, to the 'mutual-destruction' weapons of the Cold War.

rest falling short or being shot down.

From October 1944 Belgian cities came under heavy attack from V-1s, the main targets being Antwerp and Liège. Over 6,500 were fired at Antwerp, 4,000 of which landed, and over 3,000 against Liège.

The majority of V-1s were launched from inclined ramps in France, and Holland, but some were air-launched from Heinkel 111 bombers.

More than 1,100 V-2 rockets were launched from the Netherlands against London: half of these fell short, the other half killing nearly 2,750 people and injuring 6,500 more. Antwerp received 1,350 V-2 rocket attacks, Liège 98 and Brussels 65. These combined V-1 and V-2 attacks killed nearly 3,500 Belgian civilians and almost 700 Allied servicemen.

In 1939 scientists in America had become convinced that Germany was developing a nuclear weapon. When the US entered the war she co-operated with Britain and the two countries began to develop their own weapon, codenamed the 'Manhattan Project'. An international team of very prominent physicists, many being émigrés from Fascist Europe, was set up under the direction of J. Robert Oppenheimer and based at Los Alamos in New Mexico.

In the meantime, a plant in occupied Norway that was producing heavy water for the Germans was destroyed by British Special Forces and Norwegian resistance fighters in November 1942. This heavy water was necessary in the production process of a nuclear weapon. The raid set the German nuclear program back by an estimated two years. In 1944 Germany's chances of producing a bomb were finally ended by Norwegian agents, who sank the ferry containing all the remaining heavy water stocks.

Three bombs were completed at Los Alamos, the first being successfully tested on July 16, 1945. The second, called 'Little Boy', was dropped on Hiroshima on August 6, 1945 after the Japanese rejected a call for surrender. It exploded with the force of nearly 13,000 tons of TNT. Over 80,000 people were killed and 4.2 square miles of the city flattened. Still Japan refused to surrender, so the third bomb, 'Fat Man', was dropped on Nagasaki three days later, killing over 35,000. Not until August 15 did the Japanese surrender.

May 3, 1945 Rangoon secured

RUSSIAN FRONT: Germany and Berlin

Jan 1 and 7, 1945 German attempts to relieve Budapest repulsed

Jan 12, 1945 Soviet offensive in southern Poland by Konev's Front

Jan 17, 1945 Germans launch another attempt to relieve Budapest

Jan 14, 1945 Soviet offensive to encircle Warsaw by Zhukov's Front and farther north by Rokossovsky's Front

Jan 17, 1945 Warsaw liberated by Polish First Army

Jan, 19, 1945 Soviets take Cracow and Lodz

Jan 20, 1945 Konev's troops enter Germany at Namslau

Jan 31, 1945 Zhukov's Front reaches the Oder River

End Jan, 1945 There are now over 50 German divisions cut off in Courland and in East Prussia

Feb 8, 1945 Konev's Front attacks toward the Neisse River, encircling Breslau and Glogau

Feb 10, 1945 Soviets attack in East Prussia and Pomerania but gain little ground

Feb 13, 1945 Soviets take Budapest

Feb 15–17, 1945 German counterattack from Pomerania

Feb 23, 1945 Soviets take Posen

Feb 24, 1945 Rokossovsky's Front strikes north into Pomerania

March 1, 1945 Zhukov's Front also strikes north into Pomerania

March 3, 1945 German attempt to relieve Glogau fails

March 5/6, 1945 German 'Spring Awakening' offensive opens in southern Hungary but soon loses momentum

March 15, 1945 Konev's Front attacks toward Neustadt

March 17, 1945 Soviets take Kolberg on the Baltic coast

March 25, 1945 Soviets reach Gulf of Danzig

End March, 1945 German forces in Samland, north of Koenigsberg, eliminated

End March, 1945 Zhukov's Front reaches

US AIRCRAFT

In late 1939 the USAAF had 2,500 aircraft of all types, many obsolescent. By mid-1944 it had nearly 80,000, of which most were the equal of, or better than, those of its opponents.

When the US entered the war it had few state-of-the-art fighters. Many were the tubby Brewster Buffalo or the disappointing Curtiss Hawk family of fighters. Better were the Wildcat and the twin-engined Lightning, which were able to hold their own against the enemy. It was with the arrival of fighters such as the P-47 Thunderbolt, the P-51 Mustang and the US Navy F6F Hellcat that the Allies would gain the air superiority needed to bring the Axis airpower to its knees. The combination of high speed, agility, long range and fire power made the Mustang arguably the best fighter of World War II. The Hellcat was credited with 6,000 enemy aircraft shot down, 75% of the total number of US Navy air-to-air victories.

North American P-51D Mustang	
Weight	12,100lb (fully loaded)
Crew	One
Armament	Six 0.5in machine-guns
Range	1,650 miles
Engine	Packard Merlin, 1,400hp, max speed 437mph
Dimensions	Length: 32ft 3in Wing Span: 37ft 0in Height: 13ft 8in
Production	15,469 (all marks)

Grumman F6F Hellcat	
Weight	15,400lb (fully loaded)
Crew	One
Armament	Six 0.5in machine-guns
Range	950 miles
Engine	Pratt and Whitney, 2,000hp, max speed 380mph
Dimensions	Length: 33ft 7in Wing Span: 42ft 10in Height: 13ft 1in
Production	12,275

Left: F6F Hellcat.

Below: P-51D Mustang.

Bottom: B-17G Flying Fortress.

In the medium bomber role, aircraft such as the ubiquitous B-25 Mitchell and the capable B-26 Marauder would effectively carry out tactical bombing. The heavy bombers, the B-17 Flying Fortress, B-24 Liberator and the B-29 Superfortress were for the longer-range strategic bombing attacks, playing their part in the devastation of German cities and industry and the razing to the ground of numerous Japanese cities.

Lockheed P-38L Lightning

Weight	21,600lb (fully loaded)
Crew	One
Armament	One 20mm cannon, four 0.5in machine-guns
Range	450 miles
Engines	Two Allison 1,475hp V-1710-111, max speed 414mph
Dimensions	Length: 37ft 10in Wing Span: 52ft 0in Height: 9ft 10in
Production	10,037 (all marks)

Boeing B-17 Flying Fortress

Weight	55,000lb (fully loaded)
Crew	Ten
Armament	13 0.5in machine-guns, bomb-load 5,000lb
Range	3,400 miles
Engines	4 General Electric, 1,200hp, max speed 300mph
Dimensions	Length: 74ft 9in Wing Span: 103ft 9in Height: 19ft 1in
Production	12,731 (all marks)

North American B-25 Mitchell

Weight	33,500lb (fully loaded)
Crew	Six
Armament	5+ 0.5in machine-guns, bomb-load 6,000lb
Range	1,350 miles
Engines	2 Wright R-2600, 1,700hp, max speed 275mph
Dimensions	Length: 52ft 11in Wing Span: 67ft 6in Height: 17ft 7in
Production	9,889 (all marks)

Below: P-38 Lightning.

Bottom: B-25 Mitchell.

When the Germans invaded the USSR in June 1941 the majority of the firstline aircraft of the Soviet Air Force were, by German standards, obsolete. The principal fighter was the Polikarpov I-16, which was, however, woefully inferior to the Bf 109. Soviet bombers, with their meagre bomb capacity, were equally ineffective.

Gradually, better types, such as the LaGG-3 and the Yak-1 fighters, began to replace the huge numbers that had been lost in the early part of the German invasion. The Yak-1/3/7/9 family of fighters did more than any other group of aircraft in bringing about the defeat of the Luftwaffe, along with the superb Lavochkin La-5 and La-7.

The highly effective Il-2 Shturmovik ground-attack plane began to enter service in the winter of 1941–42. This heavily armored aircraft proved particularly difficult to shoot down. Then came the formidable and very versatile Petlyakov Pe-2 bomber, which was the Soviet counterpart to the British Mosquito but built in much greater numbers. The only effective heavy four-engined bomber produced by the Soviets was the Petlyakov Pe-8, but only

81 were built as Soviet efforts were concentrated on tactical air operations.

Slowly the Soviet Air Force's capability began to match that of the Luftwaffe and was then able to defeat it.

Il-2 Shturmovik

Ilyushin Il-2 Shturmovik	
Weight	14,000lb
Crew	Two
Armament	Two 23mm cannon, two 7.62mm machine-guns and one 12.7mm machine-gun, plus 1,321lb bomb-load
Range	475 miles
Engine	Mikulin, 1,770hp, max. speed 251mph
Dimensions	Length: 38ft 0in. Wing span: 47ft 11in. Height: 11ft 2in
Production	36,150

Left: The Yak-9 entered service in October 1942. Yak-9s first saw combat in late 1942 during the Battle of Stalingrad. (Kogo, via Wikimedia Commons)

Below: The Petlyakov Pe-2 bomber.

Polikarpov I-16

Weight	4,149lb
Crew	One
Armament	Four 7.62mm machine-guns or two 7.62mm machine-gunsand two 20mm cannon
Range	560 miles
Engine	Shvetsov M-63 air-cooled radial engine, 1,000 hp, max. speed 304mph
Dimensions	Length: 27ft 10in. Wing span: 30ft 2in. Height: 7ft 11in
Production	8,650

Polikarpov I-16

Yakovlev Yak-9

Weight	6,669lb
Crew	One
Armament	One 20mm cannon and one 12.7mm machine-gun
Range	560 miles
Engine	Klimov, 1,180hp, max. speed 371mph
Dimensions	Length: 28ft 5in. Wing span: 31ft 11½in. Height: 8ft 7in
Production	16,769

Petlyakov Pe-2

Weight	18,730lb
Crew	Three–four
Armament	Three 7.62 or 12.7mm machine-guns, 2,645lb bomb-load
Range	930 miles
Engine	Two Klimov, 1,100hp, max. speed 336mph
Dimensions	Length: 41ft 6in. Wing span: 56ft 3in. Height: 13ft 1in
Production	11,427 (all marks)

the Neisse River

March 30, 1945 Rokossovsky's Front takes Danzig

April 6, 1945 Soviets encircle Vienna

April 6–10, 1945 Soviets assault and capture Koenigsberg

April 12, 1945 Zhukov's Front advances from Küstrin on the Oder River

April 13, 1945 Soviets take Vienna

April 13–26, 1945 Soviets attack and take Pillau, last German outpost in East Prussia

April 16, 1945 Zhukov and Konev begin Soviet drive to Berlin

April 18, 1945 Rokossovsky's Front attacks acros the lower Oder River

PHILIPPINES

Jan 7, 1945 Japanese aircraft strength on Luzon has been reduced to 35 planes, which are flown off

Jan 9, 1945 US landing in Lingayen Gulf, Luzon

Jan 16, 1945 Japanese resistance stiffens at Rosario to the east of the beachhead

Jan 21, 1945 US forces reach San Miguel as they advance south on Manila

Jan 26, 1945 US forces reach Clark Field airbase

Jan 29, 1945 US landing at San Antonio on the east coast of Luzon to prevent Japanese retreating into the Bataan Peninsula

Jan 31 to Feb 3, 1945 US airborne forces make landing at the entrance of Manila Bay

Feb 3, 1945 US reach outskirts of Manila, which is held by 25,000 Japanese troops. Hand-to-hand urban fighting results in some of the worst destruction in the Pacific war

Feb 4, 1945 US takes San José, south-east of Lingayen Gulf

Feb 13, 1945 US forces reach Luzon's east coast, splitting the Japanese and isolating those to the north, who continue fighting in the mountains to the end of the war

Feb 15–21, 1945 US take the Bataan Peninsula, from a landing on the southern end at Mariveles

Feb 16, 1945 US air/sea landings on the

In the 27-island Bonin group, Iwo Jima – 650 miles south-east of Tokyo – was the next step after the Marianas. It would provide a base for US fighters to escort bombers striking Japan and help cut losses on the 2,800-mile round trip from the Marianas.

After a three-day preliminary bombardment, the Marines hit the beaches, initially without heavy opposition from the Japanese, whose defenses lay inland. Indeed, the island had been turned into a hellish fortress, the Japanese using caves and ravines on the volcanic island, with honeycombed hills and pillboxes.

Over 35 days of intense fighting, the Marines advanced with flamethrowers (sometimes mounted in tanks), bazookas and grenades, eradicating the defenders, who were determined to fight to the last man. On February 23 the highest point on the island, Mount Suribachi, was taken, the Marines hoisting a flag that became immortalized in Joe Rosenthal's famous photograph.

The hard and exhausting nature of the combat can be read in the Marines' names for

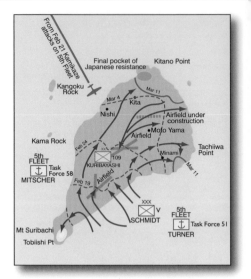

the objectives taken – such as 'The Meat Grinder' and 'Bloody Gorge'. By March 25 General Kuribayashi had been forced back to Kitano Point, the northern tip of the island. This taken, the island was declared secure,

Below: *Marines of the 5th Division inch their way up a slope on Red Beach No.1.*

prematurely, for next day a suicidal *banzai* charge provided the last significant action. Of the 22,000 Japanese on the island, 216 survived as prisoners of war. Casualties on the American side were among the heaviest of the war – over a third of the troops engaged became casualties.

Meanwhile, on March 4, a short-on-fuel B-29 had put down on one of the airstrips, the first of 2,251 bombers to use Iwo Jima's airstrips.

Above: 37mm anti-tank gun fires against cave positions in north face of Mount Suribachi. These light but extremely accurate weapons did some of their best work in the southern part of the island.

island of Corregidor

Feb, 19, 1945 US landing on north coast of Samar

Feb 26, 1945 Corregidor secured. The Japanese detonate the magazine there

Feb 28, 1945 US take the island of Palawan, to the west of the Visayans

March 3, 1945 Manila secured, but most of the city is in ruins

March 10, 1945 US land on the south-west coast of Mindanao, thereafter on Panay, Cebu, Negros and Bohol

The US plan Luzon to become the main base for the invasion of Japan

April 27, 1945 US and Filipino troops take Baguio. The liberation of the Philippines eliminates some 450,000 Japanese troops

IWO JIMA

Iwo Jima is a 5-mile long island garrisoned by General Kuribayashi's 22,000 men. Its landscape favors the defense – there are caves, tunnels and pillboxes. Iwo Jima is America's most costly battle of World War II 72 days of continuous air strikes precede the invasion of Iwo Jima. The pre-invasion bombardment lasts 3 days, less than demanded by the Marines

Feb, 19, 1945 General Schmidt's Marines go ashore on Iwo Jima. The Japanese do not attempt to prevent the initial landing; their defenses are farther inland. A rolling barrage from the ships enables the Marines to advance, but then they encounter heavy counterfire

Feb 20, 1945 The attack, in face of intense fire, gains the first of 3 airfields

Feb 21, 1945 About 50 Kamikaze suicide bombers from Tokyo strike the US invasion fleet, sinking the escort carrier *Bismarck Sea* and damaging the fleet carrier *Saratoga*

Feb 23, 1945 US take Mount Suribachi, a 500-foot high extinct volcano

Feb 28, 1945 Second airfield is taken. Then the Marines come up against strong hill defense complexes

March 3, 1945 The hill defenses are taken

YAMASHITA

Rank attained	General
Dates	1884–1946
Background	Career soldier, Kainan Military School
Commands	C-in-C 25th Army, 1941; C-in-C 14th Army, 1944

Yamashita   Imamura

IMAMURA

Rank attained	General
Dates	1886–1968
Background	Career soldier, graduated from Japanese War College
Commands	5th Division, 1938; Inspector of Military Training, 1940; 23rd Army, 1941; 8th Area Army, 1942

Out the outbreak of the Pacific War, General Tomoyuki Yamashita, the 'Tiger of Malaya', with only 36,000 men, defeated 100,000 British Empire troops in capturing Malaya and Singapore – all within ten weeks. He was one of the most formidable Japanese generals of World War II. In November 1941 he had taken command of the 25th Army. A first rate strategist, he trained his troops in the techniques of jungle warfare as well as helping to conceive the plan for the invasion of the Malay peninsula. In the course of the

campaign, Yamashita's troops overran all of Malaya and captured Singapore on February 15, 1942. He did not see active service again until 1944, when he took command of the 14th Army for the defense of the Philippines. His forces were defeated in both the Leyte and the Luzon campaigns, but he held out until after the surrender was announced from Tokyo in August 1945, not ceding to the Americans until September 3, 1945. He was charged with war crimes because of the atrocities his troops committed while under his command in the Philippines which had resulted in the deaths of 100,000 people. He was convicted and hanged in Manila in 1946.

Hitoshi Imamura, a lieutenant-general, commanded the 5th Division in China from 1938–40. He was Inspector General of Military Education from 1940 until 1941. He became Commander of the 16th Army in late 1941, leading it during the Dutch East Indies Campaign of 1942 and landing in Java. He had to abandon the ship he was on after it had been accidentally torpedoed by a Japanese cruiser, having to leap into the sea. He then commanded 8th Area Army in late 1942 which was responsible for the whole of the south-east Pacific, his HQ being at Rabaul, New Britain. He adopted quite a liberal regime, using a minimum of force while establishing order. He was promoted to full general in 1943. As the Allies went on the offensive they began to encroach on his area of command. New Britain became isolated as islands were lost to the Allies.

He had to send 6,500 of his troops to reinforce two of the New Guinea islands but their transports were sunk and most of the men were lost. At the end of the war, he was the signatory to the surrender of all Japanese forces in the area. He was also a representative at the surrender of Singapore. He was subsequently tried for war crimes and imprisoned from 1946 to 1954.

Left: Japanese General Tomoyuki Yamashita (background, center), flanked by his counsel at his trial in Manila, October 29, 1945.

after intense fighting

March 4, 1945 A B-29 short on fuel makes an emergency landing on the secured airstrip

March 8, 1945 Japanese counterattack and are repulsed next day

March 10, 1945 Japanese positions 'Amphitheater' and 'Turkey Knob', together dubbed 'The Meat Grinder' are taken

March 11, 1945 US take a strong position near the north, which becomes known as 'Bloody Gorge'

March 25, 1945 Kitano Point, northern tip of the island, is taken and the island declared secure

March 26, 1945 Japanese mount final, suicidal *banzai* charge on Iwo Jima. Of the 22,000-man garrison, only 216 survive as PoWs

RUSSIAN FRONT: Battle for Berlin

April 17, 1945 Zhukov's Front takes the Seelow Heights

April 18, 1945 Zhukov crosses the Spree River

April 25, 1945 Soviets encircle Berlin

April 26, 1945 German Twelfth Army attempts to reach Berlin

May 2, 1945 Berlin surrenders to the Soviets

April 26, 1945 Soviets take Stettin

April 26, 1945 Soviets take Brno

May 5, 1945 Prague rises against the Germans

May 7, 1945 Soviets take Breslau

May 9, 1945 Tito's forces take Zagreb

May 10, 1945 German Army Group Center surrenders to Soviets

May 14, 1945 German Army Group E surrenders to Tito's forces

NORTH-WEST EUROPE:
Rhineland and Germany

Jan 20 to Feb 5, 1945 French and US forces encircle 8 German divisions in the Colmar Pocket

Jan 31 to Feb 9, 1945 Allies secure Roer

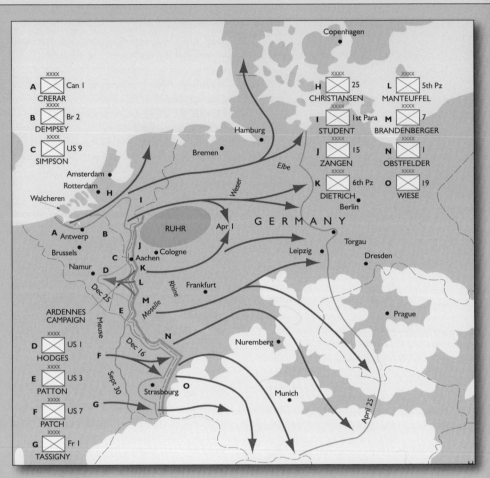

Copenhagen

A [XXXX] Can 1
CRERAR

B [XXXX] Br 2
DEMPSEY

C [XXXX] US 9
SIMPSON

H [XXXX] 25
CHRISTIANSEN

L [XXXX] 5th Pz
MANTEUFFEL

I [XXXX] 1st Para
STUDENT

M [XXXX] 7
BRANDENBERGER

J [XXXX] 15
ZANGEN

N [XXXX] 1
OBSTFELDER

K [XXXX] 6th Pz
DIETRICH

O [XXXX] 19
WIESE

Hamburg

Bremen

Amsterdam

Rotterdam

Walcheren

Elbe

Weser

Berlin

A Antwerp   **B**

Brussels

C Aachen

Namur

D

Dec 25

ARDENNES
CAMPAIGN

D [XXXX] US 1
HODGES

E [XXXX] US 3
PATTON

F [XXXX] US 7
PATCH

G [XXXX] Fr 1
TASSIGNY

RUHR

Apr 1

G E R M A N Y

Torgau

Leipzig

Dresden

Cologne

J

I

H

K

L

Rhine

Frankfurt

Prague

Meuse

Moselle

M

E

N

Dec 16

Nuremberg

F

Sept 30

Strasbourg

O

Munich

G

April 25

Left: *Men of the US Seventh Army cross the Rhine north of Mannheim.*

Right: *GIs entering a German town pass a bewildered inhabitant contemplating the devastation.*

The Rhineland Campaign

Multiple offensives during February brought the Allies to the Rhine, a series of hard-fought battles made more difficult by flooded countryside in the north and dense forests in the south. By the beginning of March the Allies were beginning to line up along the river, and on the 7th, US First Army managed to seize an intact bridge across the Rhine at Remagen. The crossing enabled the construction of two other bridges, while on 22/3rd Patton's Third Army made a surprise crossing at Oppenheim, south of Mainz. Further crossings were made during the next few days

Into Germany

At the end of March the Allies broke out of their bridgeheads over the Rhine. By April 1 Germany's principal manufacturing region, the Ruhr, was encircled, trapping a whole Army Group. Montgomery's 21st Army Group struck north-east, reaching Hanover on April 10, while the Americans thrust directly east and south. Between 11th and 19th, several units reached the Elbe, which was to be the demarcation line between the Western Allies and the Russians advancing from the east. On 25th they met at Torgau, north-east of Leipzig. Mopping-up operations continued, but local surrenders began on May 3, culminating in a formal surrender effective May 8, which was declared Victory in Europe (VE) Day.

Germany had now been conquered from west and east. From the first wave of invaders coming ashore on June 6, 1944, the forces of the Western Allies had grown to more than 4,500,000 men, of whom some two-thirds were Americans.

dams but not fast enough to stop the Germans flooding the surrounding countryside

Feb 8 to March 10, 1945 Allied 'Veritable', 'Grenade' and 'Blockbuster' offensives from the Roer to the Rhine

March 4, 1945 Reichswald cleared

March 7, 1945 US First Army captures Rhine bridge at Remagen

March, 19, 1945 Hitler orders 'scorched earth' policy; local commanders ignore it

March 22/3, 1945 US Third Army seizes Rhine bridge at Oppenheim

March 22–7, 1945 US cross the Rhine at Boppard, St Goar, near Mainz and at Worms

March 23/4, 1945 British and Canadians cross the Rhine north of the Lippe

March 28, 1945 British attack from Wesel

March 28, 1945 US encircle German LXXXIX Corps at Giessen

March 31, 1945 French cross the Rhine near Germersheim

April 1, 1945 US forces complete encirclement of the Ruhr, trapping Army Group B. 325,000 Germans surrender on 18th

April 11, 1945 US reach Magdeburg on the Elbe River, just 80 miles west of Berlin. The Elbe and the Mulde will be the agreed demarcation line between the Western Allies and the Soviets

April 15, 1945 Belsen and Buchenwald concentration camps liberated

April, 19, 1945 US take Leipzig

April 25, 1945 US and Soviet forces meet at Torgau on the Elbe River

OKINAWA

March 24, 1945 US begins main naval bombardment of Okinawa. The Japanese garrison is 77,000 men plus 20,000 Okinawa militia under General Ushijima

March 24, 1945 US land on Kerama Islands south-west of Okinawa

April 1, 1945 US forces land on the west coast of Okinawa, aiming to cut the island in two. 16,000 men go ashore during the first hour, the Japanese defenses being inland

OKINAWA

The Ryukyu Islands stretch south of Japan towards Formosa, and the last major target before Japan itself lay here, the 60-mile-long island of Okinawa. As on Iwo Jima, the Japanese had fortified intricately, the principal defenses centering on Shuri Castle in the south and consisting of tunnels, caves and mutually-supporting positions deep in the rock, practically immune to air attack and naval bombardment.

On April 1, the US troops were quickly ashore on the west coast north of Naha, with little initial opposition. By the fourth day they had pushed to the eastern shore of the narrow island and turned north against the Japanese forces in the Motobu Peninsula, and south against the main defenses. These consisted of three concentric lines around Shuri Castle and would take some seven weeks to work through, the Japanese fanatically defending each position to the death.

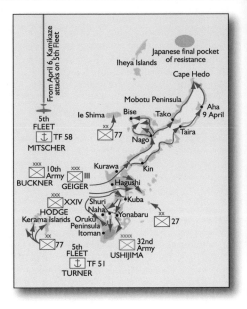

The Motobu Peninsula was cleared by April 20, and seven days later the capital, Naha, was secured. The grinding, hand-to-hand combat around Shuri continued until June 22, when General Ushijima committed suicide and all that remained were isolated pockets of resistance.

American troops were now securely ashore just 340 miles south of the Japanese homeland, but casualties were the highest of all the campaigns in the Pacific – over 7,000 dead and nearly 32,000 wounded. The most costly and complex operation of the Pacific war, involving over half a million troops and 1,200 warships, Okinawa also saw 36 ships go down, mostly to the Japanese kamikaze suicide attacks, and 763 aircraft.

Japanese losses reflect their 'fight to the end' philosophy – in addition to 107,000 killed in combat, some 27,000 are estimated to have been sealed in caves, refusing to surrender.

Above: *Tank-borne infantry moving up to take the town of Ghuta before the Japanese can occupy it. The men are members of the 29th Marines. Okinawa, April 1, 1945.*

Left: *A Marine of the 1st Marine Division draws a bead on a Japanese sniper with his tommy-gun as his companion ducks for cover. The division was advancing to take Wana Ridge before the town of Shuri. Okinawa, 1945.*

April 4, 1945 The US forces reach the east coast, cutting the island in two before turning north and south

April 9, 1945 US forces attack the formidable tri-concentric defense lines in the south of Okinawa based on Shuri Castle

April 10, 1945 US land on Tsugen Island east of Okinawa

April 16–21, 1945 US invade and clear Ie Shima island

April 12, 1945 US attack Motobu Peninsula in the north and clear it after a week's fighting

April 20, 1945 US clear north of Okinawa

May 4, 1945 Japanese launch massive counterattack but are repulsed and forced to pull back to the next line of defenses

By May 18, 1945 US breach Shuri line, and Ushijima falls back to the last line of defense on the Oroku Peninsula

May 27–9, 1945 US take Shuri Castle

June 4, 1945 US Marines go ashore on the Oroku Peninsula and secure it in 10 days

June 17, 1945 US forces face the Yuza Dake – Yaeju Dake escarpment

June 18, 1945 General Buckner, commander of US Tenth Army, killed, highest ranking officer in the US Army to die during the war

June 21, 1945 US forces reach the southern tip of the island. The only opposition now left consists of isolated pockets

June 22, 1945 Japanese General Ushijima commits suicide

ITALY: The Final Offensive

April 1/2, 4/5, 1945 British commando attacks on Lake Commachio

April 9, 1945 Opening of final Allied offensive in Italy

April 18, 1945 Argenta taken

April 21, 1945 Bologna entered by elements of Polish II Corps

April 22, 1945 Allies take Ferrara and Modena

April 25, 1945 Allies take Verona and Parma

April 26, 1945 Allies take Verona

THE HOLOCAUST

Twelve million people died in the Nazi concentration camps, of whom some 6,000,000 were Jewish. The others included gypsies, homosexuals, the mentally or physically ill and people whom, for whatever reason, the Nazis considered enemies of the German state.

A Jew was defined by the Germans in the Nuremberg Laws of 1935 as being someone with one Jewish grandparent. A quarter of the German Jews were eventually killed. Many fled before the war, many making their way to other European countries and often finding themselves back under Nazi power when that country was conquered by the Germans.

In Poland, between September and October 1939, 3,000 Jews were among more than 10,000 Polish civilians who were shot in the streets. In Russia, the shootings continued in the streets, fields and ditches as curious bystanders stood and watched. In Kiev, for example, 33,000 Jewish men, women and children were killed in just three days. The Germans also created ghettos for the Jews, where they were confined and where many starved to death or died of disease.

By 1941 the Germans had built extermination camps specifically for the purpose of mass murder by gassing. Many Jews

Left: *Bones in the ovens at the German concentration camp at Weimar, Germany, April 14, 1945.*

Below: *Inmates of the Buchenwald concentration, April 16, 1945.*

ESTIMATED NUMBERS OF JEWS MURDERED, BY NATIONALITY	
Poland	3,000,000
USSR	1,000,000
Roumania	470,000
Czechoslovakia	277,000
Hungary	200,000
Germany	160,000
Lithuania	140,000
The Netherlands	106,000
France	83,000
Latvia	80,000
Greece	69,000
Yugoslavia	67,000
Austria	65,000
Belgium	24,000
Italy	8,000
Estonia	1,000
Norway	728
Luxembourg	700
Libya	562
Denmark	77
Finland	15

were also worked or beaten to death in factories or the camps that were attached. At one of the biggest camps, Auschwitz-Birkenau in Poland, trains brought victims from all over occupied Europe who were then murdered on an industrial scale. It is estimated that between 1¼ and 1½ million died in this camp alone, including 800,000 Jews.

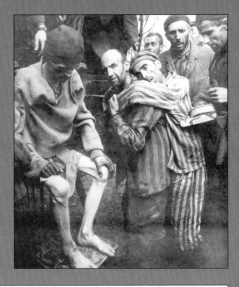

Right: Inmates of Wobbelin Concentration Camp.

Below: Bodies readied for disposal at the Buchenwald concentration camp.

BRITISH TANKS

British tank design at the early stages of World War II generally equalled that of Germany. But as the war progressed, and both tank and anti-tank weaponry improved, British tanks proved to be too lightly armed when compared with their German counterparts.

The Matilda Infantry Tank of the early war period was slow and poorly armed but heavily armoured, and proved to be difficult to knock out. The cruiser tanks were much faster but too lightly armoured and often mechanically unreliable. Later British tanks

Valentine Infantry Tank	
Weight	18 tons
Crew	Three/four
Armament	2pdr or 6pdr gun (later a 75mm gun) and one 7.92mm BESA
Armor	Max: 65mm. Min: 8mm
Engine	AEC, 135hp, speed 15mph
Dimensions	Length: 17ft 9in. Width: 8ft 7in. Height: 7ft 5in
Production	8,275

Crusader Cruiser Tank	
Weight	20 tons
Crew	Three, four or five (dependent on mark)
Armament	2pdr or 6pdr gun and two 7.92 mm BESA MGs
Armor	Max: 51mm. Min: 7mm
Engine	Nuffield Liberty, 340hp, speed 27mph
Dimensions	Length: 19ft 8in. Width: 8ft 8in. Height: 7ft 4in
Production	5,300

Above, left to right: *Valentine, Crusader and Comet tanks.* **Below:** *A Churchill infantry tank in the Western Desert. The Churchill was the basis for many specialist variants, including the Crocodile armed with a flamethower, models armed with howitzers, AVREs (Engineer vehicles), versions for clearing mines with flails and equipped with a jib for recovering other tanks from the battlefield.*

(e.g., the Cromwell) were much more reliable, but still too lightly armed and armoured. By 1941 the British began to supplement their tank stocks with American models.

During the war Britain produced more than 25,000 tanks compared with Germany's 23,500.

Comet Cruiser Tank	
Weight	35.5 tons
Crew	Five
Armament	One 77mm gun and two 7.92mm BESA machine-guns
Armor	Max: 102mm. Min: 14mm
Engine	Rolls-Royce, 600hp, speed 32mph
Dimensions	Length: 25ft 1in. Width: 10ft 0in. Height: 9ft 9in
Production	1,200

April 27, 1945 Allies take Genoa
April 27, 1945 Allies cross Adige River
April 28, 1945 Mussolini executed by communist partisans who ambush his convoy
April 29, 1945 German forces in Italy surrender, effective May 2
May 2, 1945 British advance troops reach Trieste and meet Tito's partisans
May 6, 1945 Fifth Army penetrates Alps to Brenner Pass in Austria

Western Theater General Events
Jan 30, 1945 Allied 'Argonaut' conference, Malta
Jan 30, 1945 Over 6,000, perhaps as many as 8,000 refugees drown as German liner *Wilhelm Gustlov*, out of Danzig, is torpedoed. This is the greatest loss of life at sea in history
Early February, 1945 At peak, 6 V-2 rockets are fired at London each day
Feb 13/14, 1945 Dresden bombed by RAF and USAAF. Firestorm kills c.50,000
Feb 4–11, 1945 Allied Yalta conference
March 12, 1945 Dortmund, largest RAF raid of the war
March 14, 1945 Bielefeld Viaduct, first use of 22,000lb Grand Slam bomb
April 12, 1945 President Roosevelt dies. Vice President Harry H. Truman succeeds him
April 16, 1945 Final Arctic convoy to Russia sets sail
April 20/1, 1945 Final RAF/USAAF raids on Berlin
April 26, 1945 RAF begins PoW repatriation
April 29 to May 7, 1945 Allied Operation 'Manna' drops food to starving people of the Netherlands
In the final months of hostilities between 1,500,000 and 2,000,000 refugees are evacuated by sea from Germany's eastern provinces in the path of the Soviet advance
April 30, 1945 Hitler commits suicide
May 1, 1945 Goebbels commits suicide
May 4, 1945 Montgomery receives

REFUGEES

In Poland, as soon as the war began, some civilians fled from the combat zones, and from the enemy, to safer areas. In Belgium and France, this trickle become a flood, often jamming the roads and handicapping the advancing Allied troops as they moved forward to meet the Germans. To amplify the confusion and terror for the Blitzkrieg, the Luftwaffe would sometimes machine-gun the columns of refugees, causing even more disorder for the Allied troops.

In the USSR, where the state had plans for evacuation, large numbers of refugees fled spontaneously, clogging up the transport systems,

Below and right:
Belgian refugees flee from the advancing German Army, May 1940.

thus interfering with Soviet troop movements. There were, possibly, 10 million plus 16 million official evacuees.

During the winter of 1944–45 the Allies were gradually closing in on Germany. Millions of German people began to flee, especially from the advancing Communist troops. The German rail and road system had been disrupted by bombing and the German state machinery was disintegrating; some areas were close to anarchy. The number of refugees in Europe from this period can only be estimated, but the figure has been put at 30 million.

With the collapse of the Third Reich, millions of displaced people, mostly those who had been made to work as forced labour under the Germans, criss-crossed Europe, often on foot, trying to make their way to what remained of their homes and their families.

Top: Germans expelled from the Sudetenland, Czechoslovakia, at the end of the war.

Above: A German boy, with his mother pushing from behind, pulls a cartload of possessions out of Uerdingen, Germany. They have been moved out by the Allied military seeking to prevent loss of life from the shelling by German troops from the other side of the Rhine, March 19, 1945.

German surrender in NW Germany, Netherlands and Denmark at Luneburg Heath
May 4, 1945 US take Salzburg and Berchtesgaden
May 7, 1945 Germans surrender to Eisenhower at Reims
May 8, 1945 Berlin surrender ceremony to Soviet, US, British and French representatives. This day becomes VE Day (Victory in Europe Day)

BURMA
July, 19, 1945 Japanese attack near Taungoo to re-establish contact with forces trapped on the western side of the Sittang, after a feint farther south toward Waw on 3-11th
Aug 4, 1945 Japanese Taungoo offensive repulsed. After the Japanese Taungoo offensive, there are no further major military operations, mopping up continuing until the surrender
Aug 28, 1945 Japanese Field Marshal Terauchi's chief of staff signs a preliminary surrender document in Rangoon

Far Eastern Theater General Events
June, 1945 There are so few Japanese fighters left that they are grounded to preserve them for use in the expected Allied invasion of Japan. US bombers hit 60 smaller cities and towns in Japan with incendiaries and high-level precision bombing. The Japanese oil industry is destroyed
June 6, 1945 Japanese government resolves to fight to the end and plans massive use of civilians to augment armed forces in resisting an Allied invasion
June 10, 1945 Australians take Balikpapan in Borneo. In Borneo the Allies secure the oilfields but do not attempt to clear the whole island of Japanese
By June, 1945 MacArthur has control of Luzon and most cities and towns in the Philippines have been secured. Japanese resistance continues in isolated groups in

CASUALTIES

Approximately 50,000,000 people died as a consequence of World War II, although the precise number will never be known. The USSR paid the highest price by far in terms of people who lost their lives, 50% of whom were civilians.

Of the total, the military made up approximately 22,000,000 of the war-related deaths. Of the remaining 28,000,000, 12,000,000 died in the concentration camps and 1,500,000 directly from aerial bombing. The remaining 14,500,000 died from other war-related causes, of which some 7,500,000 were in China. It is estimated that 1,000,000 German refugees died during the winter and spring of 1944–45 as they fled from the advancing Soviet armies.

In Bengal, India, during the period 1943–46, between 3,500,000 and 3,800,000 people may have died as a result of famine and the epidemic diseases that accompanied it. It was caused indirectly by the fall of Burma in 1942 and the consequent increase in local food prices. This figure has not been included in the table opposite.

Below: American soldiers, stripped of all equipment, lie dead, face down in the slush of a crossroads during the Battle of the Bulge. Note the bare feet of the soldier in the foreground. Captured German photograph. Belgium, December 1944.

APPROXIMATE NUMBERS KILLED, BY COUNTRY	
Albania	20,000
Australia	27,000
Austria	310,000
Belgium	100,000
Bulgaria	17,000
Brazil	1,200
Canada	42,000
China	10,500,000
Czechoslovakia	350,000
Denmark	7,000
Estonia	80,000
Finland	90,000
France	600,000
Germany	5,500,000
Greece	250,000
Hungary	400,000
India	36,000
Italy	300,000
Japan	2,300,000
Latvia	200,000
Lithuania	300,000
Luxembourg	7,000
The Netherlands	200,000
New Zealand	12,000
Norway	10,000
The Philippines	120,000
Poland	5,800,000
Roumania	500,000
South Africa	9,000
UK	362,000
USA	409,000
USSR	20,000,000
Yugoslavia	1,500,000

Above: Sprawled bodies on beach of Tarawa, testifying to ferocity of the struggle for this stretch of sand. November 1943.

Below: Piles of frozen dead Russian troops during the Russo-Finnish fighting, February 1940.

the mountains

June 22, 1945 Japanese Emperor Hirohito tells his government that peace must be sought

July 1, 1945 Australians land in Brunei

July 4, 1945 British agree to the use of atomic bomb

July 16, 1945 US detonates first atomic bomb at Alamogordo, New Mexico

July 16, 1945 Heavy cruiser USS *Indianapolis* sails from San Francisco for Tinian with components for two atomic bombs

July 26, 1945 From the Potsdam conference, the USA, Britain and China demand Japan's surrender. Two days later the Japanese government announce that they will ignore the demand

By end July, 1945 US bombers have practically run out of targets. Civilian casualties are over 800,000 including 300,000 dead. Some 8½ million people are homeless

July 30, 1945 USS *Indianapolis* is sunk by I-58 north-east of Leyte, returning from Tinian. Because of communications mishaps, the Navy do not know this. Of 850–900 survivors of the sinking, only 316 are left alive when they are finally spotted on Aug 2

Aug 6, 1945 US B-29 'Enola Gay' drops uranium bomb 'Little Boy' on Hiroshima, destroying 4.2 square miles and killing 80,000 people

Aug 9, 1945 US B-29 'Bock's Car' drops plutonium bomb 'Fat Man' on Nagasaki, killing 35,000 people

MANCHURIA

A constant problem for the Russians is logistics and resupplying their rapidly advancing columns with fuel and food

Aug 8, 1945 Russia declares war on Japan at midnight

Aug 9, 1945 Russian armies invade Manchuria (Manchukuo) under Marshal Vasilievsky

Aug 10, 1945 The Second Far East Front attacks unopposed across the Amur River

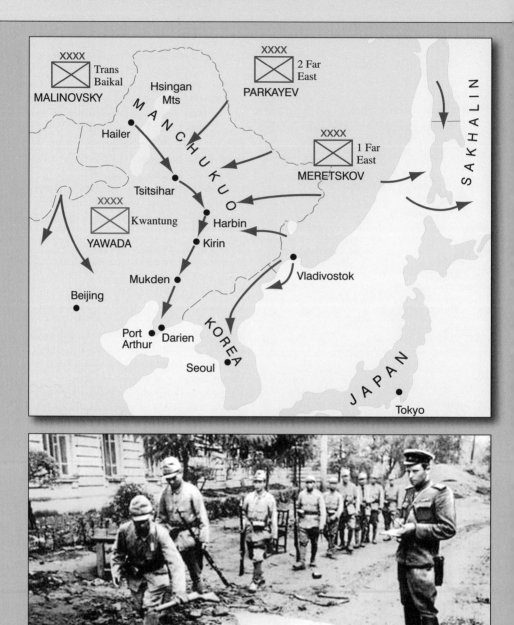

Above: *Japanese troops surrendering their arms to the Russians.*

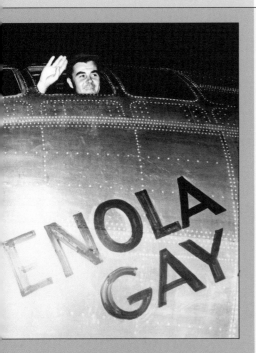

Above: Colonel Paul W. Tibbets, Jr., pilot of the Enola Gay, the plane that dropped the atomic bomb on Hiroshima, waves from his cockpit before the takeoff, 6 August 1945.

Above: Nagasaki after the bomb. The Roman Catholic cathedral can be seen in the background on the low hill.

from the north

Aug 10–11, 1945 The Trans-Baikal Front crosses the Hsingan Mountains but is then delayed by fuel and supply problems

Aug 11, 1945 Russians invade Sakhalin Island

Aug 11–16, 1945 Russians take Mu-tan-chiang, key position in the east, after a see-saw battle

Aug 18, 1945 Russians take Hailar, bypassed during the rapid advance of Trans-Baikal Front

Aug 18, 1945 Russians invade Shumshu island in the Kuriles

Aug 18, 1945 Russian airborne landing at Harbin

Aug, 19, 1945 Russian airborne landings at Mukden and Kirin. Fighting continues despite the official surrender of Japan

Aug, 19, 1945 Japanese commander in Manchukuo, General Yamada, surrenders, effective next day. But the Soviet advance does not stop and fighting continues

Aug 20, 1945 Russians secure Mukden

Aug 21, 1945 Russians take Ch'ang-ch'un

Aug 22, 1945 Russian airborne landings at Port Arthur and Dairen

Aug 22, 1945 Pu Yi, last emperor of China, is captured by the Russians. He has been Japan's puppet ruler of Manchukuo

Aug 24, 1945 Russians' armored spear-heads reach Port Arthur

Aug 25, 1945 Russians secure Sakhalin Island, taking the capital, Toyahara. Over 100,000 refugees make it across the Soya Strait to Japan

Sept 3, 1945 Russians secure the Kuriles The Soviet conquests net 600,000 Japanese prisoners, who are sent to Siberia and Mongolia as forced labor. In 1948-50, 513,139 are repatriated

Far Eastern Theater General Events
Aug 10, 1945 Emperor Hirohito tells his government that the Allies' Potsdam surrender terms must be accepted

Aug 11/12, 1945 US sends Allied response

DOUGLAS MACARTHUR

One of the most controversial generals of the US Army, Douglas MacArthur was the son of an army officer from a distinguished family. He graduated from West Point with the highest marks ever received. After service in World War I he rose rapidly through the ranks to become Army Chief of Staff. He retired in 1937, becoming a field marshal with the Philippine Army. In 1941 he was recalled to US service by Roosevelt. After his unsuccessful defense of the Philippines he escaped to Australia in March 1942, promising, 'I shall return'. From there he began the conquest of the South-West Pacific, island-hopping all the way to the retaking of the Philippines in 1945.

He had the honour of accepting the Japanese formal surrender in Tokyo Bay. He was idolised by the American public but disliked by Roosevelt and by most of the other top-ranking military men. He loved publicity and he was flamboyant, vain and egotistical. He had a total contempt for criticism and many of those who had authority over him. He was, however, charming and gracious and a bold leader with great imagination. Like a potentate, he ruled postwar Japan but the Korean War led to his downfall.

MACARTHUR	
Rank attained	General
Dates	1880–1964
Background	Career soldier; West Point Military Academy
Commands	Commander of US Forces in the Far East, 1941; South-West Pacific Area, 1942; US Army Forces in the Pacific, 1945
Campaigns	Philippines, 1941–42; New Guinea and the Solomons, 1942–44; Philippines, 1945

Below: *General MacArthur signs the articles of Japanese surrender, Tokyo Bay, September 2, 1945.*

to Japanese

Aug 14, 1945 Emperor Hirohito orders surrender according to the Allied terms, while a coup d'etat is being plotted by hard-line officers.
Formal acceptance is sent

Aug 15, 1945 Emperor Hirohito broad-casts to the Japanese, speaking in public for the first time, telling them of the surrender

Aug 28, 1945 First elements of the US occupation forces arrive in Japan

Sept 2, 1945 Japan makes formal surren-der aboard US battleship *Missouri* in Tokyo Bay. This day becomes VJ Day (Victory in Japan Day)

Sept 8, 1945 General MacArthur arrives in Japan

Sept 9, 1945 Allied landings in Malaya

Sept 12, 1945 British theater commander Admiral Mountbatten takes formal surren-der of Japanese in Singapore and South-East Asia

Top: *Watched by the officers and crew, representatives of the Japanese government arrive aboard the US battleship* Missouri *in Tokyo Bay to participate in surrender cermonies, September 2, 1945.*

Above: *Admiral Chester Nimitz adds his signature to the Japanese surrender documents.*

WAR CRIMES AND TRIALS

President Roosevelt was aware that war crimes were being committed by the Axis powers and warned them of this fact and that they would be brought to justice. These crimes were mainly concerned with breaches of the Geneva and Hague Conventions. The London Charter of the International Military Tribunal, August 8, 1945, was established to try the major war criminals, who would be tried for crimes against peace (waging a war of aggression), war crimes (violations of the laws and customs of war) and crimes against humanity (inhumanity and the persecution of civilians).

The list of people to be tried contained 24 Germans, including Göring, Dönitz, Hess and Speer. Between November 20, 1945 and October 1, 1946 the Nuremberg Trials were held. Eleven of the defendants were sentenced to hanging, three received life sentences, two 20 years, one 15 years and one 10 years and three were acquitted. Göring, who was sentenced to death, committed suicide before his execution.

An International War Tribunal was also set up to try 28 leading Japanese for war crimes. The Tokyo War Crimes Trials were held between May 3, 1946 and November 6, 1948. The most prominent defendant was General Tojo. By the conclusion of the trial two defendants had died, one had been found to be mentally unfit, and the rest were found guilty. Seven, including Tojo, were sentenced to hang, sixteen to life imprisonment, one to 20 years and one to seven years.

In the Far East over 2,000 regional trials were held by the USA, Britain, Canada, France, the Netherlands and the Philippines, and these continued until 1951. The majority of indictments were for the maltreatment and murder of prisoners of war and civilians. The high number of convictions arose from the fact that, for example, 4% of Anglo-American POWs died in German prison camps while 27% died in Japanese camps. Overall 5,700 were indicted, some 3,000 of whom were convicted and imprisoned for varying terms, and 920 were sentenced to death.

Below: Overview of the dock at the Nuremberg Trials, US military police lining the back of the court, while the defendants listen to the proceedings on headphones.

Right: *The defendants at the International Military Tribunal for the Far East Ichigaya Court, Tokyo.*

Below: *Nuremberg Trials. Defendants in the dock: Göring, Hess, von Ribbentrop, and Keitel in the front row.*

Alanbrooke, Field Marshal Lord, (ed. Alex Dancher and Daniel Todman), *War Diaries 1939–1945*, 2002

Allen, Colonel Robert S., *'Lucky Forward'*, 1947

Ambrose, Stephen E., *Eisenhower: Soldier and President*, 2003

— *Pegasus Bridge*, 2003.

Arnold, James R., *Ardennes 1944 – Hitler's Last Gamble in the West*, 1990

Avon, The Rt. Hon. the Earl of, *The Eden Memoirs: Facing the Dictators*, 1962

Bagnasco, E., *Submarines of World War Two*, 1973; translation 1977

Baker, David. *Adolf Galland: The Authorised Biography*, 1996

Barnett, Correlli (ed), *Hitler's Generals*, 1989

— *The Desert Generals*, 1960

Bateson, Charles, *The War with Japan*, 1968

Baudot, M., et al, *The Historical Encyclopedia of World War Two*, 1989

Beevor, Anthony, *Stalingrad*, 1999

— *Berlin: The Downfall, 1945*, 2003

Bender, Roger James, and Law, Richard D., *Uniforms, Organization and History of the Afrikakorps*, 1973

Bergot, Erwan, *The Afrika Korps (Corps d'élite)*, 1975

Bidwell, Shelford, *The Chindit War*, 1979

Black, Jeremy, *World War Two: A Military History*, 2003

Black, Conrad, *Franklin Delano Roosevelt: Champion of Freedom*, 2003

Bodle, Peter and Boulter, Bertie, *Mosquito to Berlin: Story of 'Bertie' Boulter DFC, One of Bennett's Pathfinders*, 2007

Bradley, Omar N., *A Soldier's Story*, 1951

Brown, David, *Warship Losses of World War Two*, 1990

Bull, Stephen and Dennis, Peter, *World War II Infantry Tactics: Company and Battalion*, 2005

Bullock, Alan, *Hitler and Stalin: Parallel Lives*, 1998

Burt, R. A., *British Battleships 1919–1939*, 1993

Calvocoressi, Peter, and Wint, Guy, *Total War*, 1972

Carver, Michael, *El Alamein*, 1962

Chamberlain, Peter, *Churchill Tank*, 1971

— and Chris Ellis, *British and American Tanks of World War II*, 1969

— *Pictorial History of Tanks of the World 1915–45*, 1972

Chamberlain, Peter, Doyle, Hilary L., and Jentz, Thomas L., *The Encyclopedia of German Tanks of World War Two*, 1978

Chambers, John Whiteclay, *The Oxford Companion to American Military History*, 1999

Chandler, David G., *Battles and Battlescenes of World War Two*, 1989

Channon, John, and Hudson, Robert, *The Penguin Historical Atlas of Russia*, 1995

Chant, Christopher, *Battle Tanks of World War II*, 1997

Chronicle of the Second World War (1990), reissued as *World War II Day by Day*, 2001

Chronology and Index of the Second World War, 1975

Churchill, Winston S., *The Second World War*, 6 vols, 1948–54

Clark, Alan, *The Fall Of Crete*, 1962

— *Barbarossa: The Russian German Conflict, 1941–45*, 1963

Clarke, Jeffrey J., and Smith, Robert Ross, *United States Army in WWII – Riviera to the Rhine*, 1993

Cobban, Alfred, *A History of Modern France. Vol. 2: 1799–1945*, 1963

Cole, Hugh M. *United States Army in WWII – The Ardennes: Battle of the Bulge*, 1965

Connell, J. Mark, *Ardennes: The Battle of the Bulge*, 2003

Costello, John, and Hughes, Terry, *The Battle of the Atlantic*, 1977

— *The Pacific War, 1941–45*, 1981

Craig, Gordon A., *Germany 1866–1945*, 1984

Cressman, Robert J., *The Official Chronology of the U.S. Navy in World War II*, 1999

Crookenden, Napier, *The Battle of the Bulge*, 1978

Davidson, Edward, and Manning, Dale, *Chronology of World War Two*, 1999

Davis, Brian L., *German Army Uniforms and Insignia, 1933–1945*, 1971

— *British Army Uniforms and Insignia of World War Two*, 1983

— *Uniforms and Insignia of the Luftwaffe*, 2 vols, 1991, 1995

Dear, Ian, and Foot, M. R. D., *The Oxford Companion to the Second World War*, 1995

Delaney, John, *The Blitzkrieg Campaigns*, 1996

Delve, Ken, and Jacobs, Peter, *The Six-Year Offensive: Bomber Command in World War Two*, 1992

Doherty, Richard, *A Noble Crusade: The History of the Eighth Army, 1941–45*, 1999

Douglas-Home, Charles, *Rommel*, 1973

Doyle Hilary L., *Tiger 1*, 1993

— *Panther Variants, 1943–45*, 1997

— *Sturmgeschutz Ausf F, F/8, G, Sturmhaubitze and Sturmgeschutz IV 1942–1945*, 2001

— and Jentz, Thomas L., *Panzerkampfwagen IV Ausf G, H and J 1942–1945*, 2001

Dunn, Dennis J., *Caught Between Roosevelt and Stalin: America's Ambassadors to Moscow*, 1998

Edmonds, Robin, *The 'Big Three': Churchill, Roosevelt and Stalin in Peace and War*, 1991.

Edwards, R., *Panzer: A Revolution in Warfare, 1933–1945*, 1989

Eisenhower, Dwight D. *Crusade in Europe*, 1948

Ellis, John. *World War II Data Book*, 1994

Elstob, Peter, *Hitler's Last Offensive*, 1971

Essame, H., *The Battle for Germany*, 1969

Este, Carlo d', *Eisenhower: A Soldier's Life*, 2002

Ethell Jeffrey, L., and Isby, David C., *G.I. Victory: The U.S. Army in World War II in Color*, 1995

— *Eagles Over North Africa and the Mediterranean, 1940–43: Luftwaffe at War*, 1997

Evans, Anthony A., *World War II, An Illustrated Miscellany*, 2005

Evans, Tom Parry, *Squadron Leader Tommy Broom DFC: The Legendary Pathfinder Mosquito Navigator, 2007*

Feis, Herbert, *Churchill, Roosevelt and Stalin: The War They Waged and the Peace They Sought*, 1957

— *Between War and Peace: The Potsdam Conference*, 1960

Fiorani, Flavio, (ed), *A New Illustrated History of World War II: Rare and Unseen Photographs 1939–1945*, 2005

Fletcher, David, *Crusader: Cruiser Tank 1939–1945*, 1995

— *Cromwell Cruiser Tank 1942–50*, 2006

— and Sarson, Peter, *The Matilda Infantry Tank 1938–1945*, 1994

Ford, Roger, *Sherman Tank*, 1999

Ford, Ken and Gerrard, Howard, *El Alamein,*

1942: The Turning of the Tide, 2005

Forty, George, *Patton's Third Army at War*, 1990

— *The Armies of George S. Patton*, 1996

— *Tank Aces from Blitzkrieg to the Gulf War*, 1997

— *The Armies of Rommel*, 1999

— *The Reich's Last Gamble*, 2000

— *The Desert War*, 2002

— *Tanks of World Wars I and II*, 2006

Francillon, Rene J., *Japanese Aircraft of the Pacific War*, 1987

Freeman, Roger A., *The Mighty Eighth*, 1970

Gelb, Norman, *Ike and Monty: Generals at War*, 1994

Gibbons, David, *The Timechart History of World War II*, 2003

Gilbert, Martin, *Churchill at War*, 2003.

— *Holocaust: A History of the Jews of Europe during the Second World War*, 1987

— *The Day the War Ended: VE-Day 1945 in Europe and Around the World*, 2004

— *Second World War: A Complete History*, 2004

Glenny, Misha, *The Balkans 1804–1999: Nationalism, War and the Great Powers*, 2000

Goralski, Robert, *World War II Almanac, 1931–1945*, 1981

Görlitz, W., *The German General Staff*, 1953

Griehl, Manfred, *German Bombers Over England, 1940–44: Luftwaffe at War*, 1999

— *Air War Over the Atlantic: Luftwaffe at War*, 2003

Grove, Philip D., *Great Battles of the Royal Navy*, 1997

— *The Price of Disobedience: The Battle of the River Plate reconsidered*, 2000

— *Midway*, 2004

Gudgin, Peter, *The Tiger Tanks*, 1991

— *With Churchills to War: 48th Battalion Royal Tank Regiment at War, 1939–45*, 1996

Hamilton, Nigel, *Monty: The Making of a General, 1887–1942*, 1984.

— *Monty: Master of the Battlefield, 1942–1944*, 1985.

— *Monty: The Field Marshal, 1944–1976*, 1987

Hart, Stephen Ashley and Laurier, Jim, *Panther Medium Tank 1942–45*, 2003

Hastings, Max, *Bomber Command*, 1979

— *Overlord: D-Day and the Battle for Normandy, 1944*, 1999

— *Armageddon: The Battle for Germany, 1944–1945*, 2004

FURTHER READING

— *Nemesis: The Battle for Japan, 1944–45*, 2007

Heckmann, W, *Rommel's War in Africa*, 1981

Hogg, Ian V., German Artillery of World War Two, 1975

— *British and American Artillery of World War Two*, 1978

— and John Weeks, *Military Small Arms of the 20th Century*, 6th edition 1991

Hoffman, Karl, *Erwin Rommel*, 2004

Holmes, Richard, *World War Two in Photographs*, 2000

Hood, Jean, (ed.), *Submarine*, 2007

Irving, David, *The Rise and Fall of the Luftwaffe*, 1973

— *The Trail of the Fox: The Life of Field Marshal Erwin Rommel*, 1977

— *Hitler's War*, 1991

Jackson, Robert, *Through the Eyes of the World's Fighter Aces: The Greatest Fighter Pilots of World War Two*, 2007

Jackson, W. G. F., *The Battle for Italy*, 1967

Jenkins, Roy, *Churchill*, 2002

Jentschura, Hansgeorg, Jung, Dieter, and Mickel, Peter, *Warships of the Imperial Japanese Navy, 1869–1945*, 1970; English translation 1977

Jentz, Thomas L., *Germany's Tiger Tanks: Tiger I and Tiger II – Combat Tactics*, 1997

— *Tank Combat in North Africa*, 1998

— and Doyle, Hilary L., *Germany's Panther Tank: The Quest for Combat Supremacy, Development Modifications, Rare Variants, Characteristics, Combat Accounts*, 1995

— *Germany's Tiger Tanks: Germany's Tiger Tanks DW to Tiger 1 Design, Production and Modifications*, 2000

Jewell, Derek, (ed.), *Alamein and the Desert War*, 1967.

Johnson, Brian, *The Secret War*, 1978

Jones, R. V., *Most Secret War*, 1978

Kaplan, Philip, *Fighter Aces of the Luftwaffe in World War 2*, 2007

Keegan, John (ed), *Who Was Who in World War II*, 1978

— *The Times Atlas of the Second World War*, 1989

— *Churchill's Generals*, 1991

Keilig, Wolf, *Die Generale des Heeres*, 1983

Kemp, Paul, *U-Boats Destroyed*, 1997

— *Convoy*, 1999

Kershaw, Ian, *Making Friends with Hitler: Lord Londonderry, the Nazis and the Road to World War II*, 2004

— *The Nazi Dictatorship: Problems and Perspectives of Interpretation*, 1996

Kochan, Lionel, *The Making of Modern Russia*, 1962

Koenig, William J., *Americans at War: From the Colonial Wars to Vietnam*, 1980

Lagarde, Jean de, *German Soldiers of World War Two*, 2005

Latimer, John, *Burma: The Forgotten War*, 2004

Lavery, Brian, *Churchill Goes to War: Winston's Wartime Journeys*, 2007

— *In Which They Served*, 2008

Le Tissier, Tony, *Berlin: Then and Now (After the Battle Publications)*, 1992

Leckie, Robert, *Okinawa: The Last Battle of World War II*, 1995

Lewin, R. *Rommel as Military Commander*, 1968

— *Montgomery as Military Commander*, 1971

— *Ultra Goes to War*, 1978

Liddell-Hart, B. H., *The Other Side of the Hill*, 1948

— *History of the Second World War*, 1971

Loewenheim, Francis L., Langley, Harold D., and Jones, Manfred, (eds), *Roosevelt and Stalin: Their Secret War Correspondence*, 1975.

Lucas, James, *Germany's Elite Panzer Force: Grossdeutschland*, 1979

— *War in the Desert: The Eighth Army at El Alamein*, 1982

— *Kommando: German Special Forces of World War Two*, 1985

— *Storming Eagles: German Paratroopers in World War Two*, 1988

— *The Last Year of the German Army*, 1994

— and Matthew Cooper, *Panzer: Armoured Force of the Third Reich*, 1976

MacDonald, Charles B., *United States Army in WWII – The Last Offensive*, 1973

— *The Battle of the Bulge*, 1984

Macksey, Kenneth, *Rommel: Battles and Campaigns*, 1979

— *Afrika Korps*, 1968

— *Military Errors of World War Two*, 1987

Mather, Carol, *When the Grass Stops Growing*, 1997

McDonald, Charles. *The Battle of the Bulge*, 1984

Merriman, Robert E., *The Battle of the Ardennes*, 1958

Messenger, Charles, *'Bomber' Harris and the*

Strategic Bombing Offensive, 1939–1945, 1984
— *Hitler's Gladiator: The Life and Times of Oberstgruppenführer and Panzergeneral-Oberst der Waffen-SS Sepp Dietrich*, 1988
— *The Chronological Atlas of World War Two*, 1989
— *The Second World War in the West*, 1999
Michulec, Robert, *Luftwaffe Aces of the Western Front: Luftwaffe at War*, 2002
Miller, David, *The Cold War: A Military History*, 2001
Miller, Merle, *Ike: The Soldier As I Knew Him*, 1987
Milsom, John, *Russian Tanks, 1900–1970*, 1970
— *German Armoured Cars of World War Two*, 1974
— *German Halftrack Vehicles of World War Two*, 1975
— *German Military Transport of World War Two*, 1975
Mitcham, Samuel W., *Hitler's Legions. The German Army Order Of Battle, World War II*, 1985
Montefiore, Simon Sebag, *Stalin: The Court of the Red Tsar*, 2003.
Montgomery of Alamein, Field Marshal Viscount, *Memoirs*, 1958
Nafziger, George F., *The German Order of Battle: Panzers and Artillery in World War II*, 1999
— *German Order of Battle: Infantry in World War II*, 2000
— *German Order of Battle in WW II: Waffen SS, Fallschirmjagers and Foreign Troops in German Service*, 2001
Neillands, Robin, *Eighth Army: From the Western Desert to the Alps, 1939–1945*, 2004
Pallud, Jean Paul, *Battle of the Bulge Then and Now (After the Battle)*, 1984
— *Blitzkrieg in the West: Then and Now (After the Battle)*, 1991
Parker, Danny S. *The Battle of the Bulge*, 1999
Payne, Michael, *Messerschmitt Bf109 in the West, 1937–40: Luftwaffe at War*, 1998
Perrett, Bryan, *Churchill Infantry Tank*, 1993
Pimlott, John, *The Viking Atlas of World War II*, 1995
Pitt, Barrie and Frances, *The Chronological Atlas of World War II*, 1989
Preston, Antony, *Decisive Battles of Hitler's War*, 1978
— *Super Destroyers*, 1978

— *U-Boats*, 1978
— *Decisive Battles of the Pacific War*, 1980
— *An Illustrated History of the Navies of World War II*, 1985
Price, Alfred, *Instruments of Darkness*, 1967
— *Spitfire at War*, 1974
— *Last Year of the Luftwaffe: May 1944–May 1945*, 1991
— *Spitfire in Combat*, 2003
— *Battle Over the Reich: The Strategic Bomber Offensive Against Germany 1939–1945: Vol 1*, 2005
— and Mike Spick, *Great Aircraft of WWII*, 1997
Raven, Alan, *Man o' War 2: 'V' and 'W' Class Destroyers*, 1979
— and John Roberts, *British Battleships of World War Two*, 1976
— *British Cruisers of World War Two*, 1980
Ray, John, *The Second World War: A Narrative History*, 1999
Reynolds Michael. *Men of Steel*, 1999
The Rise and Fall of the German Air Force, 1933–1945, HMSO, 1948; reprinted 1983
Roberts, Andrew, *Hitler and Churchill: Secrets of Leadership*, 2003
Rohwer, Jürgen, and Hümmelchen, Gerhard, *Chronology of the War at Sea, 1939–1945*, 1972, 1974, 1992
Rolf, David, *The Bloody Road to Tunis*, 2001
Rommel, Erwin (ed. B. Liddell Hart). *The Rommel Papers*, 1953
Rooney, David, *Burma Victory*, 1992
— *Wingate and the Chindits*, 1994
Rössler, Eberhard, *The U-Boat*, 1975; English translation 1981
Schmidt, H., *With Rommel in the Desert*, 1951
Scutts, Jerry, *War in the Pacific 1941–1945*, 2000
Schneider, Wolfgang, *Tigers in Combat*, vol 2, 2005
Short, Neil, and Taylor, Chris, *German Defences in Italy in World War II*, 2006
Shulman, Milton, *Defeat in the West*, 2004
Sixsmith, E. K. G. *Eisenhower as Military Commander*, 1973
Skorzeny, Otto, *Skorzeny's Special Missions*, 1997
Smith, Albert and Ian, *Mosquito Pathfinder: Navigating Ninety World War II Operations*, 2003
Smith, Peter C., *Dive Bomber*, 1988

— *Stuka Spearhead, The Lightning War from Poland to Dunkirk, 1939–1940: Luftwaffe at War*, 1998

Snyder, Louis, *Encyclopedia of the Third Reich*, 1976

Speer, Albert, *Inside the Third Reich*, 1970

Spick, Mike, *Luftwaffe Fighter Aces: The Jagdflieger and Their Combat Tactics and Techniques*, 1996

— *Allied Fighter Aces: The Air Combat Tactics and Techniques of World War II*, 1997

— *Defeat in the West, 1943–45: Luftwaffe at War*, 1998

— *Luftwaffe Bomber Aces: Men, Machines, Methods*, 2001

Stewart, Adrian, *The Early Battles of the Eighth Army: Crusader to the Alamein Line*, 2002

Strawson, John, *The Battle for the Ardennes*, 1972

— *The Italian Campaign*, 1987

Summersby, Kay, *Eisenhower was my Boss*, 1949

Swanston, Alexander and Malcolm, *The Historical Atlas of World War II*, 2007

Tarrant, V. E., *The U-Boat Offensive, 1914–1945*, 1989

Thomas, David A., *Japan's War at Sea*, 1978

Thompson, W. H., *I Was Churchill's Shadow*, 1955.

Thompson, R. W., *Battle for the Rhine*, 1959

Thompson, Sir Robert, (ed.), *War in Peace*, 1981

Toland, John. *Adolf Hitler*, 1976

— *The Battle of the Bulge*, 1959

Weal, Elke C. and John A., and Barker, Richard F., *Combat Aircraft of World War Two*, 1977

White, Graham, *Night Fighter Over Germany: Flying Beaufighters and Mosquitoes in World War 2*, 2006

Whiting, Charles, *Battle of the Ruhr Pocket*, 1972

— *The March on London*, 1992

— *The Battle of the Bulge: Britain's Untold Story*, 1999

Whitley, M. J., *Destroyer! German Destroyers in World War II*, 1983

— *German Cruisers of World War II*, 1985

— *Destroyers of World War Two*, 1988

— *German Capital Ships of World War Two*, 1989

— *Cruisers of World War Two*, 1995

— *Battleships of World War Two*, 1998

Whittell, Giles, *Spitfire Women of World War II*, 2007

Wilks, J. and E. *Rommel and Caporetto*, 2001

Winterbotham, F. W., *The Ultra Secret*, 1974

Wisniewski, Richard A., *Pearl Harbor and the USS Arizona Memorial*, 1986.

Young, Desmond, *Rommel*, 1950

Zaloga, Steven J., *The Sherman Tank in United States and Allied Service*, 1982

— *T-34/76 Medium Tank, 1941–45*, 1994

— *T-34-85 Medium Tank, 1944–94*, 1996

— *KV-1 and 2 Heavy Tanks, 1939–45*, 1996

— and Ramiro Bujeiro, *D-Day 1944: Omaha Beach*, 2003

Zaloga, Steven J. and Brian Delf, *US Anti-tank Artillery, 1941–45*, 2005

Zaloga, Steven J. and Hugh Johnson, *M3 Lee/Grant Medium Tank 1941–45*, 2005

Zaloga, Steven J. and Peter Sarson, *IS-2 Heavy Tank 1944 to 1973*, 1994

Zitemann, Rainer, *Hitler, The Policies of Seduction*, 1999

INDEX

INDEX

INDEX

INDEX